SERENDIPITY
ENCYCLOPEDIA

BY LYMAN COLEMAN

EDITORS: Andrew Sloan, Cathy Tardiff, Steve Sheely
PRODUCTION TEAM: Maurice Lydick, Sharon Penington, Christopher Werner, Erika Tiepel
Author of the last two sections on Customizing and Planning: Steve Sheely

SPECIAL THANKS: To Cherry Hills Community Church, Highlands Ranch, Colorado for the use of their photos in the *Group-Sharing Bible Studies*, *Customize Your Event* and *Planning Your Event* sections of this book.

SERENDIPITY HOUSE / Box 1012 / Littleton, CO 80160 / 1-800-525-9563 / www.serendipityhouse.com

SERENDIPITY IS
WHAT HAPPENS WHEN
TWO OR THREE GET
TOGETHER AND SHARE
THEIR LIVES AND THE
HOLY SPIRIT DOES
SOMETHING BEAUTIFUL
WHEN YOU
LEAST EXPECT IT.

TABLE OF CONTENTS

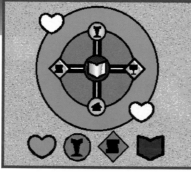

HISTORY OF SERENDIPITY......7

The story of the evolution of Serendipity over the last 40 years, from a ministry primarily to youth to a ministry to the whole church.

'60s—THE COFFEE HOUSE YEARS. The hootenanny. Folk nights. Coffee houses. Happenings. Light and sound shows. Film-making. Serendipity develops programs for the church to use in reaching kids.

'70s—ON THE ROAD. The Serendipity work-shop introduces thousands of church leaders to the Serendipity group-building process in a one-day, double-time eight-hour experiential retreat in the ballroom of a hotel.

'80s—TRAINING OTHERS. Serendipity gets involved in teaching the method behind the madness in schools and seminaries, and developing a system for small group ministry in a local church.

'90s—PREPARING FOR THE 21ST CENTURY. Serendipity targets four specific audiences in the church; develops a model to reach all four audiences; and moves beyond the small group model into family ministry, pulpit groups and special events.

GROUP-BUILDING THEORY..........47

Behind the techniques, the theory for building relationships. Basic theological assumptions. Educational philosophy. Group-building princi-ples and church growth strategies.

VISION. In the average church, there are four lev-els of commitment. The 10% CORE. The 30% CONGREGATION. The 60% CROWD who attend twice a year. And the COMMUNITY at the door. The small group program should target each of these audiences based on their felt needs.

DESIGN. A small group is like a living organ-ism: It has a lifetime. In the beginning stage, the focus is on becoming a group, which requires a certain approach to Bible study. It is called Scripture sharing—or "telling your story through stories in Scripture."

SKILLS. Leading a small group is crucial, but not difficult, if the leader will stick to a three-part tight agenda: gathering, study and caring. Starting on time, keeping to the agenda, and giving priority to the caring time at the end makes for a healthy and effective group.

CROWD BREAKERS........59

When a large group comes together, it is important to help them "unpack" and relax. Here are some fun, simple crowd breakers to help them do so.

WARM-UP CALISTHENICS. Slap-downs and shoulder rub-downs. Things you do in aero-bics class to get the blood circulating.

TENSION BREAKERS. Quick, 30-second ice-breakers to help a group relax.

MIXERS. Three ideas to open a meeting and get the crowd moving—fast.

NONSENSE RHYMES. Short diddies used in kindergarten and Vacation Bible School still work.

FUN SONGS. Sing-a-long rounds, put to motions. Get the crowd singing and moving together.

CELEBRATION DANCES. The Cancan. The Bunny Hop put to new words. It's the celebra-tion of the child and the Spirit with a large group. Great for starting a meeting.

COMMUNICATION ACTIVITIES......67

For small groups who don't know one anoth-er, here are strategies that help the group get acquainted and share their story.

GROUP-BUILDING GAMES. Fun, active small group exercises to enjoy together.

SENSORY EXERCISES. Three activities to get groups better acquainted by using their physical senses.

CONVERSATION STARTERS. Simple ways to talk about yourself with others.

POP QUIZZES. Quick and easy self-exams, as well as deeper, more thought-provoking exer-cises.

GUESSING GAMES. See how much you know about the members of your group.

SHOW-AND-TELL and GROUP SHOW-AND-TELL. Learn more about yourself and your group through creating simple works of art.

NONVERBAL STATEMENTS. Share how you feel without using words.

AFFIRMATION GAMES. Once you know the others in your group, reverse the sharing process and let others give positive feedback.

INTERACTIVE EXERCISES 105

Here are can-openers. Simple 5- to 30-minute discussion starters. Some fun, some serious.

KICK-OFF SENTENCES. Half-finished sentencesfor you to finish—about who you are.

MULTIPLE-CHOICE OPTIONS. Questions with forced choices to choose from.

SPECTRUMS. Share about yourself by choosing between two extremes.

INTERVIEWS. Questions to ask your partner—like a news reporter.

PERSONAL INVENTORIES. Interesting "psychological tests" to take and share with your group.

RANKING. Have fun ranking yourself on a variety of issues.

BIBLICAL INVENTORIES. Measure your growth against some standards set in the Bible.

CASE STUDIES. Discuss what you would do in certain critical situations.

SERIOUS AFFIRMATION. Give the gift of affirmation to the people in your group.

GROUP-SHARING BIBLE STUDIES ...141

Here are guided questionnaires to help a group share their own stories through stories in Scripture—45 stories in nine categories.

IDENTITY. My uniqueness. My personality. My values. My abilities. My future.

RELATIONSHIPS. Friendships. Being Real. True Friends. Peer Pressure. Family Expectations.

CARING. Tough Love. Down and Dirty. Friendly Fire. Sharing Your Faith. I Appreciate You.

VALUES. Priorities. Possessions. Responsibility. Morality. Bottom Line.

PRESSURES. Stress. Worries. Shattered Dreams. Old Habits. Shame and Blame.

ISSUES. Moral Anger. Racism / Prejudice. Violence / Apathy. Sexual Desires. Cults / Occult.

SPIRITUAL FORMATION. My Spiritual Journey. Forgiveness of Sins. Turning Around. Dealing With Doubt. Heavy Stuff.

BELIEFS. God the Father. Jesus Christ. The Holy Spirit. The Church. Resurrection.

DISCIPLESHIP. Mountain Training. Spiritual Calling. Pot Holes. Rebounding. Miracles.

CUSTOMIZE YOUR EVENT 233

Here's how to design your own program using the resources in this encyclopedia.

SMALL GROUP EVENTS. Specific ideas for special events and types of groups. Outreach groups. Support seminars. Leaders' retreats. Intergenerational groups. Small group kick-off.

FAMILY EVENTS. Family fun nights. Retreats. Father-Son rallies. Mother-Daughter celebrations. Home devotionals. Here's how to do it.

YOUTH EVENTS. Ideas for your youth ministry. Weekly meetings. Retreats. Outreach parties. Prayer and share groups. Parents' nights.

SINGLES EVENTS. Bible studies. Valentine's banquets. Mingling parties. Spiritual growth retreats. Here's how.

SUNDAY SCHOOL EVENTS. Turn a typical class into a caring community. New class kick-off. Retreats. Outreach dinners. Multi-class rallies. Intergenerational Sunday schools.

OTHER EVENTS. Tips for various other occasions. New member orientations. Recognition banquets. Weeknight prayer suppers. Committee meetings. Apartment outreach parties. Interactive worship services.

PLANNING YOUR EVENT 295

For your next meeting, here is a checklist of things to do and ways to adapt the resources in this encyclopedia to create your own agenda.

PLANNING PROCESS. How to: • create a planning calendar • organize a team • host an introductory meeting • conduct a trial run • evaluate and improve • delegate tasks • survey your target group • gather materials • monitor your teams and say "thank you."

PROMOTING YOUR EVENT. Here are some suggestions to use in publicizing your project in church meetings, publications, sermons, pulpit interviews, skits, slide shows, phone teams, display tables and brochures.

PREPARING FOR FUTURE EVENTS. Here are some ideas for follow-up after your project is over. Use evaluation forms. Interview participants. Hold an evaluation meeting. Record ideas for your next event. Recognize team members.

HISTORY OF SERENDIPITY

Every person and every family has a story. So does every church and every movement. The story of Serendipity has a lot to do with my own story. The story of my family, my church, my schooling and my struggle to find an authentic way of becoming a Christian community.

I grew up on corn bread, collard greens, black-eyed peas, fried chicken and the Bible. My brother and I used to fight over the wishbone and the gizzard. He usually won. He won at everything he did. Sports. Studies. Girls. And religion. He went on to be an evangelist. A professor. The author of *The Master Plan of Evangelism*. My brother was a hard act to follow—and I didn't even try. This may have something to do with the way Serendipity got started. The story of Serendipity is the story of my struggle to carry on the tradition of my godly, old-fashioned, pietistic Methodist family—but I had to do it in a different way.

When I went off to college at Baylor, I majored in philosophy, not religion. In seminary, when they asked for an exegesis of a Scripture passage, I turned in doodles, expressionistic designs, driftwood, and free-verse poetry. A few of my teachers saw through this rebellious streak to a genuine spirit that was trying to find new ways of expressing the Gospel. To these mentors, I have dedicated this encyclopedia.

There may be another reason why I had to find new wineskins. Behind my usual professional bluff, I am an introvert. In the Myers-Briggs personality inventory, I am an INFJ—which means that, although I am drawn to others, I am by nature a reserved, private person. In graduate school (New York University), we sat around and "observed" how we assumed typical roles in a group: talker, listener, gatekeeper, blocker. I was often tagged as the doormat—unless I took over the group in self-defense and was accused of being the dominator. An egg timer was passed around the group and we were expected to talk for three minutes when we got the egg timer. By the time the egg timer got to me, my mouth had turned to sawdust and my armpits were dripping blood. It was in those days that I decided to find another way for shy people like me to get acquainted.

This history section will share some of the struggles I have had to find new and better ways for helping people like me to belong to a group: To tell our story with simple, nonthreatening conversation starters. To affirm the beautiful things we discover about one another. And to become a community of love. A true Christian fellowship—where "serendipity" happens when we least expect it.

A three-legged stool. A 35 mm slide projector. A "Peter, Paul and Mary" album on the record player, and the stage is set for a coffee house in the early sixties.

The '60s—The Coffee House Years

As I fidgeted through endless hours of family devotions, religious instruction and Bible lectures, I had a gnawing feeling that there must be a better way. Surely the greatest story ever told could be a little more exciting.

In the late '50s the church renewal movement was coming in, causing a lot of us getting out of seminary to see a ray of hope for the years ahead. John Castell, in his book *Spiritual Renewal Through Personal Groups*, told about six churches that started small sharing groups for the people who wanted to grow in their faith. I remember feeling that I had found a niche in the church where I could give myself.

I announced to the world that I was available to go into a church and teach the people how to accomplish church renewal.

To my chagrin, we had few takers. In fact, in the first year we had a grand total of three invitations and all three were for youth retreats.

We finally sold our home to make ends meet and used the extra time to read everything possible in the personal growth and motivation field, all the way from Dale Carnegie to my brother's new book, *The Master Plan of Evangelism.*

These were the years of the hootenanny. Bob Dylan was the idol of the teen world, and the guitar was its newfound toy. Since I had nothing else to do, I started creating exercises to help young people relate Scripture to the folk generation.

That summer a camp in New Jersey asked me to lead the senior highs in Bible study for a week. I tried our "folk expression" technique. Each morning the kids explored a passage in Scripture and put their responses into a simple creative piece—a drawing, a free-verse poem or a diary. In the afternoons, they would put their expressions into a folk medium—wall poster, pop sculpture, ballad, reading or interpretive dance. Each evening we staged

Entertainment in the coffee house in the early days usually consisted of a folk group singing Woody Guthrie ballads and Mitch Miller sing-a-longs. The atmosphere was quiet. When electric guitars and heavy amplification came in around 1965, the coffee house atmosphere changed into a spectator sport.

9

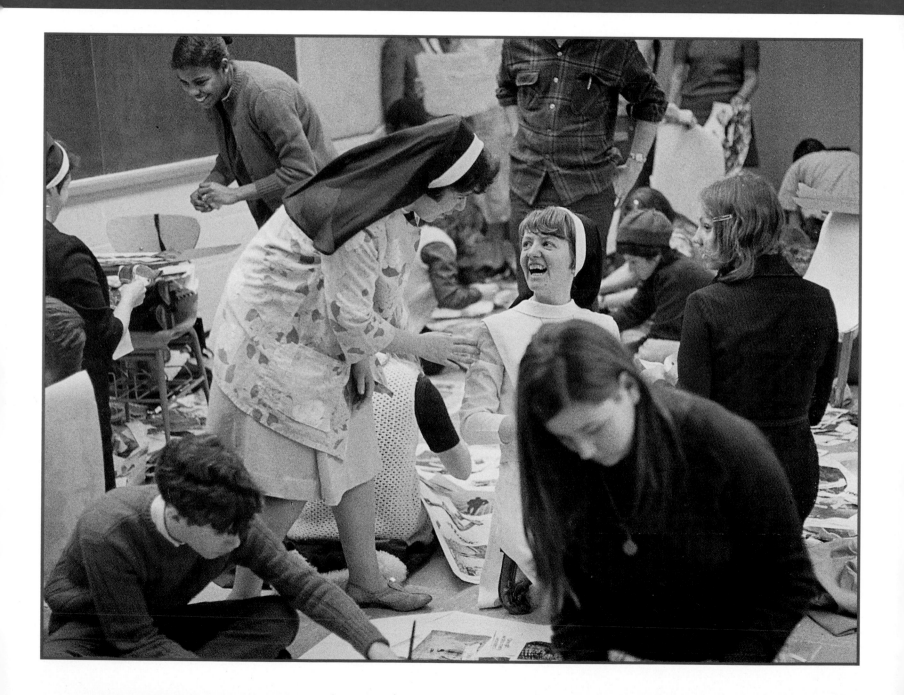

OPPOSITE PAGE: *Participants at the Youth Education Day in Wilmington, Delaware, make wall murals out of magazine tear-outs to describe their feelings and prepare for a folk night in the evening.* TOP LEFT: *A teenager explains his self-portrait to his group at the Dayspring Retreat Center in Germantown, Maryland.* BOTTOM: *Students from a Catholic high school in Brooklyn, New York, turn their self-portraits into full-scale murals. Some paint with brushes, others with their feet.* NEXT PAGE: *A folk night concludes the week-long senior high camp in Lebanon, New Jersey, with teenagers sharing their original free-verse poetry, ballads and sculpture that they created through the week in folk-expression workshops.*

a hootenanny with the kids performing their masterpieces.

It worked! Kids who had been turned off to the Bible were suddenly engrossed. A sense of community slowly emerged. And the evening hootenannies, while not very professional, were beautiful times together.

The word spread. Invitations started to come in, and Gene Herr, Youth Secretary for the Mennonite Church, asked me to write a program for their denomination. It grew into a full-scale pictorial study book based on the book of Acts. We sold our house again to get money to print it and came out with our first Serendipity book, *Acts Alive.*

The book had a mixed reception, particularly in the Mennonite Church. One of the bishops called the book a "heap of educational garbage."

The next few years were exciting, but hardgoing. At some meetings I would be met with great hostility and opposition; while at others people accepted my ideas.

The rhythm of the Serendipity process began to take shape: the wedding of self-discovery and self-expression with Scripture, the short creative exercise to prime the pump, a continuing support group

(continued on page 15)

"... It was a night I shall never forget.
That night, something in me came alive—
A creative part of me that I never knew I had.

"When they told me that I
had an unlimited potential of creative energy
just waiting to be tapped,
I laughed.
I just wasn't the type for
that creative stuff.

"But on that night,
something wonderful happened.
I found myself, for the first time in my life,
coming alive! Really alive ..."

CREATIVE EXPRESSION IN BIBLE STUDY:
The first Serendipity book, *Acts Alive*

In my last year of college I took a course that really got me excited, but it was not in the religion department.

At every "Integration of Ability" class we were given a creative exercise to get in touch with an area of our creative self. We took our initials and doodled until we had the makings of an expressionistic design. Then we walked out our doodles in our imagination and wrote a free-verse poem. Finally we developed the doodles into a symbolic self-portrait by coloring our feelings. We even played our feelings on the piano with our arms and elbows.

Back in 1954 this was radical. And for me, it was doubly radical. But it opened up something in me that I didn't know I had. I was a creative being with vast reservoirs of untapped potential and God-given gifts.

In my own private study of Scripture, I started to "feel" the passage. I put my meditations in diary form, adding color and texture and sound. In my years at seminary I tried to help my Young Life kids discover the Scriptures through creative techniques. And with one professor (Howard Hendricks), I turned in crazy, expressionistic drawings for Bible interpretations, and he was crazy enough to accept them.

But the years had much trial and error, with many more failures than successes. Most of my teachers and a great many of my associates thought the ideas a little weird and even dangerous. And maybe they were, but that's the way Serendipity started out.

APPROACHING STORM   ANXIETY   CRISIS   PEACE

The story of the storm in Mark, chapter four, in existential doodles.
Some of my teachers in seminary thought I was crazy.

A storefront in the small farming community of Hesston, Kansas, gets ready for a coffee house at the end of a mission retreat.

"The Coffee House Itch" came out in 1966. It was a how-to-start-your-own coffee house training guide with six sessions for the coffee house team to get ready.

(continued from page 11)

to share results, and the occasional special program to share with the larger community.

The Vietnam War was raging. Young men were being drafted out of college and sent overseas to fight in an increasingly unpopular war. The music turned to protest, and a new forum was discovered for young people to get together and share their broken dreams with each other—the coffee house.

Many saw the coffee house as a den of iniquity, but a few churches (like the Church of the Savior in Washington, D.C.) were proving that the coffee house was an effective marketplace for the church to minister in the world, earning the right to share their faith in Christ.

I started to put on workshops for youth groups to prepare for their mission to the community. The group skills of listening and caring were perfectly suited to coffee house dialogue, and the creative techniques were great for developing good folk entertainment.

These were the wild years in my own development. It was as though I had to get something out of my system—to prove something. The elders in the church often got upset by the way-out ideas, and I took a weird sort of satisfaction in upsetting them. I regret this now.

Nevertheless, this period was crucial in my own spiritual development as well as in the Serendipity process. During those years, we developed the creative exercise into the show-and-tell techniques that were to become more and more introspective and therapeutic.

If it is true that every person goes through a time of rebellion, these years could be considered my most rebellious, but they were also the prelude to a spiritual breakthrough just around the corner.

Coffee house decorations in Hesston were quite basic. Card tables. Candles in coke bottles. Paper tablecloths with crayons to scribble if you want to. A chessboard or two. Maybe pipe cleaners. Play-doh and pizza. Total budget was under $50.

In my opinion, the coffee house movement was radically altered in 1965 when the electric guitar and powerful amplification systems came in. Suddenly the emphasis switched from dialogue to entertainment—from "rapping" to listening.

We continued to put on coffee house workshops at Christian education conferences, but times were changing, and a new form was coming in—and it required another shift on our part.

ABOVE: *Every coffee house had a grafitti wall where you could scribble your thoughts. Here a student at the ecumenical coffee house in Butler, Pennsylvania, adds her comments to the communal board.* OPPOSITE: *Before the electric guitar and the heavy amplification system came along, the heart of every coffee house was dialogue or "rapping." Here students at the coffee house in Hesston, Kansas, share their feelings about the war in Vietnam.*

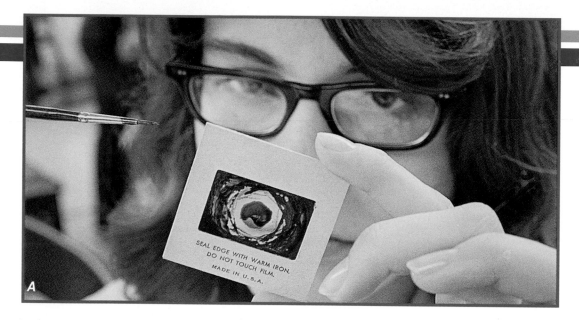

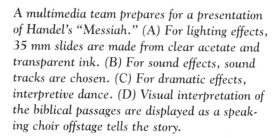

A multimedia team prepares for a presentation of Handel's "Messiah." (A) For lighting effects, 35 mm slides are made from clear acetate and transparent ink. (B) For sound effects, sound tracks are chosen. (C) For dramatic effects, interpretive dance. (D) Visual interpretation of the biblical passages are displayed as a speaking choir offstage tells the story.

In the late '60s the fad was light and sound shows—with fluorescent paint, whirling lights and psychedelic music. Marshall McLuben coined the phrase, "The medium is the message." The medium included all five senses: hearing, seeing, touching, tasting and smelling. And the events were called "happenings."

This gave us an opportunity to involve students in a new approach to Bible study and sharing. We called it Scripture happenings. We used the text of Handel's *Messiah*—the Christmas and Easter portions. And we involved students in the process of creating a modern-day *Messiah*—as a light and sound show, with narration, interpretive dance, and in some cases a speaking choir.

For low-budget lighting effects, we used 35 mm slides, painted with impressionistic designs on acetate. With the lens of a projector turned out of focus, these slides flooded the room with swirling light. The final performance was an exciting event for the church, but the real transformation was in the lives of the participants who got to internalize the story of the *Messiah*.

At the same time that we were developing our youth models, another experiment was taking place in the academic world through the influence of Sidney Simon. It was called "values clarification." Sid Simon and I would often be teaching at the same event. I would be leading coffee house experiments for youth leaders while he would be leading a values workshop for school teachers. I was fascinated with his strategies for getting people to share. Before long, I had incorporated his techniques in the study of Scripture. I called it Scripture sharing strategies.

(continued on page 22)

Interpretive dance is used to interpret the Scripture passages in Handel's "Messiah" in preparation for the performance that weekend.

FOLLOWING PAGES: The barn at the United Church of Christ retreat center in Allentown, Pennsylvania, is turned into a primitive theater for the final performance of Handel's "Messiah." All the decorations, program, light and sound effects have been created by the young people in one week.

19

(continued from page 18)

This, in turn, led to the guided questionnaire approach to Scripture sharing. The guided questionnaire allowed the group to move across the "disclosure scale" from no-risk questions about "things outside" to high-risk questions about "things inside."

In the late '60s, a lot of things came together for me, in particular the art of group building and the approach to Scripture study and Scripture sharing. I will say more about this in the section in the encyclopedia on theory. It would be another 20 years before I learned a way of getting a church to incorporate these ideas into religious education in the church—but most of the essential ideas which are called the Serendipity process were first experienced in the radical '60s.

Youth at the Butler, Pennsylvania, "happening" work on music to go with their free-verse poetry in preparation for the performance of Handel's "Messiah." OPPOSITE PAGE: The final scene of Handel's "Messiah" is presented—with light, sound, interpretive dance, and music created by the young people. ABOVE RIGHT: "Kaleidoscope" and "Man Alive" came out of our experiments in the late '60s, based on the interpretation of Handel's "Messiah."

THE TIME IN MY LIFE WHEN SERENDIPITY HAPPENED

In the late '60s, a new movement in group experience started to sweep across the country. It was variously called sensitivity training, encounter groups, or the human potential movement. I was frightened by the emphasis on physical touch. I had been trained in seminary to keep a safe distance from people, and I was naturally reserved. Even in a group situation I hid behind a professional air for fear that someone might "get to me" if they got too close. Like a pro, I knew when to excuse myself from a group and busy myself when things started getting deep.

In these years, the big, bluff exterior started to crumble and I discovered a whole new dimension to group experience that radically changed my life as well as the programs I was writing.

I was in Atlanta for the first of a series of National Clergy Conferences being put on by a team that I was part of. Lloyd Ogilvie said the team would meet together at least once a day to report in on how we were feeling—and that we would plan the agenda around our own needs. This scared me to death. The thought of revealing my needs to my peers was bad enough—I had had a bad "team" experience before—but the idea of going before the whole world "in weakness" was worse. (I had explained away the words from the apostle Paul about that as psychologically unsound.)

The first day or two when we met together as a team, I faked it. I said something about my frustrations in the ministry—a subject that was safe to talk about. But some of the men opened up about their personal needs. They really got to me.

On the last morning of that conference, I was to lead the experimental worship. This was my professional bag, but I was not ready for worship that morning—and I decided not to fake it. So I refused, and Ralph Osborne took over.

After the session I got together with Ralph and said, "I'm sorry, but I just can't pretend that everything is fine with me. This idea about being a team and ministering to each other is tearing me up, because I was on a team once that wasn't a team and I just don't want to go through that again."

I talked and talked and Ralph just sat there. When I was completely talked out he said, "Lyman, how would you like for me to pray that God will erase those memories and give you a new start in building some deep relationships?"

My first thought was, "These guys are a bunch of fanatics!" But after a moment, I said yes. He stood up, laid his hands on my head and prayed that God would erase the hurt and pain of my bad experience and give me a clean start. And do you know what? It worked. It worked!

The next 27 days in conferences were something else. I was like a little child, starting all over again. I led the same relational games and talked about the same in-depth relationships in small groups, but I did it as a learner instead of a teacher. Leading from weakness and being vulnerable were more than theories. They were a whole new lifestyle of leadership for me.

When I got home I had some homework to do before I could finish the book I was writing at the time. I had always looked upon small groups as an educational tool for a learning activity, but now I had discovered that a small group can be much more if the members are willing to give themselves completely to each other. When Jesus refers to the church, he is saying that people who are lonely and hurting can get together and really find healing for their hurts.

For me, spiritual growth has been a series of extremes, like a pendulum gone wild. For most of my years, I was a people-isolationist, a group con artist with a bag of tricks for every occasion, as long as it didn't involve me. Then the dam broke and I swung completely in the opposite direction. For two years, I gave myself so much to people that I was emotionally spent.

The encounter movement opened me up to my own feelings for the first time in my life. I learned to laugh and cry—to reach out and touch, to show my feelings and to feel for others. I experienced the joy of sharing with fellow-strugglers, of caring for the hurts and needs of each other—in a community of love, trust and acceptance. Beautiful things happened to me that changed my life ... and my lifestyle.

When I discovered this relational lifestyle, I went overboard on relationships. I tried to give myself away to every person with whom I came in contact. Every weekend I was in a new city, starting all over with a new group—before the hurt and the pain of the previous weekend's good-byes had been healed.

Suddenly, I found myself feeling a terrible loneliness in the midst of caring people, and I didn't know why.

What had happened to me? Where did Christ fit into all of this? These were the questions that troubled me in these years as I sought to get myself together—as a whole person with a whole Gospel for the world.

I remember going to a theologian whom I respected and asking him to explain what had happened to me. He referred me back to the ministry of Christ and the "incarnational" way in which he shared himself with people.

The Gospels became very precious and comforting to me. I discovered that Jesus talked very little *about* theology, but constantly invited people to reach out, touch, and experience him. And it was very often a nontheological experience. In fact his followers probably would have flunked the average catechism test given in the church today.

I put together a rationale for group experi-ence. I described it as going around a baseball diamond, with home plate being depth Christian community. In the first stage (first base), I went along with the encounter movement in saying a group must begin with history-giving. Members of a group need to get to know about one another.

For the second stage (second base) in the development of a group, I broke with the clinical ideas of feedback in the encounter program and substituted the word affirmation (positive feelings). The use of confrontation or attack as a group technique may be all right in a contract group with a qualified leader, but for amateurs to use such methods on unsuspecting people is almost criminal.

To be honest to my own experience, I had to incorporate a deeper dimension in a group building process for the time when the members are willing to minister to each other through the presence and power of the Holy Spirit. I called this step goal setting, and symbolized it with a cross in the center of the group.

These two distinctions: (a) affirmation instead of confrontation, and (b) ministry to each other through the Holy Spirit, were to become the foundation of the Serendipity model.

The real story of these years is that of my spiritual homecoming. For many years I had been living in a spiritual "no man's land" of secular humanism. I had abandoned my conservative upbringing as stuffy and uncomfortable, and not found anything to take its place.

Secular humanism had a lot of integrity to it, and I owe a great deal of my personal growth to it. But down deep inside, I found an inner hunger for spiritual wholeness that could not be satisfied on the human level.

I have come almost full circle in my spiritual pilgrimage, but this time it is my own experience ... and it feels right.

This is your invitation to reach out, stretch, grow, become the new thing God has for you.

It's SERENDIPITY! Eight hours of frog kissin'— in a riot of interpersonal relationships. Outrageously childlike and profoundly Christlike.

Where God meets you when you least expect it.

The '70s—On The Road

The National Clergy Conferences in 1970 were a breakthrough for me personally (see the previous story). They were also a breakthrough for the Serendipity ministry. Twenty-six hundred pastors and church leaders showed up for the conferences—to hear such leaders as Bruce Larson, Keith Miller and Ralph Osborne talk about the "emerging church." Unlike the typical conference, the speakers were asked to share the struggles in their lives—especially the gut issues in their marriage, their family and their church.

Over the three days of a conference, hundreds of pastors tasted the "new wine" of depth sharing in a caring group. And these pastors returned home with a whole new style of doing church:

- people, not programs
- relationships, not religion
- Christ, not creeds
- the future, not the past

Suddenly I had more invitations than I could handle—for adult as well as youth retreats. I decided to condense the three-day retreat format into an eight-hour marathon, and to hold the one-day retreat in a hotel ballroom.

Up to this time, all of our work had been on the East Coast—within driving distance from our home in Newtown (Bucks County), Pennsylvania. With a little faith, hope and a shoestring, I booked hotels in 30 cities—the same cities as the NFL (National Football League). I figured if a city was crazy enough to support a football team, they might go for Serendipity.

The bank loaned us the money to print a brochure and send it to our friends. Faith At Work helped us pass the word to their churches

LEFT: *The Serendipity workshop in Omaha, Nebraska, begins with an introduction to the eight-hour, fast-moving retreat in the Hilton Hotel.* TOP RIGHT: *Dave Stone warms up the crowd with fun sing-along camp songs.* BOTTOM RIGHT: *The audience joins in singing the drinking song from "The Student Prince."*

and the Mennonite Publishing House offered to do the office work. We hoped for 200 in each city. Our board was skeptical and apprehensive about the venture.

I decided to conduct the one-day workshop like a small group retreat. In the first session, we divided the large crowd into small groups of 8, and had each small group stay together for their entire time. This would mean leading 16 groups simultaneously through the day from up front.

In the last week before the Newark workshop, registrations started to go over 200, 250, 300, 350. I started to panic. The hotel ballroom was not big enough to hold the meeting and feed everyone in the other half. I remember taking my son, Tudor, and driving up to Newark the night before—not knowing what might happen.

What happened was the beginning of something that continued for seven years—until I burned out in 1979 and had to quit. In the first year, 8,000 people showed up. The next year, 14,000. The next year, 18,000, etc.

GROUP BUILDING

The people came to the Serendipity workshop to learn the techniques—what some people call the "bag of tricks." But I had another agenda. I wanted these people to experience what I had experienced in a caring group. (See the story on pages 24–25.) This meant involving a person in the process of telling their story and helping the people in their group to affirm this story. Then, encouraging them to go deeper into telling their story (their needs) and letting the group affirm this deeper story and pray for them. I call this process going around the bases of a ball diamond. (See page 51.)

To get to home plate in the baseball diamond as a group takes about eight hours—moving through a series of story-sharing communication games.

We started out with a series of crowd breakers. Dave Stone, my partner and musician, would introduce two or three celebration dances—like *One in the Spirit* to the cancan, *It's a Small World* to the bunny hop, and *Jesus Loves Me* to the side-step. Before they realized it, the crowd was involved in a profoundly childlike way.

Then we introduced the first and basic group—a group of two people—and asked everyone to find a partner and sit down face-to-face. We explained that shy people will talk if they are paired off with one other person.

To get acquainted with their partner, we asked everyone to explain the name tag which they had created. Then, we had them sit back-to-back and guess three more things about their partner—such as their favorite TV show, magazine and vacation spot. Without realizing it, they were getting involved in listening skills as well as learning a lot about one another.

(continued on page 31)

ABOVE: *Workshops began with everyone making a name tag.* RIGHT: *A group of 8 tries to keep in rhythm with each other in the game of nonverbal rhythm.*

(continued from page 28)

"Now take your partner. Get together with two others whom you do not know and introduce your partner to your group of 4." Simple. Easy to do. Nonthreatening. In the first hour, total strangers had started on a journey that would eventually become a depth community.

After the break, the groups of 4 joined with another group of 4 to form a group of 8. We used the old-fashioned game of rhythm to get the groups of 8 working together. Then, a couple of concentration games were introduced to help the group work together. This was followed by the first serious exercise of the day.

"With this paper cup, in silence do to the paper cup what you would like to do to the institutional church. You can do anything you wish—bless it, tear it, kiss it—but you must be honest. And when you are through, pass it in silence to the next person in your group."

As the cup went around, feelings about the institutional church started to surface. The teenager often stomped on the cup. The next

Various group configurations are used to facilitate sharing. Here the group of 8 is rearranged into a wagon wheel—four as the hub in the center and four as the outside ring—with the outside ring rotating every two minutes.

Group-Building Strategies

C ertain communication exercises work best in groups of 2; others in groups of 4; and others in groups of 8. This is the reason for the suggestions given for the structuring of each group session.

CONFIGURATION	BEST USE
TWOSOME **Face-to-face**	**Beginnings** **Introductions** **Conversation starters** **Interviews** **Deep sharing**
FOURSOME **Kneesie-nosey**	**Getting acquainted** **Discussions** **Affirmation**
WAGON WHEEL **Four back-to-back in center.** **Four on outside, rotating** **every two minutes.**	**Quick, multiple introductions** **Conversation starters**
GROUPS OF 8 **Circle of 8**	**Nonverbal exercises** **Celebrations** **Affirmation** **Team spirit** **Group projects** **Worship / Commissioning**

Crayons are needed for drawing your childhood table—the shape of the table, the color to represent each person, and the lines of communication between you and the others at the table.

person would bless it. The next would tear it apart. The next would put it together. When they were through, the silence was broken; the people in the group leaned forward, and the sharing began.

Now it was lunch time. If there was another room, the group of 8 gathered there to relax and eat together. If there was not another room, the group sat on the floor and had a picnic. And while they were eating, butcher paper, colored tissue and masking tape were passed out—for each group to create a wall banner to express what they had experienced in the morning session. The banners, in turn, were put on the walls for decorations.

After lunch, the calories were burned up with one more celebration dance and a few crowd breakers to reestablish the groups. Crayons were passed out and everyone was asked to describe their spiritual pilgrimage or childhood table in a simple drawing. I went first to show how to do it. Then, crayons were dumped into

the group and everyone was on their own.

Ten minutes later, instructions were given: "Hold your drawing so the other three people in your group can see it, and tell the story of your spiritual pilgrimage or your supper table to your group. When you are finished, let the other three finish this sentence: 'The gift that you gave to me in your story was ... .' "

I don't understand what happened in the next 30 to 45 minutes. I do know that God became very real to these groups of four strangers when they started to share their stories—and hear how their stories became a gift to another person. It was like ... "serendipity."

After one more break, the groups of 4 regathered for the giving game. This is a simple little communication game—but sometimes beautiful things happened. Each person was asked to look through their wallet or purse for things they could make into gifts for the others in their group. "Something personal ... that expresses how you feel about this person ... and what you would like to give this person to keep as a token of the time you have been together."

One at a time, each person shared their gifts with the other three members of their group. Those who were receiving gifts were instructed to simply receive them in silence.

Twenty-five years later I still carry in my wallet some of the gifts that I received in this crazy game. A Band-Aid from Sister Mary from Buzzards Bay, Massachusetts, "for the little hurts you get on your journey." A blood card from a pastor in Albany, New York, "for a pint of blood

In groups of 4, one person explains his childhood table and the relationship he had with the members of his family when he was 7 years old. Then, the group gets to affirm something beautiful they learned about this person from this story.

For many, the high point of the Serendipity workshop was an exercise we called the "giving game." Each person in the group of 4 (who had gotten to know one another through six hours of intentional storytelling) is given a gift from the others in the group as a token of their appreciation. It was a beautiful way to say "thank you" and "this is something I want you to keep as a reminder of our brief time together."

BELOW: In the group of 8, each person receives the Serendipity cross from their community and a prayer for the next step in their spiritual life. NEXT PAGE: The eight-hour workshop comes to a close with the whole crowd joining in a celebration of life.

if you ever need it." A hug coupon from a teenager in Texas—"good for one hug from me."

It is 4 p.m. now. The groups have been together for about six hours, including their lunch and making their banner. They have laughed together. Played together. Shared their stories with each other. Now it is time to pray together.

The final celebration started out as a repeat of the morning celebration dances—only this time they were ready to celebrate. Then, as the lights in the ballroom fade, the groups pull up their chairs one more time. A cup containing Serendipity crosses on string necklaces are given to each group. Each person has five minutes to talk about the next step in their spiritual life. Then, this person's cross is passed around the group and anyone who wishes gives a word of affirmation to support them. The person kneels and receives the cross from their group. This continues until everyone has received their cross.

I don't know what the Day of Pentecost was like when the disciples burst out of the Upper Room to tell their story on the streets, but I think we experienced a little of what that day must have been like at the close of the workshop. The celebration of the child and the spirit—hilarity and healing—childlikeness and Christlikeness.

The '80s—Training Others

Two events occurred in 1980 that impacted the future course of Serendipity. First, I burned out from all of the travel. Keith Miller explained it this way:

"When you lead out of your own story, you run the danger of getting your zipper stuck ... with your guts exposed and no way to get them back in."

This is what happened to me. For seven years, I had led meetings by going first in sharing my life in the large meeting—first about my past before the groups shared their past; then about my present; and finally about my hopes and dreams for the future. By the end of the day, I was into sharing the heavy stuff in my life. The groups, in turn, would get into their heavy stuff and find healing in their community. Oftentimes, this gradual disclosure process was therapeutic—even life changing for people in the group.

But I was left on the stage psychologically drained and emotionally naked. After the meeting, I would put my guts back into the suitcase, fly to another city and start all over again the next morning with 500 to 700 people.

I did this for 300 meetings in seven years. At the end, I had given away all of my emotions. There was nothing left. For two years I did very little. My wife and kids held on to me for dear life as I went through the slow process of coming back to life.

The second event was even more scary. Back in the midseventies, a graduate student at New York University (my old school) asked if he could write his doctoral dissertation around the Serendipity phenomena. In a moment of weakness, I consented and gave him access to everything in my life—including the evaluations from 10,000 people who had attended the Serendipity workshops in 1978. He created a 12-page questionnaire and asked a random selec-

tion of these participants about the impact of the Serendipity day on their lives.

On a scale from 1 to 10, these participants gave us an 8 on behavior change. This was exceedingly high. But on understanding what they had experienced, these same people gave us a 3. In other words, in the eight-hour intensive workshop, there was a lot of emotional impact—but very little understanding.

The graduate student (Frank Fowler) was awarded a doctorate for his study, but his doctoral committee predicted on the basis of his results that the Serendipity movement would likely turn into a cult—attracting followers through high impact meetings without rational explanation.

(continued on page 40)

37

8 Critical Decisions That Will Determine the Future of Your Church

You will be carefully guided to make a fundamental decision in each of these 8 strategic areas as you create your own one-of-a-kind Master Plan.

1. Defining Your Vision: Quit bouncing from crises to crises! Learn how to set foundational goals custom-tailored to your church. Every church is driven by something: Traditions? Personalities? Maintaining the institution? What is your church in business for? What's its driving purpose?

2. Targeting Your Audience: Make every effort count. Grasp how to quickly and accurately assess people's needs in your community. Your church is made up of three kinds of people: (1) 10%-Dedicated Few, (2) 30%-Congregation, and (3) 60%-Inactive Crowd. There's 50% to 80% of the people in your "parish" who do not attend church. How is your program designed to target these audiences?

3. Choosing Your System: Master the art of networking your people and their myriad of gifts together. What is your system for bringing people on the fringe of the church to the center, and from the center out into ministry? How can you design a system that integrates your purpose, people and programs?

4. Selecting Your Model: You'll never have to feel or look disorganized again! Discover how to skillfully design a model that fits your unique situation. Study four strategic group models: (1) Covenant; (2) Meta; (3) Cho and (4) Serendipity. Each has strengths and weaknesses. Which will work best in your church or should you customize your own model with the best qualities of all four paradigms?

5. Training Your Leaders: Small groups put ministry back into the hands of the people. Everyone agrees a trained leader is the key to a healthy group. When and how are they trained? The academic model puts the training UP FRONT (especially for "special" needs or recovery groups). For most share/care groups, you may want to consider less training UP FRONT and more ON-THE-JOB.

6. Supervising Your Leaders: People with a vision, a plan and proper skills succeed! Insure successful community-wide ministry through effectively focusing your people on target needs. As you diversify, you may require differing levels of supervision—more for special needs and recovery groups and less for share/care groups. The Covenant, Meta, Cho and Serendipity models all recommend supervision. How much control do you need and when is it required?

7. Structuring Your Lifecycle: Don't lose them, use them! Growing people have changing needs. Build growth into your ministry without abusing volunteer leaders by "automatically" cultivating and equipping future leaders. Unlike all other models, Serendipity believes a group must go through a three-stage lifecycle: (1) Birthing, (2) Growing and (3) Releasing. Each has a different purpose and agenda.

8. Planning Your Calendar: Planning is not putting all you did last year on a new calendar. Choosing your own model is the easy part, carrying it out is another matter. When you leave, you will have a complete, executable game plan. Launch out and watch your people and your church grow!

In the Advanced Training Conferences in the '80s, we created a decision-making format to help pastors design a model for their own church in which relationship could be built into every event in their church.

Growing the Church through Small Groups

March 10-13, 1987

SPONSORED BY

FULLER THEOLOGICAL SEMINARY

Institute for Continuing Education

STEPHEN MINISTRIES
and
SERENDIPITY

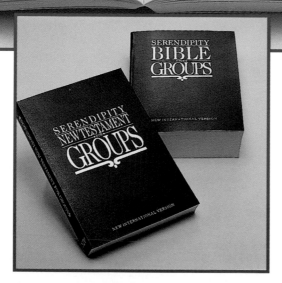

(continued from page 37)

When Frank Fowler told me this, I said: "I will never lead another meeting without building all of the sharing process around the Scriptures that the people can take back and rebuild in their church."

This helps to explain the direction in the '80s in my own life. When I started back on the road in the early eighties, my focus was on group building through Scripture study and sharing your story through stories in Scriptures, and the building of an ongoing caring group in and through the local church.

In the early '80s, the church growth movement was attracting a lot of attention. Pastors who had never taken small groups seriously because they didn't consider it their job discovered a new reason for building small groups into the church program to "close the back door."

The challenge for us in the '80s was to come up with a system to help churches in the formation of groups, the training of group leaders, and the ongoing supervision of leaders to keep them healthy and growing. We developed a model to build the small group program in a church around the teaching of the pastor at the Sunday service or Sunday school class. We called this new series *Mastering the Basics*—three looks at a Scripture passage: (a) with your pastor; (b) by yourself; and (c) with your small group. Richard Peace, a teacher at Gordon Conwell Seminary, wrote the material and I put together the process for groups.

The major work that we developed in the '80s was the *Serendipity Bible for Groups*. I had dreamed about this project for years, but didn't have the time to work on it. When I burned out and had nothing to do, I found the time.

I came up with the idea of running a column of questions next to the text. The questions would be on three levels: (a) OPEN—fun, open-ended, right-brain questions to start off the sharing; (b) DIG—observation questions about the text; and (c) REFLECT—questions about personal application. I asked Richard Peace and Denny Rydberg to help me find writers. Together we came up with 50 writers around the world. It took us nearly four years for the New Testament and another two years for the Old Testament. Dietrich Gruen did a great job on the editing.

In my own life, I was trying to figure out what God was wanting me to do. I tried teaching in graduate schools, but the heavy academic emphasis was too stifling. I passed out the grade book in the first session of the semester and asked the students to put down the grade they wanted to live up to. I gave each student an hour of my time at the end of the semester (in lieu of a final exam) to tell me what they were going to do about what they learned in the course. The administration had problems with my tactics. I had problems with their head trips.

With my friend, Roberta Hestenes, we did help to sponsor a series of National Conferences on Small Groups with Fuller Seminary and Stephen's Ministry.

In the '80s, the new thing that we helped create for the church was a new paradigm for reaching out to broken people and hurting people in the community through support and recovery groups.

Early in my training I was drawn into the ministry of Sam Shoemaker, the rector of Calvary Episcopal Church in New York City. He had a heart for the "door" people.

Sam Shoemaker and his Faith at Work ministry had a big influence on my life in my student days in New York City.

As the small group movement became more popular in the '80s, we lost touch with the original vision of reaching out to people at the "door," and by the end of the eighties, we were largely a navel-gazing, head-shrinking, mutual admiration society content with being the people of God in the ivory tower.

It became my new passion to get the small group movement back to its roots—back to helping the broken people at the door. We started to create support programs for:

- divorce
- grief and loss
- addictions and compulsions
- codependency
- unemployed and unfulfilled
- stress management
- compassion fatigue
- waist watchers
- engaged couples
- newly married
- infertility
- parents of preschoolers
- parents of adolescents
- parents of children with learning disabilities
- single parents
- blended families
- midlife crisis
- golden years

Altogether, we created over 30 special courses for special needs in the community. And we devoted the majority of the time at the training seminars to their emphasis.

By the end of the '80s, we had over 10,000 churches involved in Serendipity programs. But I was restless and struggling to find out what God was going to do with the institutional church.

The '90s—Preparing for the 21st Century

Don Quixote has always been my hero. I have a collection of Quixote statues. Some on his trusty horse Rosenette. Chasing windmills. Wearing his helmet, lance extended. With Sancho at his side and *The Impossible Dream* in the background.

Call it madness if you wish, but I see God doing a whole new thing in the '90s to prepare his church for the next century.

Sure, there is a lot to be concerned about. The three building blocks for our society are gone: (a) the guaranteed job; (b) the extended family; and (c) the secure neighborhood. But this makes the local church all the more important, and the need to build relationships in everything we do as a church is crucial.

Serendipity has always targeted the people at the "door," especially the baby boomers. In the '60s this led us into the hootenanny, the coffee house, the light and sound shows and film festivals to reach the "flower children."

In the '70s this meant going into personal growth issues, encounter groups and psychological testing to reach out to people in the "me generation."

When the baby boomers became parents in the '80s, we offered support and recovery groups, "back to basics" Bible study and the extended family in the church for people who needed the church to help raise their children.

In the '90s, our target is much more diverse. We still have baby boomers on their way back to God reading *Victoria Magazine* and looking for an institutional church like the "good ole days" when they grew up. And we have the baby busters and the Generation X kids who will have nothing to do with the old institutional church.

Someone identified four audiences in every community.

UNCHURCHED AND UNCOMMITTED	UNCHURCHED BUT COMMITTED (parachurch)
CHURCHED BUT UNCOMMITTED	CHURCHED AND COMMITTED

Some churches appeal to one audience. For instance, the "seeker" church is targeted for the UNCHURCHED and UNCOMMITTED audience. Most traditional mainline churches target the CHURCHED but UNCOMMITTED audience. The parachurch movements reach the UNCHURCHED but COMMITTED audience, and the typical evangelical mainline church targets the CHURCHED and COMMITTED audience.

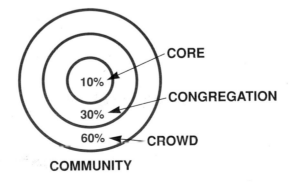

I am personally committed to targeting all four audiences with four different models for groups. Using Rick Warren's diagram of the four levels of commitment, we have developed Discipleship Groups for the 10% CORE who are ready for high commitment; Pulpit Groups for the 30% who attend church and are willing to go to a small group if they do not have to do homework; Special-Interest Groups for the 60% CROWD to appeal to their felt needs, and Seeker Groups for the COMMUNITY who are willing to come to a special event and work on their felt needs.

Over the last 40 years, it has been my privilege to be on the front line of the shaping of the church in general, and the small group movement in particular. Throughout those years I must admit to feelings of frustration with the institutional church—wondering if I was really making any significant impact. As Moe Pierce said to me: "The only difference between a rut and a grave is the dimensions."

On one hand, I cannot help but look back at "the good ole days" in the '60s when the baby boomers came alive in the coffee house scene. They were so creative. So open to change. So idealistic. But on the other hand, those of us who rebelled at the institutional church in the '60s are often the most resistant to change in the '90s.

And I have learned, not without pain and regret, that raising our fists in anger toward the church is not the answer. Because we are imperfect people, God's church is not perfect. But we *are* God's church!

With the remaining influence I will have on the church, I am dedicated to helping local congregations do their best to reach out to all four audiences. As I get older, I grow more appreciative of the saints in my life who represent each

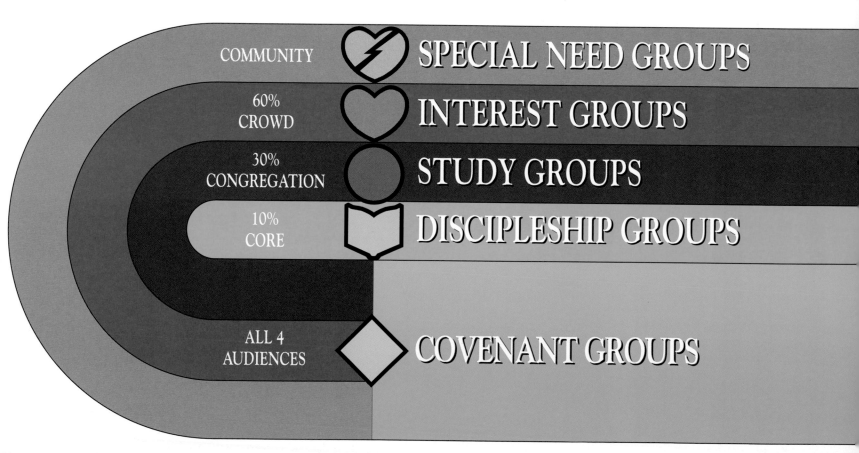

COMMUNITY — SPECIAL NEED GROUPS

60% CROWD — INTEREST GROUPS

30% CONGREGATION — STUDY GROUPS

10% CORE — DISCIPLESHIP GROUPS

ALL 4 AUDIENCES — COVENANT GROUPS

congregation's committed CORE. I truly hope Serendipity can help build your church's core both spiritually and numerically.

One way I envision the mainstay of most churches—the CONGREGATION who attend church regularly—to move into the CORE is through Pulpit Groups. Serendipity is offering a brand-new resource, *Exploring the Sermon,* which is a series based on the Scripture readings of the church year. Hopefully this will help involve those who typically attend only the Sunday worship service. I'm excited to think of multitudes of people joining a small group based upon the pastor's teaching from the pulpit Sunday morning.

Again, my heart has always gone out to the CROWD and the COMMUNITY, who still need to be introduced to the "reality" of Christian fellowship. Recent research shows that the churches in America, with few exceptions, simply are *not* growing. Yet, we all know that those people at the "door" certainly are not without needs. May God's Holy Spirit give us creative strategies for inviting those persons to join us. Serendipity will always attempt to provide resources for congregations to tastefully and effectively meet people "at the door."

I feel in a real sense that I have come full circle in my life. My beginnings were steeped in the organized church. In my younger years I moved away from those structures, challenging the church to open its eyes to the new things God was trying to do. Now the desire of my heart is to "make peace" with the institutional church, and to exert my energies (from within the church) to help God's people move forward with hands raised up to God and out to others. Here's to the dream!

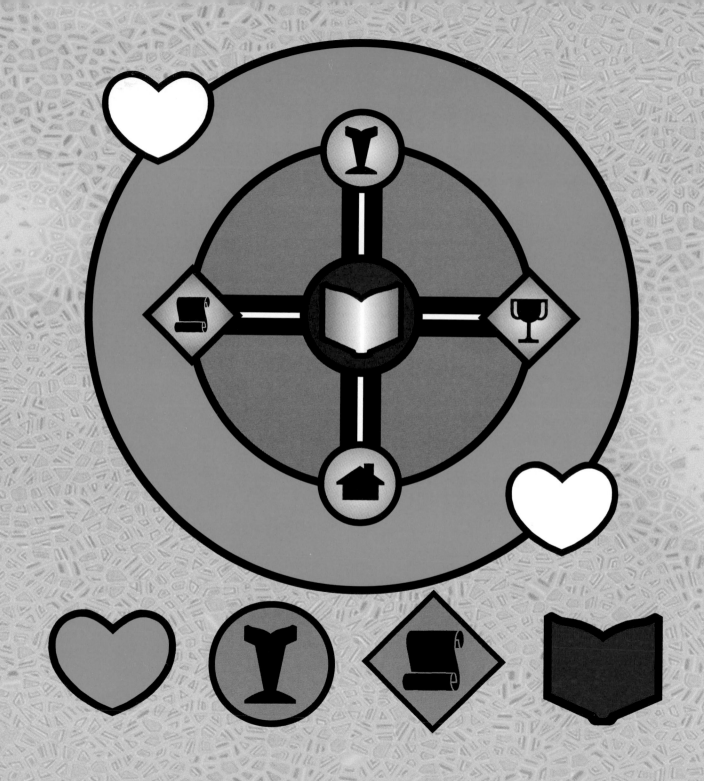

THEORY

The word "serendipity" means surprise. Unexpected, happy chance discoveries. When we were looking for a word to describe what can happen in a group when two or three people get together and share their lives, we stumbled onto this word.

Serendipity, as we use the word, is a fusion of group-building exercises, self-discovery Bible study and spiritual community. It takes place in a blending of interpersonal relationships that are mischievously revealing and outrageously healing. It is childlikeness and Christlikeness, laughter and tears, all mixed up together. It is frogs and frog-lovers, losers and sinners, caterpillars and Dulcineas on their way to becoming the people of God.

It is the super cool teenager and the little old lady finding out about each other. It is the joy that comes from personal discovery, the inner warmth that comes from honest, sincere praise.

It is mother and daughter, father and son, finding they are not so far apart. It is a fellowship of strugglers—sharing, caring, growing and discovering the new thing that God has for them.

It is the high-collared pastor and the low-collared layperson discovering that down deep inside each is a scared little child wanting to be known—but afraid to be found out.

It is a handful of people honestly wrestling with the purpose and meaning of their lives, open to the Spirit and the Bible, without fear of being stupid or wrong. It is the cup of cold water offered as fellow ministers of Christ, calling forth the best in one another.

It is the call in the middle of the night, the touch of an understanding friend, the mysterious, unexplainable bond that draws people together in Christ.

It is the "serendipity" of the Holy Spirit, setting us free to be the persons we were meant to be. One in the Spirit—holy, holey, wholly FREE.

In the next few pages, we have tried to introduce the concept of Serendipity under three categories: VISION—to see the potential of Serendipity in the church; DESIGN—to understand the process of Serendipity for building relationships; SKILLS—for leading groups with the Serendipity process.

VISION

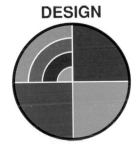

DESIGN

SKILLS

---

8 Assumptions Behind the Serendipity Group Model

1. *We* are created in the image of God and endowed with amazing potential.

2. This *potential* can be realized through Jesus Christ, in the company of a supportive Christian community.

3. To become a truly *supportive Christian community* we need to get to know one another in depth, and this takes time, effort and a common commitment to life together.

4. Personal *growth* begins with inner change—as we respond to the invitation of God for newness of life.

5. The *Holy Spirit* has endowed us with *spiritual gifts* for ministering to others within our supportive community, and through the community to the church and world at large.

6. *Scripture* is the living account of God's redemptive activity, and the primary guide to his will for right now.

7. Spiritual *wholeness* includes our whole being—our emotions, relationships, values and lifestyles.

8. *Celebration* happens naturally and spontaneously when we are set free in a supportive Christian community to discover and express the beautiful persons we are in Christ.

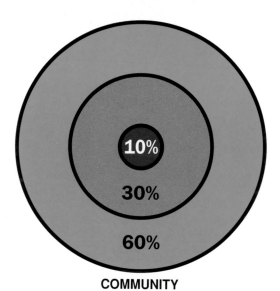

10%

30%

60%

COMMUNITY

VISION

Bill Hybels, the pastor of Willow Creek Community Church in Barrington, Illinois, tells the story of canvassing the neighborhood before starting a church and asking the people if they did not attend church to please explain why. He heard three common reasons: (1) you are boring; (2) you use language that nobody understands; and (3) all you do is ask for money.

When he started his church he vowed *not* to be boring, *not* to use religious words and *not* to ask the guests for money.

They do a lot of market research at Willow Creek—to find out who their audience is, and how to meet their felt needs. The same is true of any church that wants to be serious about their calling.

If you expect to hit all the people in your church, you will have to target these four audiences based on their felt needs. When it comes to a program for small groups, you need to offer four dif-

ferent kinds of groups. For the 10% CORE—Discipleship Groups; for the 30% CONGREGATION—Pulpit Groups; for the 60% CROWD—Special-Interest Groups, and for the COMMUNITY—Support and Seeker Groups. Though these groups vary in entry level and length of duration according to the particular audience they serve, they are all short-term. These groups can be offered anytime in the church year and they can meet at church.

There is one more kind of group, and it is the only group that targets all four levels of commitment in the church. It is a COVENANT GROUP. This is a long-term group.

I will use symbols from now on to describe these four groups: a *HEART* for SUPPORT groups; a *CIRCLE* for PULPIT

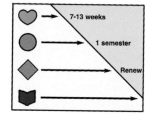

groups—to symbolize the link of the pulpit to a sharing group after the sermon; a *DIAMOND* to represent COVENANT groups—because diamonds are forever; and a *BOOK* to represent DISCIPLESHIP groups—because of the heavy emphasis on study.

SUPPORT GROUP

The purpose of a Support Group is to offer mutual support around a common need or concern, such as: divorce, grief and loss, unemployed or unfulfilled, single parents, parents of preschoolers, adoptive parents, newly married, blended families, caregivers of Alzheimer's, and victims of abuse, violence, SIDS, AIDS, etc.

This group is short-term—seven to 13 weeks, with low-level entry—that is, all that is required of a group member is to show up. After the initial period is over, the group can dismiss or switch to another, longer, group model.

All you need to be a leader of a Support Group is life experience. If you are a single parent, you would make a good leader of a short-term support group for single parents.

STRENGTHS:
1. Starts where people feel a need or concern.
2. Entry or reentry point for people to come back to the church.
3. Life experience is all the leader needs to have.

WEAKNESSES:
1. "Felt need" is no substitute for spiritual formation.
2. Short-term duration not long enough for many needs.
3. Life experience for the leader is not enough for some deeper needs.

PULPIT GROUP

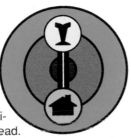

The purpose of this group is to link the teaching of the pulpit to a sharing group after the sermon. This is the easiest group to launch and lead.

The CONGREGATION who attends regularly will like this kind of group because it requires no homework and very few skills to lead the group. A handout in the Sunday bulletin gives the group the questions to start the group meeting, to discuss the Scripture passage and to apply the passage to their lives.

The group can meet immediately after the worship service during Sunday school, Sunday evening, or any other time during the week.

All you need to be the leader of a Pulpit Group is an interest in people and attendance at the Sunday morning worship service.

STRENGTHS:
1. One integrated system for the whole church family.
2. Pastor becomes the cheerleader—utilizing the power of the pulpit.
3. Leader's role made easy because the pastor's sermon prepares everyone to share.

WEAKNESSES:
1. Rules out people who do not come to church.
2. Dependent upon a good teaching pastor.
3. Group can become ingrown.

DISCIPLESHIP GROUP

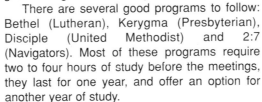

The purpose of a Discipleship Group is to offer a group for the 10% highly committed people in the church to do heavy-duty Bible study and grow through accountability.

There are several good programs to follow: Bethel (Lutheran), Kerygma (Presbyterian), Disciple (United Methodist) and 2:7 (Navigators). Most of these programs require two to four hours of study before the meetings, they last for one year, and offer an option for another year of study.

Hopefully, everyone in a church will get to the place in their spiritual journey that they feel the need to be in a year-long Discipleship Group. But our experience has found that only 10% of a church will sign up for this group—so if you only offer this kind of a group you will write off 90% of your people.

STRENGTHS:
1. Spiritual discipline of an in-depth study with homework.
2. Accountability to a committed group.
3. Master-Teacher component.

WEAKNESSES:
1. Will appeal to only 10%.
2. Closed group.
3. Saps energy of pastor.

COVENANT GROUP

The purpose of a Covenant Group is to become an extended family over a long period of time. Unlike the other three group models, the Covenant Group is targeted for all four levels of commitment—the 10%, 30%, 60% and people at the door.

The symbol for a Covenant Group is a diamond—because "diamonds are forever."

The Covenant Group begins by people making a "covenant" for six weeks. After this trial period, the group can renew their covenant for the rest of the year (or school year) ... and for another year if they wish.

In the next two sections we will discuss the Covenant Group in greater detail. The leader of a Covenant Group needs to know a little more about group process and caregiving, which is what the next two sections are all about.

STRENGTHS:
1. Long-term relationships.
2. Six-week trial / renewal options.
3. Democratic / adjustable agenda.

WEAKNESSES:
1. Danger of burnout if it lasts too long.
2. Danger of becoming ingrown.
3. Risk of getting stuck on leader's hobbyhorse.

DESIGN

In the previous section, we introduced the four kinds of groups and described the fourth group, the Covenant Group or Diamond Group, as the only one that is long-term—because diamonds are forever.

In this section, we want to focus on the Long-Term Group in three ways: key strategies; the lifecycle of a Long-Term Group; and the approach to Bible study during that lifecycle.

THE BIG THREE

If you can remember these strategies, you will understand our whole philosophy of ministry for small groups in the church: • The Three-Legged Stool • The Flying Wedge • The Baseball Diamond. The three are interconnected and each builds upon the one before.

STRATEGY 1:

The Three-Legged Stool.

This strategy pertains to the essentials for a healthy small group. There was a time in the early '50s that people believed you could build a small group completely around the disciplines of Bible study and prayer. Then, in the '60s, the emphasis changed to mission and service; and finally, in the '70s, to group building and support.

All of these movements failed, and we have today a whole lot of churches that are turned off because they tried groups with a single focus and the groups went sour.

We need all three emphases to make a healthy group: (a) Bible study (BOOK); (b) group building and support (HEART); and (c) service or mission (ARROW). We call this "The Three-Legged Stool" for healthy small groups.

Bible Study / Content: Bible study is the most important element in the life of a healthy small group, but it cannot stand alone anymore than a one-legged stool can stand alone. You've got to have two more legs!

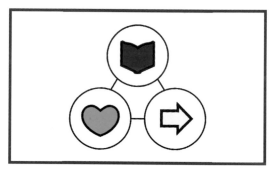

Group Building / Support: This is the process of "becoming" a group and caring for one another, like they did in the Upper Room. This takes time. Effort. Commitment. And unless a group is committed to this—and works at it—the group will probably fall apart. On the other hand, if a group does nothing but group building (like in so many support groups today) the group will become codependent, which is most unfortunate.

Service or Mission: The thing that will save a group from becoming ingrown and codependent is service or mission—reaching out to others. Alcoholics Anonymous really pushes Step 12: "Having had a spiritual awakening as the result of these steps, we tried to carry this message to alcoholics, and to practice these principles in all our affairs." To reach out in love to others is not just for their sake. It is essential for the health of a group.

But to build a small group strictly around service or mission is also very dangerous, because it will lead to burnout. Elizabeth O'Connor was very prophetic when she said: "The journey outward without the journey inward is the road to burnout." This is what is happening to so many "mission" groups today.

Dawson Troutman, the founder of the Navigators, said: "The greatest danger to any chain is its *strongest* link." This is especially true when it comes to small groups.

STRATEGY 2:

The Flying Wedge.

In the first strategy, we learned that there are three essential elements in a healthy group. Now, in the second strategy, we will learn how to shuffle these three elements to get the most "miles out of every gallon." Basically, you can choose between two options:

- *Static Agenda:* Every meeting is split into three equal parts, like a three-layer cake; (a) 30 minutes for Bible study; (b) 30 minutes for group building and support; and (c) 30 minutes for decision making about the service or mission. This is the old system of InterVarsity in the '50s and it keeps a group in balance—but it tends to be monotonous.

- *Dynamic Agenda:* The period that the group is going to be together is seen as a package. For instance, if the group is going to meet for a school year—from September to May—you have nine months to play with.

Then you ask the question: "If we are going to be together for nine months and we want to keep a balanced diet with the three essentials of Bible study, group building and service, what do we need to major on first?" If you ask this question, you can divide the nine months into three stages ... and concentrate on group building in stage 1.

LIFECYCLE

Then, after the group has really become a group, you can shift the formula to allow for greater time for Bible study and decision making. And by the end of the year, all three essentials have received equal time.

Understood correctly, the Flying Wedge Strategy will help pastors and small group trainers see how the goal of "spiritual formation" can be accomplished best in a small group format when the priority is given over to group building at the beginning.

STRATEGY 3:

The Baseball Diamond.

In the first strategy, we have the big picture—the three essentials. In the second strategy, we see how group building takes priority in the beginning stage of a group.

Now, we are ready to ask the questions, "What does group building look like?" and "What is the process for becoming a group?"

The best illustration we can use is a baseball diamond, with home plate being "koinonia" or depth Christian community. This is what a small group needs to become ... like the Upper Room gathering in the 50 days leading to Pentecost. And to get to home plate, you have to go around three bases like the three bases of a baseball diamond.

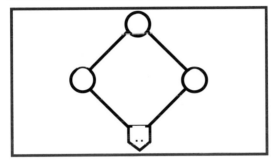

First Base: History Giving. Some people call this "unpacking." Others call it "getting acquainted." We call it "history giving" because we want you to tell your spiritual story to one another.
• YOUR PAST: Your roots. Early memories. Significant people and places. Milestones in your spiritual development. • YOUR PRESENT: Where you are right now in your spiritual pilgrimage. • YOUR FUTURE: Where you want to be. Your hopes and dreams.

Your "story" is important to your group if you are ever going to be a caring community. The GREATEST GIFT you can give your group is the gift of your story.

Second Base: Affirmation. Some people call this "feedback," but feedback could mean negative response and we do not believe a group should ever engage in negative feedback.

WHAT IS A GROUP?

So what is a small group, anyway? Roberta Hestenes, one of the great pioneers of the small group movement, has defined a small group in this way:

"A Christian small group is an intentional, face-to-face gathering of 3 to 12 people on a regular time schedule with the common purpose of discovering and growing in the possibilities of the abundant life in Christ."

Consider the elements of this definition:

"intentional"
This refers to the covenant or agreement which the group establishes at the beginning to identify the responsibilities and accountability of the group members. Group members *choose* to be involved.

"face-to-face"
When people meet face-to-face, the gathering can produce honesty, freedom, trust, evaluation and growth uniquely found in interpersonal relationships. Besides, 90% of all communication is nonverbal.

"3-12 people"
With less than three people, you don't have a group, and with more than 12 you begin to lose intimacy.

"regular time schedule"
This is essential to foster loyalty and consistency among group members. Many small groups meet weekly, especially at the beginning, so bonding can occur.

"common purpose"
If a group does not share a common vision and common goals, it will eventually fail. People follow clearly understandable ideas and direction.

"discovering and growing"
A small group is an ideal place for a non-Christian to discover what following Jesus is all about. It is also a place for believers to grow in their faith.

"the abundant life in Christ"
Small groups have the capacity to make Christianity come to life through prayer, discussion, study, fellowship and ministry.

We prefer the method that Jesus used when he called Simon a "Rock," and changed his name and his life with this affirmation; or when he said to Zacchaeus, "I see you as a son of Abraham"—that is, somebody of value. (He, in fact, was a son of Abraham, but he wasn't acting like one ... and it took the affirmation of Jesus to help him see this.)

Second base is saying something like, "Thanks for sharing ..."; "I appreciate what you shared ..."; "Your story became a gift to me ..." Every group needs to learn how to do this, and we specifically work on this in the group-building process.

Third Base: Goal Setting. Once affirmed, the group is ready to move on and share on a deeper level. This is sometimes called the need level. Ask the group members to explain this in the positive: "Where do you need to move on ... ?" "What is God saying to you?" "What is keeping you from ... ?"

Third base is what the disciples must have shared when they returned to the Upper Room after Christ's ascension—scared, frightened, confused and hurting. Can you hear the disciples in the room saying, "I can't believe that God has left us"; "I'm afraid"; "I'm angry"? And can you imagine the Holy Spirit beginning to reach out to these hurting people and "bind up their wounds" as he had promised? The Holy Spirit was discovered in this atmosphere of broken people.

Home Plate: Koinonia. Nowhere in the Bible is the Greek word *koinonia* defined. It defies definition. But the disciples must have experienced something in the Upper Room, because they were empowered with a new kind of power. The "walking wounded" became the "wounded healers" in this community of love and support.

Some have tried to describe this as bonding, as catharsis, as a symphony orchestra of individual instruments—each contributing their gift. But once a group reaches this level of being, lives are changed and the church comes alive! The power and ministry of the Holy Spirit is released. This is what the first six to eight weeks in a small group are all about birthing and bonding.

LIFECYCLE OF A LONG-TERM / COVENANT GROUP

In the previous sections we talked about the four models of groups and the strategies for group building and group process. Now, we want to focus in particular on one of the four models of groups—the COVENANT GROUP—and in particular on the lifecycle or life stages of this kind of group.

Unlike the other models for groups in the church, the Covenant Group is designed to last a long time. In fact, the purpose of the group is to become an extended family to one another.

Like any other living organism, a Covenant Group has a birth, an adolescence, a maturity, and a declining period. (We don't call the last period a death.) We call the four periods in the life of a Covenant Group a four-stage lifecycle.

STAGE 1: *Birth Stage.*

The first stage in a Covenant Group is the beginning period—generally six to seven weeks. The purpose of this stage is to get acquainted and to bond as a group.

SIX PRINCIPLES FOR BIBLE STUDY FOR BEGINNER GROUPS / BIBLE STUDY 101

1. **Group vs. Personal Bible Study:** Group Bible study is different from personal Bible study. The purpose is different, particularly in the beginning stage. The purpose of GROUP Bible study in the beginning stage is "to become a group"—and the way you become a group is by sharing your spiritual stories with one another.

2. **Disclosure Scale:** Sharing your spiritual story with anybody is scary (particularly with people you do not know), but it is easier if you can start off by talking about somebody else's spiritual story first. Then you don't feel so bad comparing "your story" to the story in Scripture. This is called moving across the disclosure scale. Applied to Bible study, it looks this way:

DISCLOSURE SCALE	
Start with low risk	End with high risk
STORY IN SCRIPTURE	MY OWN STORY
How Simon Peter met God	How I met God
What's going on in Peter's life	What's happening in my life

3. **Open Questions / Right Brain:** Open-ended questions are better than closed questions. Open questions allow for options, observations and a variety of opinions in which no one is right or wrong.

Closed questions shut down discussion in a group.

"Right-brained" questions are better than "left-brained" questions. Right-brained questions seek out your first impressions, color, tone, texture, motives and subjective "feelings" about the text. Right-brain oriented questions are especially good in narrative stories where you are asked to share what you would do in that situation.

4. **Multiple-Choice Options:** Multiple-choice options encourage people who know very little about the Bible. Given a set of multiple-choice options, a young Christian is not threatened, and a shy person is not intimidated. Everybody has something to contribute.

5. **Tight Agenda:** A tight agenda is better than a loose agenda for beginner groups. The engineer in your group was goosey already about this group when he arrived. Now, he's terrified at the thought of sharing.

6. **The Fearless Foursome:** Groups of 4 are better than groups of 10 or 12 for sharing and discussion. In your group, you've got three engineers, an accountant, a lawyer and a preacher. Who do you think is going to do the talking? And how long do you think it is going to take to finish the Bible study?

You're right. If you keep those people together, you've got problems. But if you split into groups of 4, everyone will be able to participate and BE THROUGH WITH THE BIBLE STUDY IN 30 MINUTES.

How to Decide On a Beginner Group Covenant

Go around your group on the first half-finished sentence below and ask everyone to finish the sentence. Take notes and write down what the group agreed upon as the purpose. Then, go around on the second sentence, etc. until you have worked out your group covenant together.

1. The purpose of our group is ...
2. Our specific goals are ...
3. We will meet _____ times, every _____ week, after which we will evaluate our group before continuing.
4. We will meet on _____(day) from _____ (time) to _____, and strive to start on time and close on time.
5. We will meet at _____ (place) or rotate where we meet.
6. We will agree to one or more of the following disciplines:
   ❏ Attendance: To give priority to the group meetings.
   ❏ Participation: To share responsibility for the group.
   ❏ Confidentiality: To keep anything that is said strictly confidential.
   ❏ Accountability: To give permission to group members to hold each other accountable ... to the goals you set for yourself.
   ❏ Accessibility: To give one another the right to call upon one another in time of need—even in the middle of the night.
   ❏ Empty Chair: To keep an empty chair for others and seek to reach out to people like us who need this place of caring.

In the previous section, we have already discussed two of the three parts of the birth stage of a Covenant Group: The HEART and the ARROW. Now, we are going to look at the BOOK—the Bible study approach in the birth stage.

It is important to remember that the purpose of the birth stage is to get acquainted. This requires that the approach to Bible study be designed to fulfill this purpose.

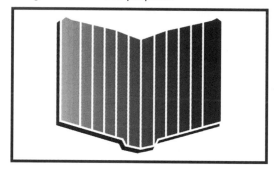

We call the beginner Bible study approach Scripture sharing or story sharing or 101 Bible study. The purpose is to share your story through stories in Scripture.

We have discovered the best way to accomplish this is to provide a guided questionnaire that has a built-in disclosure scale—from light questions at the beginning to heavy questions at the close.

And there is a certain way to ask questions—which we call the Serendipity formula.

The question must be:
• open-ended
• no right or wrong answers
• multiple-choice options

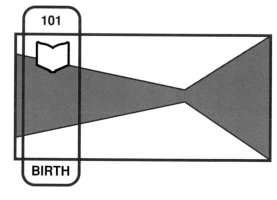

The questions should be framed so that anyone in the group can answer—without previous Bible knowledge—and share how the story or lesson in the Scripture intersects their own life story. For instance:

• Who do you identify with in this story—the Prodigal Son, the older brother or the father?
• Where are you right now in your own relationship with your father?
• How did the way you "left home" or "stayed home" compare with the two brothers in the Bible story?

If you could place a dollar price on the questions, based on the amount it will cost you to answer the question, the first question should cost you in disclosure about 25 cents and the last question should cost you about 10 dollars.

STAGE 2: *Growth Stage.*

After a few weeks, the group should be ready to move to a deeper level of Bible study—what we call 201.

The group needs to remember that the overall purpose of the group includes MISSION—bringing new people into the group. Often, the

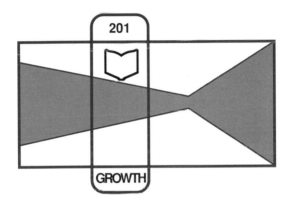

deeper approach to Bible study will keep people from entering the group.

So how can a group go deeper in Bible study and still bring new people into the group? Here are two options: Start off the second period with a three-week open period, when new members are brought into the group—when the Bible study approach is like 101. The second option is to use a two-track Bible study course like the Serendipity 201 Focus Group courses—which have two options for each session: light and heavy tracks. The leader calls the "option play" whenever a new member comes to the group—and uses the light track.

STAGE 3: *Depth Stage.*

When the Covenant Group is ready for heavy-duty Bible study, the group needs to keep in mind the biblical background of all of the members of the group.

If you have people in the group with little or no biblical background, we recommend using a

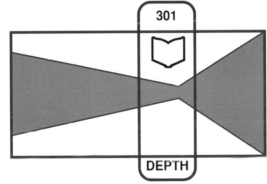

Serendipity 301 Group Study series course. These courses have reference notes on the same passage as the questions—to help a novice in the Bible keep up to speed. These notes, which are a running commentary on the Scripture text, contain definitions of terms and background information on key people, places and events to go along with each session.

STAGE 4: *Graduation.*

The most difficult stage in the life of a group is the release stage. A good group will find it hard to quit, but if they don't they will run the risk of burnout.

We recommend three things. First, hold annual graduation events when all of the groups in the church meet together for a banquet to celebrate

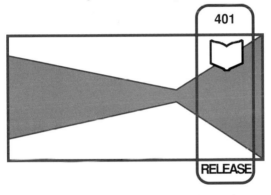

their year. The month of May is a good time for this because everyone is thinking graduation.

Second, prepare the groups for disbanding by going through a debriefing period. Provide the groups with a questionnaire to follow that asks the group to:
- remember the good times
- affirm one another—the gifts that you have come to recognize in one another
- discuss God's leading—what God would have you do as a group
- share how you feel about giving up your life together

Third, become a reunion group that still meets twice a year to celebrate the new thing that God is doing in your lives.

SKILLS

In any kind of Serendipity event or group, the role of the leader is crucial, but not difficult, as long as the leader will keep to the basic principles of group building and group process that we discussed in the last section.

Here is one more important strategy to keep in mind: the level playing field. In the old days, we used to classify people in a relationship as talkers or listeners, introverts or extroverts, givers or receivers, thinkers or feelers, etc. And in group relationships, we would describe these people as dominators, preachers, gatekeepers, doormats, etc. And in church groups, we have those who are familiar with church language or the Bible and those who have no religious or biblical background.

It is important at the beginning of a meeting to start the sharing where all of these kinds of people can start even. We call it "leveling the playing field" or starting at the "child" level—where everybody is equal. Then, like a pendulum, you can swing from the "child" level to the "spirit" level—from light to heavy, from hilarity to healing, from childlikeness to Christlikeness.

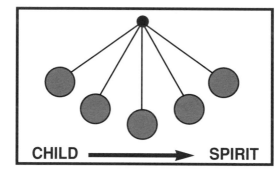

CHILD → SPIRIT

THE THREE-PART AGENDA

To apply this principle of leveling the playing field to a small group, we recommend that a meeting be built around a three-part agenda with specific time limits for the first two parts.

GATHERING: 15 Minutes

The first part of the agenda is the gathering time. The purpose of this time is to "unpack" as latecomers arrive. While coffee or refreshments are served, these things should be addressed:

- Welcome to any new members
- Reporting in on any old business—such as a prayer request from the former meeting
- Ice-Breaker question or interactive exercise
- Opening prayer

In the center of this encyclopedia, there are nearly 100 interactive exercises for various topics. A question or exercise should be chosen that roughly relates to the study or topic of the meeting; remember the principle to "level the playing field" and "to meet at the child" in framing this question—so that everyone can share a little about themselves.

For instance, if the topic or study for the meeting is about family, a good ice-breaker question might be:

- Where were you living when you were 7 years old?
- When you were a child, what was the longest trip you took with your family?
- Who was your hero when you were a kid?

The leader should go first and "set the pace" by answering the question so the rest of the group will know how much time to take and how deep to go.

Keep time, and at the end of the allotted time in the agenda call time and open the meeting, if it is appropriate, with a short prayer. This will focus the group and prepare the group to move to the next phase—that is, the study or business of the meeting.

STUDY: 30 Minutes

The middle section of a meeting will vary according to the nature and purpose of the group. For small group meetings where the focus is on nurture or Bible study, the middle portion of the meeting is the "meat of the sandwich."

In planning the approach to the study time, it is important to decide where the group is in their lifecycle as a group. (The lifecycle was described in detail in the previous section.)

If a group is in the formative or birth stage (just getting started), the way the group approaches the study must focus on group building—or story sharing. For instance, if the topic is spiritual formation, or the story of Creation in the Bible, you might ask everyone to share when they first felt the tug of God on their lives or when the story of Creation took on special meaning to them.

In the previous section, we recommended the use of subgroups for more participation in discussion. Simply ask the group to divide into groups of 4 by counting off—1,2,3,4 ... 1,2,3,4, etc. Rearrange chairs so that each group can sit close together.

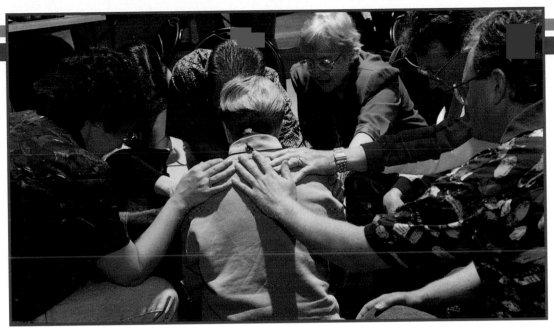

CARING: 30–45 Minutes

The third stage in the three-part agenda is the closing or caring time. In process language, this might be called congruence, catharsis, or closure. This is the time when the personal stuff is dealt with.

We recommend this part of a small group meeting start out with prayer requests: "How can we help you this week in prayer?" This is a very open-ended question. Anyone can answer this.

In the first few meetings, a group will probably give "football and weather" prayer requests. A good rule to follow is that the prayer requests must deal with something you are facing in your own life or family or job situation.

When a group has built some confidence, the prayer requests will go deeper—like "Please pray for our son." At this point, the leader will have to make a judgment call. You can either come back with a follow-up question—like "Would you explain?"—or you can simply jot down the request and go on to the next person. You cannot do both.

We recommend this rule when somebody opens up and needs more time. If this is the first time this need has been shared in the group, the leader gives the person more time to share—the rest of the time in the meeting if necessary. But the leader will do this only once for that need. In the next meeting, the person with this need may be asked to "report in" on the situation briefly at the beginning of the meeting, before the opening prayer. Then, the meeting continues with the purpose at hand. YOU MUST NOT BUILD A GROUP AROUND THE NEED OF ONE PERSON!

What do you do if the person needs more time? We recommend that the leader say this: "We are going to stop on time and conclude with a closing prayer ... but I am going to stay after the meeting with this person. If you can stay for a few minutes, you are welcome." Again, the rule is to close on time. But if there is someone who needs more time, the leader stays after the meeting—and everyone else is invited to stay.

Now, how do you move into the closing prayer time? Here are some suggestions for the leader to follow:

WEEK 1: The leader says, "I will pray," and closes the meeting with prayer.

WEEK 2: The leader asks for volunteers: "Who will take Mary's request?"; "Who will take Bob's request?"; etc. Those who are comfortable praying out loud will volunteer.

WEEK 3: Now some in the group will be ready for more spontaneous prayer. So the leader says, "Two or three of you please pray, and I will close."

WEEK 4: The leader says, "Let's go around and let everyone finish this sentence: 'God, this is _____ (your name); I want to thank you for _____.'"

But even here, we would recommend saying, "If anyone would like to say their prayer in silence, just say 'Amen' at the close so that the next person will know when to start."

CROWD BREAKERS

FOR LARGE GROUPS

WARM-UP CALISTHENICS

SLAP-DOWNS

Stretch your left arm straight out and slap it down with your right hand—from the shoulder to the finger tips and back again. Do the same with your right arm, using your left hand. Then stand up and, with both hands, slap down your left leg. Do the same to your right leg.

SHOULDER RUB-DOWN

Stand, turn to the right, and rub the shoulders of the person to your right. Then, turn toward the person on your left and rub their shoulders.

HEAD, SHOULDERS, KNEES, TOES

To the tune of *There's a Tavern in the Town*, sing the following and touch the corresponding parts of the body.

> *Head and shoulders, knees and toes,*
> *   knees and toes.*
> *Head and shoulders, knees and toes,*
> *   knees and toes.*
> *Eyes and ears and mouth and nose.*
> *Head and shoulders, knees and toes,*
> *   knees and toes.*

TENSION BREAKERS

FINGERS UP

Pair off in 4s. Put your hands behind your back. On the word GO, everyone brings their hands out in front of them with any number of fingers up. The first person to call out the correct total number of fingers up (between you and your partner) wins. Repeat as needed for the best-two-out-of-three.

MIRROR

In 2s: One person puts their hands up, fingers out, and proceeds to hand-dance, moving their hands as against a glass. The partner, with his or her hands about an inch away, should try to keep up with the movement exactly, as though they were the reflection in a mirror. Then reverse the roles and do it again. In 4s: Two pairs of partners get together, crisscross from each other. Each pair tries to hand-dance as though the other pair were not there. (For added fun, allow body and feet movements as well.)

MORAH (Italian Karate)

The same as "Fingers Up" except each person puts just *one* hand in front of them with any number of fingers up and calls out a total as they bring their hand around *before* seeing any fingers! Keep playing until one of the partners guesses the right number.

WHO STOLE MY CHICKENS AND MY HENS?

Sit in groups of 2, facing your partner. Put to the motions of patty-cake, this song and the motions go as follows:

Who (slap your legs) *stole* (clap) *my chickens* (right hand to partner's right hand)

and (clap) *my hens* (left hand to partner's left hand) *and* (clap; pause; both hands to partner's both hands)

Who (slap your legs) *stole* (clap) *my chickens* (right hand to partner's right hand) *and* (clap) *my hens?* (left hand to partner's left hand; *and* clap; pause; both hands to partner's both hands) Repeat three times ... going faster and faster.

61

MIXERS

FIND YOUR SONG MEMBERS

Using as many song titles as there will be groups, put each title on eight slips of paper. Mix up and pass out slips. Everybody sings their song until their group of 8 is formed.

FIND YOUR PUZZLE MEMBERS

Using as many pictures as there will be groups, cut each into eight pieces. Mix up and distribute. Each person, having one-eighth of a puzzle, will look for the puzzle pieces corresponding to theirs to put the picture together.

SERENDIPITY BINGO

Question one person on a point. If they answer "yes," put their name in the square. Let that person question you. Then ask someone else a question. Keep going until someone has six "yes" answers in a row—horizontally, vertically or diagonally.

Uses mouthwash regularly.	Can whistle *Dixie.*	Watches cartoons.	Has hole in sock now.	Plays chess regularly.	Takes bubble baths.
Sleeps in church.	Has walked into wrong restroom.	Has broken a bone.	Refuses to walk under ladders.	Loves raw oysters.	Is an only child.
Can touch palms on floor.	Detective story fan.	Watches soap operas.	Has been expelled from school.	Has milked a cow.	Has been to Hawaii.
Has TP'd a house.	Writes poetry.	Weighs under 100 pounds.	Loves broccoli.	Can do back bend.	Reads *Peanuts.*
Never changed a diaper.	Owns a motor-cycle.	Sleeps on a water bed.	Loves classical music.	Has scar three inches long.	Has played hooky.
Can touch tongue to nose.	Still has tonsils.	Can wiggle ears.	Eats health foods.	Overdrew bank account recently.	Moved last year.

NONSENSE RHYMES

To get the crowd on the edge of their chairs, try doing the same thing at the same time in rhyme and rhythm:

RABBIT

Slap your legs, then clap your hands.

> Rabbit in the bean patch
> Possum in the pot
> Try to stop the fiddler
> While the fiddler's hot.

Try it again. This time slap your left knee with your right hand and your neighbors knee with your left hand. Then clap ... and reverse it.

HARRY

Oh (make O with fingers), *I* (point to eye) *say* (point to mouth) *have you heard* (ear) *about Harry* (hair) *who just* (chest) *got back* (back) *from the front* (stomach) *where he was needed* (knee) *at the foot* (foot) *of the army* (arm). *Everybody's* (hands up) *heard* (ear) *about Harry* (hair). *Hip* (hip) *Hip* (hip) *Hurray* (hands up)!

DUM DUM

Slap your knees twice as you say the words *Dum Dum*. Then grab your nose with your left hand and your left ear with your right hand while you say *Diddy Diddy*. Slap your knees twice again to the words *Dum Dum*. Now grab your nose with your right hand and your right ear with your left hand while you say *Da Da*. Go faster and faster. *Dum Dum Diddy Diddy Dum Dum Da Da. Dum Dum Diddy Diddy Dum Dum Da Da,* etc.

FUN SONGS

LOVE ROUND

Divide the "crowd" into three groups. Start one group on the first line. When they begin the second line, bring the next group in on the first line. As the first group moves to the third line, bring in the last group. Sing through the song twice, cutting out each group as it concludes.

Love, love, love. That's what it's all about.
'Cause God loves us, we love each other,
Mother, father, sister, brother,
Everybody sing and shout!
'Cause that's what it's all about!

ROW, ROW, ROW YOUR BOAT

To the words, use four motions: (a) rowing, (b) gently, (c) merrily, (d) dream. Sing as a round, faster and faster.

Row, row, row your boat,
Gently down the stream.
Merrily, merrily, merrily, merrily,
Life is but a dream.

HOKEY POKEY

Act out the motions of the song.

Put your right hand in.
Put your right hand out.
Put your right hand in and shake it all
about.
You do the hokey pokey.
And turn yourself around.
That's what it's all about.

Then continue with: (a) left hand; (b) right foot; (c) left foot; (d) your whole self.

CELEBRATION DANCES

WE ARE ONE IN THE SPIRIT

Stand in rows; put your arms over the shoulders of those on either side; step out with your left foot in the left direction—three steps and a kick with your right foot. Then reverse direction—three steps and a kick ... like the *Cancan.*

We (step) *are* (step) *one* (step and kick) *in* (step) *the* (step) *Spirit* (step and kick) ...

LORD OF THE DANCE

Sing with the steps of the *Bunny Hop*—same as *It's a Small World* on the next page.

"I danced in the morning when the world
was begun,
And I danced in the moon and the stars
and the sun.
I came down from heaven and I danced on
the earth,
In Bethlehem I had my birth."

CHORUS:
"Dance, dance, wherever you may be,
I am the Lord of the Dance," said He.
"And I'll lead you on wherever you may be.
"And I'll lead you all in the Dance," said He.

"I danced for the scribes and the Pharisees,
But they would not dance, and they would
not follow me.
I danced for the fishermen, for James and
John,
They followed me, and the Dance went
on." (Repeat CHORUS)

There are some other steps which a Jewish expert can teach if you know someone.

Ha-va • na-gi-la
Ha-va • na-gi-la
Ha-va • na-gi-la • v'-nis-m'cha (repeat)
Ha-va • n'-ra-n'-na
Ha-va • n'-ra-n'-na
Ha-va • n'-ra-n'-na • v'-nis-m'cha (repeat)
U-ru
U-ru • a-chim
U-ru • a-chim • b'-lev • sa-may-ach
U-ru • a-chim • b'-lev • sa-may-ach
U-ru • a-chim • b'-lev • sa-may-ach
U-ru • a-chim • b'-lev • sa-may-ach
U-ru • a-chim
U-ru • a-chim
B'-lev • sa-may-ach

IT'S A SMALL WORLD

Here is an enchanting, childlike song that goes perfectly with the *Bunny Hop*. Have the group turn in rows and form a conga line with their hands on the hips of the person in front of them. Do the steps of the *Bunny Hop* to the beat of the music: right foot—two kicks to the right; left foot—two kicks to the left; one hop forward; one hop backward; three hops forward. Repeat.

> *It's a world of laughter, a world of tears;*
> *It's a world of hope and a world of fears.*
> *There's so much that we share*
> *that it's time we're aware.*
> *It's a small world after all.*
> > *It's a small world after all.*
> > *It's a small world after all.*
> > *It's a small world after all.*
> > *It's a small, small world.*
> *There is just one moon and one golden sun,*
> *and a smile means friendship to everyone.*
> *Though the mountains divide*
> *and the oceans are wide.*
> *It's a small world after all.*
> > *It's a small world after all.*
> > *It's a small world after all.*
> > *It's a small world after all.*
> > *It's a small, small world.*

HA-VA NA-GI-LA

This is a Jewish song danced to the square dance grapevine step. Have everyone circle up and join hands around the group. Start out by walking to the left in this fashion: STEP 1—right foot in front of the left foot; STEP 2—left foot slides back in place; STEP 3—right foot behind left foot; STEP 4—left foot back in place.

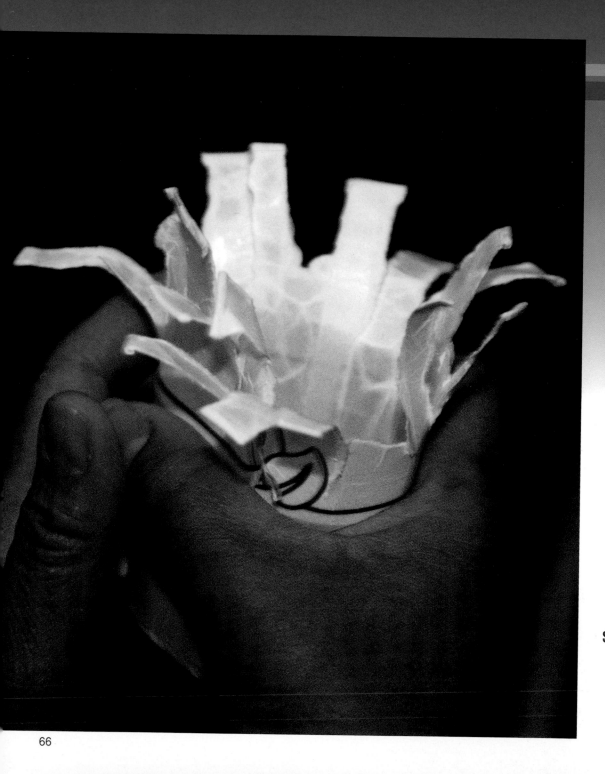

FOR SMALL GROUPS

COMMUNICATION ACTIVITIES

GROUP-BUILDING GAMES

IMAGINARY BALL

Make believe there is an imaginary ball in your group and throw it back and forth. To add excitement, ask everyone to change the shape and weight of the ball before tossing it. When it gets going, holler out, *"It's hot—move it fast!"*

MOTORMOUTH

Make believe your small group is a motor. See how much speed you can achieve. At the word GO, the first person turns their head to the right, making the sound for the specified motor; then the next person turns their head to the right, repeating the sound, etc. The first group to finish the specified number of laps should cheer.

Round One:

  Go-carts ... for five laps ... and the sound is "putt."

Round Two:

  Motorcycles ... for seven laps ... and the sound is "rrrrrr."

Round Three:

  Racing cars at the Indianapolis Motor Speedway ... for 10 laps ... and the sound is "zooooommmm."

CHARADES

Place a name tag *(Little Red Riding Hood, Goliath, Romeo or Juliet, Dallas Cowboy Cheerleader, John Wayne,* etc.) on the back of each person in a group of up to 8. First person stands and turns around so the others in the group can see the tag. Then, in silence, the group members act out this thing or person until the one with the name tag guesses who they are. When that person guesses correctly, the next person stands and turns around. The group acts out this thing ... etc. until everyone in the group has guessed.

RHYTHM

First, count off around your group: *one, two, three,* etc. Then, altogether, slap your knees; clap your hands; snap your right fingers; and then your left fingers. This is the rhythm to keep repeating. Then, after everyone gets the hang of it, the number one person calls out their number (*"One"*) as they snap their right fingers ... and then somebody else's number (such as *"Three"*) as they snap their left fingers.

When your number is called, you respond with your number when you snap your right fingers ... and somebody else's number when you snap your left fingers.

NONVERBAL RHYTHM

Same rhythm as above, except you use signs instead of numbers. First, everyone thinks of a crazy action and demonstrates it to the group. You could *scratch your ear,* another might *rub their stomach,* another *pull their hair,* etc.

Now, after your group has slapped their

knees twice and clapped their hands twice, the number one person does their sign (such as pulling their hair) ... and somebody else's sign (such as scratching their ear). Then, everybody slaps their knees and claps their hands in rhythm and the one whose sign was given shows his or her sign ... and someone else's sign, etc.

If anyone breaks the rhythm or fails to come in when their sign is given, they go to

the end of the line and everyone moves up a seat, *but keeps their own sign.*

CATEGORIES

Same rhythm as above, except that instead of numbers or actions you use categories: *football players, famous singers, nursery rhymes,* etc., and a little different procedure.

First, everyone thinks of a category, preferably one that has two words or syllables. Everybody slaps their knees and claps their hands, and then the number one person calls out *"Cate"* as they snap their right fingers and *"gory"* as they snap their left fingers. Everybody continues the rhythm while, the next person in the group (going clockwise) responds by calling out a particular category, such as *auto ... mobiles as* they snap their fingers. Again, everyone continues the rhythm and the next person must answer by naming something within the category, such as *Chev ... rolet,* as they snap their fingers.

The group keeps going until someone cannot think of an auto. Then the person simply says, *"Cate ... gory,"* and the next person must call out a new subject. Repeat the procedure.

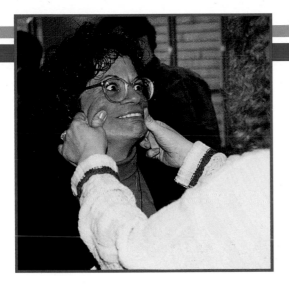

SCULPTURING

In 2s: One person is the modeling clay and one is Michelangelo. Sculpture feelings like fear, joy, tension, despair. *In 4s:* Two people are the clay and two are Michelangelo. Sculpture relational words like distrust, trust, confrontation, affirmation. *In 8s:* Four are clay; four are Michelangelo. Sculpture collective terms like celebration. *In 8s:* Everyone can be clay—or any substance! Sculpture a Rube Goldberg Machine (a complex machine doing a simple task) ... and then Christian community.

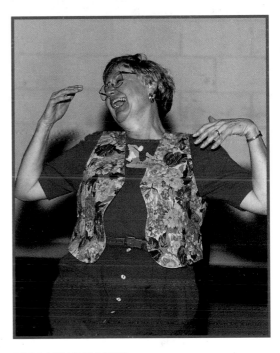

PASS THE BALLOON

Form groups of about 10 people and give each group a balloon. The object of the game is to throw the balloon to each other as quickly as possible so that you are empty handed when the whistle blows. If you are caught, here are the penalties. *First offense:* must stand up and sit down before you pass the balloon. *Second offense:* must stand up, turn around and sit down before you pass the balloon. *Third offense:* must stand up, turn around, laugh like a hyena and sit down before passing the balloon. *Fourth offense:* must stand up, turn around, laugh like a hyena, flap your arms like a bird and sit down before passing the balloon. The leader blows the whistle after about 10 seconds of play and enforces the penalty to those caught holding the balloons.

Remember, you need one *"In the pond"* and two *"Kerplunks"* for every frog. Here's the catch! If you mess up, you have to go back to *one frog.* So it is a race of skill as well as against time.

BUZZ-FIZZ
Count up to 50 as fast as you can, but instead of saying, *"five,"* or any multiple of five, call out, *"BUZZ."* Instead of saying, *"seven,"* or any multiple of seven, call out, *"FIZZ."* For example, each person, in turn, around the group will sound off with *"one," "two," "three," "four,"* and the next person will say, *"BUZZ,"* the next, *"six,"* the next, *"FIZZ,"* etc.

When you get to 35, which is a multiple of both five and seven, say *"BUZZ-FIZZ."* If you mess up, start over again at *one.* The first group to reach 50 should cheer.

ONE FROG
Work together on a riddle about a frog: first, one frog; then, two frogs, etc., until you get up to 10 frogs. Here is the first riddle:

> One frog.
> Two eyes.
> Four legs.
> In the pond.
> Kerplunk.
> Kerplunk.

One person in the group says, *"One frog,"* the next person says, *"Two eyes,"* the next *"Four legs,"* the next, *"In the pond,"* the next, *"Kerplunk,"* and the next, *"Kerplunk."*

Then the next person says, *"Two frogs,"* the next person, *"Four eyes,"* the next, *"Eight legs,"* the next, *"In the pond,"* the next, *"In the pond,"* the next, *"Kerplunk,"* the next, *"Kerplunk,"* the next, *"Kerplunk,"* and the next, *"Kerplunk."*

THIS IS A CUP! A WHAT?

Form groups of 8 to 12. Pass a cup and a saucer around the group at the same time in opposite directions. One person holds the cup; the person on their left holds the saucer. At the word GO, the person with the cup turns to the person on their right, passes the cup and says, *"This is a cup!"* That person asks, *"A what?"* The first person answers, *"A cup!"* Then the second person turns to the one on their right, passes the cup and says, *"This is a cup!"* The third person asks, *"A what?"* Then the second person must turn back to the original person and ask, *"A what?"* The original person replies, *"A cup!"* and the second person turns again to the third person and says, *"A cup!"*

In other words, each time the cup is passed, the *"A what?"* must be asked all the way back to the original person, and the answer, *"A cup!"* must be returned all the way.

At the same time the cup is going to the right, the saucer is being passed to the left. *"This is a saucer!" "A what?" "A saucer!"* etc.

Do this as fast as you can, but beware—you must start over if anyone makes a mistake. The first group to finish should cheer.

PASS THE FEETBALL

Form groups of 6 to 8. Each group passes a balloon around their circle five times ... using only feet and ankles. The first group to finish sits on the balloon and pops it.

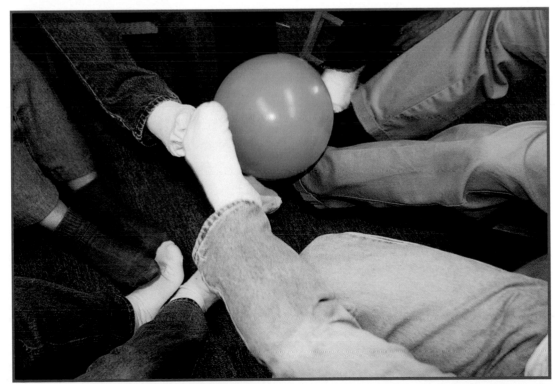

SENSORY EXERCISES

TRUST WALK

Pair off with someone you don't know very well. One person keeps their eyes closed while the other leads them around for 5-10 minutes in the room, in the hall and even outside. Ask questions to stimulate the imagination, such as: *"What does this texture make you think of?" "What kind of music comes to your mind now?" "What does this remind you of?" "Do you feel safe?"* Reverse roles and go for another trust walk.

Take a couple minutes to fill out the questionnaire. Partners share their answers and explain the reasons behind them.

Trust Walk Questionnaire

1. How would you describe the inner feelings that you had on the trust walk?

2. What was the most significant moment for you during your walk?

3. How would you describe your partner if your only experience with them was the trust walk?

4. What did you discover about yourself during this time?

5. What experience out of your past did this walk bring to mind?

SENSORY ROCK

Have twice the number of rocks and pieces of driftwood as there are people. The group divides into 4s. Put an assortment of rocks and driftwood in the center of each group.

Choose one and, with your eyes closed, feel it with your fingers, in the palm of your hand and against your cheek. Put it back and choose another. Get acquainted with the characteristics of several pieces, taking about 30 seconds for each one. Do not talk.

Select two that portray your personality—the way you are now and the person you want to be.

Go around the group, giving each person a turn to explain their feelings.

CHOOSE YOUR APPLE

Have a selection of apples—one for each person. Have groups of 4 to 8 people sit in circles. Everyone examines their group's pile of apples and picks out one particular apple that reminds them of themselves—because of certain marks and characteristics. Everyone studies their apple, polishes it and puts it back.

Mix the apples up. Ask everyone to find their apple and explain to someone why they chose that one. Then each person explains: (a) one area of their life where they shine; (b) one area where they need a little polishing.

CONVERSATION STARTERS

WALLET SCAVENGER HUNT

Get together with one to three people and work on this exercise together. With your wallet or purse, use the set of questions below. This is run like a scavenger hunt. You get two minutes in silence to go through your possessions and think about your answers. Then you break the silence and "show-and-tell" what you have found. For instance, "The thing I have had for the longest time is ... this picture of me when I was a baby." Now take two minutes in silence to find the items on this scavenger hunt list.

LIST OF ITEMS (finish the sentence):

1. The thing I have had for the LONGEST TIME is ...

2. The thing that has SENTIMENTAL VALUE is ...

3. The thing that reminds me of a FUN TIME is ...

4. The thing that causes me a lot of CONCERN is ...

5. The thing that means a lot to me because of the PERSON who gave it to me is ...

JOHN WESLEY QUESTIONNAIRE

The founder of the Methodist Church, John Wesley, started the sharing at the weekly class meeting with the question: "How is it with your soul?" How would *you* answer? Try describing your spiritual condition right now in one of the following ways.

1. Choose a COLOR and explain. *(For instance, you might say, "I feel bright orange, because I know God took care of the details for my getting here—and I'm thankful!")*

2. Choose a WEATHER CONDITION and explain. *(You might say, "I feel cloudy, because I've got a problem I just can't cope with.")*

3. Choose a number from 1 to 10. Assume that "1" is the lowest you could possibly feel and that "10" is the highest. *("I feel like a 7 today because ...")*

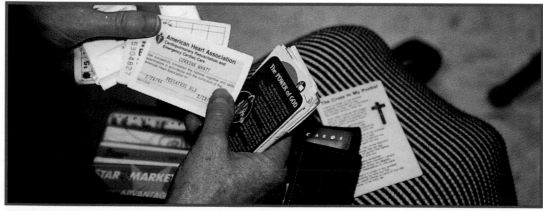

REMINISCING CHOICES

Choose one of the four experiences below and complete the sentence. Include interesting anecdotes or significant lessons you learned from the experience.

1. The first time I tried to swim ...

2. The first time I tried to dance ...

3. The first time I tried to smoke ...

4. The first time I tried to play hooky ...

WARM MEMORIES

Get together with one to three others. Each of you answer the first question. Then, go around and take turns answering each of the other questions.

1. Where were you living between the ages of 7 and 12, and what was your favorite thing to do on a warm summer day?

2. What is the worst storm you can remember? Where was your favorite place to hide during bad storms?

3. What was the center of warmth in your life when you were a child? (It could be a place in the house, a time of year, a person, etc.)

4. When did God become a "warm" person to you, and how did that happen?

FIND YOURSELF IN THE PICTURE

In this drawing, which child do you identify with—or which one best portrays you right now? Share with your group which child you would choose and why. You can also use this as an affirmation exercise, by assigning each person in your group to a child in the picture.

OLD-FASHIONED AUCTION

Just like an old-fashioned farm auction, conduct an out loud auction in your group—starting each item at $50. Everybody starts out with $1,000 and you have to bid something on every item. SELECT AN AUCTIONEER by deciding the person in your group who most resembles a used-car dealer. This person can also get in on the bidding. Remember, start the bidding on each item at $50. Then, write the winning bid in the left column and the winner's name in the right column. Remember, you only have $1,000 to spend for the whole game. AUCTIONEER: Start off by asking, "Who will give me $50 for a 1965 red MG convertible?" ... and keep going until you have a winner. Have fun!

YOUR BID   **WINNER**

$_____ 1965 red MG convertible in perfect condition   _____

$_____ Winter vacation in Hawaii for two   _____

$_____ Two Super Bowl tickets on the 50-yard line   _____

$_____ Three months of skydiving lessons   _____

$_____ Nightly back massage for one year   _____

$_____ Holy Land tour hosted by your favorite Christian leader   _____

$_____ Season pass to ski resort of my choice   _____

$_____ Two months off to do anything I want, with pay   _____

$_____ Home theater with surround sound   _____

$_____ A chance at a role in a major motion picture   _____

$_____ Breakfast in bed for three months   _____

$_____ Two front-row tickets at the concert of my choice   _____

$_____ Two-week Caribbean cruise with spouse in honeymoon suite   _____

$_____ A week of golf lessons with Tiger Woods   _____

$_____ Shopping spree at Saks Fifth Avenue   _____

$_____ A deluxe Sea-Doo jet ski   _____

$_____ Six months of maid service   _____

$_____ All-expense-paid family vacation to Disney World   _____

$_____ One year of no hassles with my kids/parents   _____

79

POP QUIZZES

To bring out information in a hurry that can be used as a basis for a sharing experience, one of the best approaches is the Pop Quiz. It gives people a chance to collect their thoughts for a few seconds before having to share.

FIRE DRILL
Jot down the items you would grab and take with you if your house caught on fire. In your imagination, run through every room and jot down the specific items that you would try to take. (Assume the children and pets are safe.) After 30 seconds, in groups of 4, share the three most important items on your list and explain why.

1. _____
2. _____
3. _____
4. _____
5. _____
6. _____
7. _____
8. _____
9. _____
10. _____

SUCCESS ANALYSIS
Jot down your biggest accomplishment for each of the age periods given. For instance, when you were between 7 and 12 you may have won a hopscotch contest or placed in a soap box derby.

Then, in groups of 4, share your accomplishments and explain how they reveal your changing values.

Age 7–12: _____

Age 13–17: _____

Age 18–30: _____

Recently: _____

FAMILY FUN TIMES

Quickly try to jot down 10 things your family enjoys doing together, such as camping, playing ball, eating popcorn, etc. Now, beside each activity, put the symbols that apply.

$—if it requires more than $10

T—if it requires traveling over 100 miles

O—if it brings your family closer together

†—if it brings your family closer to God

✔—if your family has done it in the last three months

Next, put a circle around your three favorite activities. Then, get together with one to three others and share your choices.

MY FAMILY LIKES ...

_____ 1. _____

_____ 2. _____

_____ 3. _____

_____ 4. _____

_____ 5. _____

_____ 6. _____

_____ 7. _____

_____ 8. _____

_____ 9. _____

_____ 10. _____

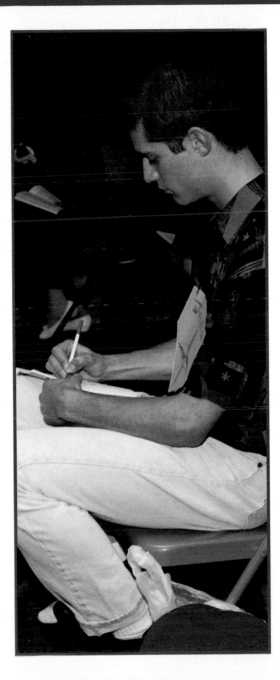

MOON TRIP

Close your eyes and imagine yourself packing for a trip to an uncivilized planet to start life over. Think of 10 things you would want to take with you.

You might list a stack of books, a microwave oven, your guitar, a textbook on organic gardening, a motorcycle with a solar-powered engine, golf clubs, your scrapbook, your dog, etc. You are free to use literary license and put down things that are impractical in a primitive society.

Now the load must be lightened, so you can only take half the number of items. Check the five things most important to you. Then get together with a couple of others and share what you chose.

TEN THINGS I'D LIKE TO TAKE:

1. _____

2. _____

3. _____

4. _____

5. _____

6. _____

7. _____

8. _____

9. _____

10. _____

GOAL SETTING WITH A PLAN

In this exercise, you can sort through the major concerns in your life and come up with specific goals and plans of action.

In the first column below, jot down the major concerns in your life—such as deciding where to go to college ... what to major in ... looking for a new job ... paying off your debts. Then, rank these concerns, 1, 2, 3, etc., in order of priority.

Next, take the number 1 concern and write in the middle column the things you wish you could do about this. Don't let lack of time, money, ability or opportunity deter you from jotting something down. For instance, if "building a bridge of communication between the black and white community" is your number 1 concern, you might put down: I wish I could get some of these people together in my home for a talk; I wish I could convince the news media to report on the good things that are going on; I wish I could get on the school board; etc. Now rank these 1, 2, 3, etc., in order of urgency or procedure.

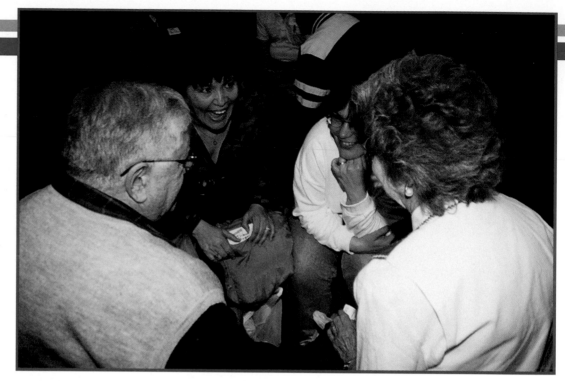

Finally, in the last column, write down the plan you would like to follow in carrying out these priorities. Where appropriate, include quotas, deadlines, dates, etc. Get together with two or three others and share how you arrived at your plan of action.

MY MAJOR CONCERNS	I WISH I COULD	MY PLAN OF ACTION

PROJECTION EXERCISE

Jot down in the space provided what you recall as your major (a) interest, (b) problem, and (c) hope or dream when you were in the sixth grade.

Next, consider your life right now and fill in the same three categories. Then, project yourself 10 years into the future and jot down what you feel will be true then.

In groups of 2 to 4, share your feelings about those areas when you were in the sixth grade. Go around the group again and share your present feelings and then your future outlook.

WHEN I WAS IN THE SIXTH GRADE

Interest:_____

Problem: _____

Hope: _____

RIGHT NOW IN MY LIFE

Interest:_____

Problem: _____

Hope: _____

TEN YEARS FROM NOW

Interest:_____

Problem: _____

Hope: _____

HERO ANALYSIS

Jot down one or two heroes for each of the age periods given below. For instance, when you were between 7 and 12 years old your heroes may have been Mighty Mouse and Abraham Lincoln.

Then, in groups of 4, share your heroes and explain what they reveal about your changing values.

Age 7–12: _____

Age 13–17:_____

Age 18–30:_____

Right now: _____

GUESSING GAMES

To make the process of getting acquainted exciting, reverse the procedure of describing yourself and have the others guess your answers. This increases the interest and multiplies the group involvement.

BACK-TO-BACK

Get together with one other person. Sit with your back to theirs and try to recall the following information or predict how your partner would answer the following questions. Then turn around and check out your answers.

1. Color of eyes?

2. Height?

3. Shoe size?

4. Favorite TV program?

5. Favorite magazine?

6. Favorite hobby?

7. The thing that gives them the greatest fulfillment?

8. The word that characterizes their outlook on life right now?

MY PARTNER

Sit back-to-back and let one person guess out loud what their partner would do in each situation: Yes ... No ... or Maybe. Give yourself 10 points for every correct guess. Then reverse roles and let your partner guess about you in these situations.

MY PARTNER IS SOMEONE WHO WOULD:	YES	NO	MAYBE
1. Yell at a referee?	Y	N	M
2. Ask for directions if lost?	Y	N	M
3. Go to the restroom if the movie got scary?	Y	N	M
4. Spend instead of save?	Y	N	M
5. Take a day off just for fun?	Y	N	M
6. Buy the latest fashions?	Y	N	M
7. Rather participate in a sport than watch one?	Y	N	M
8. Choose vanilla ice cream over jamoca almond fudge?	Y	N	M
9. Rather ride a motorcycle than a horse?	Y	N	M
10. See a movie more than once?	Y	N	M
11. Choose ESPN over CNN?	Y	N	M
12. Prefer to own a Jeep more than a Mercedes Benz?	Y	N	M
13. Rather be a great moviemaker than a U.S. president?	Y	N	M

THREE FACTS / ONE LIE

Get together in groups of 4. Complete the following statements truthfully—except for one. Yet make that one believable! Then one person at a time reads their answers and lets the others guess where they are lying. Finally, they confess which "fact" was a lie and what would be their honest answer.

1. My favorite game as a child:

2. My favorite TV show at age 12:

3. My favorite music when I was a teenager:

4. My favorite pastime right now:

SALVADOR DALI

Each person creates a verbal picture of someone else in the group by comparing them to the following:

1. A BODY OF WATER. (If the person I am thinking of were a body of water, they would be a deep-flowing stream, a rushing river, or ...)

2. AN INSTRUMENT in a symphony orchestra (kettledrum, French horn, piccolo ...)

3. A FLOWER in a garden (violet, morning glory, red rose ...)

4. A PERFORMER in a circus (lion tamer, clown, tightrope walker ...)

5. A PLAYER on a football team. (If our group were a football team, this person would be quarterback, offensive tackle, coach ...)

Begin by having each person in the group write their name at the top of a sheet of paper and put it in the center of the circle. After mixing up the sheets of paper, everyone draws one and jots down a comparison for that person in the five categories above.

Then one person at a time reads their list aloud, and the others try to guess who the subject is. After the person is identified, the one describing them explains their answers for the first two: BODY OF WATER and INSTRUMENT OF THE ORCHESTRA. You might say, "I put down a deep-flowing stream because I see Jim as a deep-thinking person."

MYSTERY PERSON

Form groups of 6 to 8. On a blank sheet of paper, answer the questions below. Fold the slips of paper and place them in a bowl in the center of the group. One person takes out a slip, reads the clues aloud, and everyone tries to guess which group member matches the answers. Finally, the mystery person confesses and explains one or two of their answers.

1. A COLOR that reveals your personality.

2. An ANIMAL that portrays the way you see yourself.

3. A SONG that illustrates your philosophy of life.

4. A CAR that symbolizes you in some way.

5. A COMIC STRIP or TV CHARACTER that you identify with.

TWENTY QUESTIONS

Form groups of about 8. Someone in the group thinks of a person in the circle. Then each group member asks one question (do not ask about age or sex, though) that will give a clue as to who it is. For instance:

1. What movie star does this person remind you of? *(Robert Redford)*

2. What would this person do between halves at a football game? *(watch the band)*

3. If our group were a zoo, which animal would this person be? *(a tiger)*

4. How would this person dress for a masquerade ball? *(Superman)*

5. What character out of history (or the Bible) does this person remind you of? *(Jonah)*

After everyone has asked a question, go around again, each one trying to guess from the clues who the person is. Then the one who began reveals the name and explains why they see the person as they do. Repeat the procedure until everyone has been the subject.

SHOW-AND-TELL

For sheer enjoyment and universal appeal, there is nothing like making something with our hands. It helps us collect our thoughts, surface our feelings, and create a piece of art that we can use to explain our feelings to others.

Here are a number of different approaches to self-discovery crafts.

MAKE YOUR NAME TAG

Instead of having prepared name tags, make your own. Tear a piece of colored construction paper into a shape symbolic of you—a heart, a butterfly, etc. Write your first name on it, punch two holes in it, and wear it on a string around your neck like a medallion.

When groups are formed, explain your name tag to your group.

MAGAZINE COLLAGE

Leaf through a magazine or newspaper and tear out titles, pictures, words, slogans, want ads, etc. that portray you in some way—such as: (1) the concerns in your life at the moment; (2) the important things in your world; (3) your hopes and dreams for the world. Then paste your tear-outs together on a sheet of newsprint and add color, design or graffiti with poster paints or markers.

TIME LINE / TURNING POINTS

On a sheet of paper, draw your personal time line. Divide the line into the major periods of your life, such as childhood, adolescence, college, young adult and adult. Think back over your life and try to pinpoint on this line the major turning points. A turning point can be considered anything that has significantly influenced or altered your life, or shaped your present values. It can be a happy or painful experience, but it is one which you now view with great meaning. It may be the death of your mother when you were 12, a spiritual commitment you made while in high school, etc.

DRAW YOUR FAMILY TREE

Draw a tree to symbolize the life of your family. Choose: (1) a type of tree that represents your family, such as a tall elm or a scrub oak; (2) colors for the foliage to represent mood, such as red and orange because your childhood was bright and cheerful, or color in no leaves at all because your childhood was painful; (3) roots to represent your spiritual formation, such as straight and deep or shallow and barren; (4) additions to represent your dominant childhood memories, such as a bird because your family sang a lot.

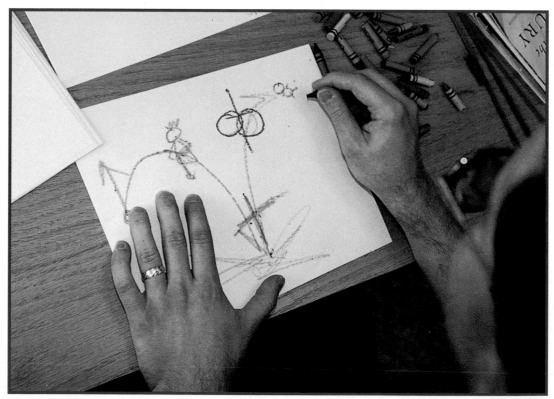

WIRE SCULPTURE

Using wire or pipe cleaners, make a sculpture that describes your spiritual ups and downs ... or your spiritual life at the moment.

When you are in your small group, share the meaning behind your sculpture.

DRAW YOUR SPIRITUAL PILGRIMAGE

Think about the ups and downs in your life from as far back as you can remember to this moment. Draw a design symbolizing the low and high points with color and shape. For instance, early adolescence might be portrayed by a sunburst because everything was sunshine. The high school years might be portrayed by clouds because it was a period of doubt and frustration.

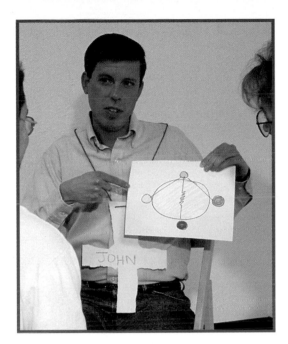

DRAW YOUR CHILDHOOD TABLE

Remember back to the time you were between 7 and 12 years old. Draw the shape of the table where you ate most of your meals. Then for each person who was at the table pick a color that suggests their personality and draw them where they usually sat. You might use blue for your father because he was serious and draw him at the head of the table; orange for your cheerful mother, next to your father, etc. Finally, color the center of the table to represent your childhood. The table might be black and brown with splashes of purple to indicate the somber tone and the times of fun.

THIS IS YOUR LIFE

Create a TV special on the places where you have lived. Think of the various moves you have made. What was significant about each place for you? How did they contribute to the person you are today?

Then, make a drawing of each location and feature something that symbolizes your feelings during that period in your life. For instance, for a time in your childhood, you might draw a simple frame house with a tall oak tree—the oak tree symbolizing the strength and stability in the home, etc.

YOUR FAMILY CREST

If you could design a crest or shield to represent your family, how would you do it?

Divide the crest into as many parts as there are members in your family. Put their names in the various sections. Describe each person with an animal—such as a lion for Dad, a mother hen for Mom, a teddy bear for Johnny, etc. In the ribbon across the top put three words or phrases that your family stands for—such as honesty, loyalty, God, or a motto like "One for all and all for one."

GROUP SHOW-AND-TELL

GROUP BANNERS

Each group of 8 makes a banner with materials from a paper sack. In the sack are: one balloon, four different colors of tissue paper, a strip of white wrapping paper six feet long, and some masking tape. Your group decides upon a theme that expresses what you are experiencing together. You work out the design with the materials available and hang the banner on the wall.

COMMUNITY CONSTRUCTION

In groups of 4 assume that you can create a new church and community for your area. Consider the master plan for the community as well as the architectural design for the church.

Focus on the kind of church you would want in this community—the building, with the arrangement of the sanctuary, education rooms, etc. Don't worry about matters of tradition, negative reactions or cost.

Put everything into the model that you feel is important; leave everything out of the building that you feel is unimportant.

It would be helpful at the beginning for the leader to show a rough sketch of what they consider to be an ideal community and also a half-finished model of their ideas for a church building.

NONVERBAL STATEMENTS

There is more than one way to express yourself ... and sometimes the best way is not with words. This is especially true when it comes to explaining how you feel about something important, how you feel about yourself, or how you feel about God.

We have discovered that you can help a person get in touch with their feelings by giving them an inanimate object with which to role-play. By action, without saying a word, they can share what they are feeling on the inside about a given subject.

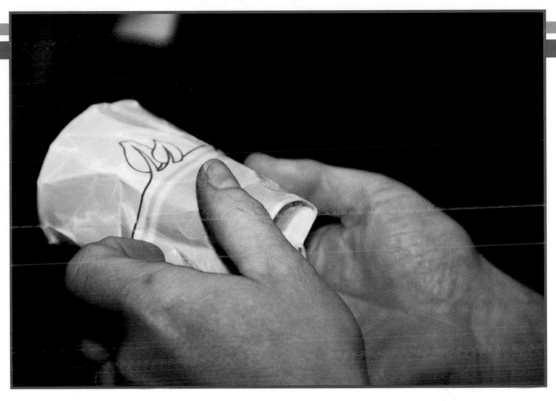

PASS THE CUP

Give each group of 8 a paper cup. Ask one person in the group to do to the cup what they would like to do to the institutional church (anything from kissing it to ripping it open). Then, without comment, that person passes the cup to the next person. The second person considers the state in which they receive the cup (the church) and does what they would like to do. The cup is passed around until everyone in the group has expressed their feelings. Then break the silence and talk about your feelings during the activity.

PASS THE COAT

Give each group of 8 a heavy coat. Ask one person to take the coat and do something with it that represents what they would like to see happen to themselves during the group time.

Then, without comment, they pass the coat to the next person, etc., until everyone has treated the coat according to what they would like to see happen to themselves. Then pass the coat around a second time and let each one explain what they did.

PASS THE CHALICE

Pass a chalice around the group, having each person do with it as they would like to do with Jesus Christ. Pass the chalice a second time and let everyone explain what they did.

Another possibility is to have a towel, a hard roll and a cup of juice. Each person, in turn, uses the three articles to minister to the others in the group in the way they feel Jesus would minister to them.

AFFIRMATION GAMES

Affirmation games are designed for the members of a group to share their positive feelings for each other, to recognize the strengths and gifts in each other, and to express their concern and love for each other.

Affirmation games are best used after a group has had time to get to know each other—to listen to each other's past history, present concerns and future hopes.

You will notice that Serendipity typically uses affirmation exercises with similes. We have found that it helps most people to affirm one another by sharing their impressions and appreciation in symbolic ways. For additional affirmation activities, see the Serious Affirmation exercises on pages 136-139.

COLORS
One person is silent while the others try to think of a color that would best describe their personality. For example, one person might think of the color bright orange to describe Bill, because he is outgoing. Another person might think of the color deep blue because he is strong and outspoken. A third might see Bill as light green because he appears so fresh and springlike.

Then, go around and let each person share the color that came to mind and why. Finally the person explains the color they would choose to describe themselves. Bill might have chosen light brown because he sees himself as quiet, timid and conservative.

Repeat for each person in the group.

STRENGTH BOMBARDMENT

One person in the group sits in silence while the others think of a particular strength they see in his or her life. Each member of the group then shares the strength they have selected and explains why. For instance, one might say, "Jim, I see in you the quality of compassion—because you have a tremendous ability to care." Another might say, "I see in you a quality of childlikeness—because you are beautifully honest and transparent." A third might say, "I have appreciated your sense of humor—and freedom of lifestyle; they are refreshing." Repeat the procedure for each person in the group.

RECOGNITION CEREMONY

Award time! If you could give an award to each member of your group for their contribution or growth during your time together, what would it be? Jot down the name of each group member beside their award.

_____ GOLDEN HELMET: *For the Don Quixote who saw in us only beautiful things and called forth the best in all of us.*

_____ GLASS SLIPPER: *For the Cinderella who came to the party and discovered she was a princess.*

_____ PURPLE HEART: *For the one who shared our hurts and gave of themselves for our healing.*

_____ ROYAL GIRDLE: *For the one who drew us together.*

_____ THE VELVET EAR: *For the one who patiently listened, giving the rest of us the chance to unload.*

_____ MEGAPHONE: *For the person who cheered us on.*

_____ NOBEL PEACE PRIZE: *For the one who harmonized our differences of opinion without diminishing anyone.*

_____ ATLAS TROPHY: *For the person who undergirded the group with their inner strength and care.*

CHILD PRODIGIES

For each person in your group, pick one of the categories below—the area in which you think they might have excelled as a "child prodigy." Ask one member to listen while the others share what they chose for this person. Then, ask another to listen while the others focus on this person, etc., around the group.

_____ smuggling stray animals into the home

_____ having and surviving childhood accidents

_____ making up imaginative excuses for misbehavior

_____ talking at an early age

_____ climbing the highest trees in the neighborhood

_____ inventing imaginative games that the other children wanted to play

_____ wearing out the most clothes in a year

_____ embarrassing their parents by telling family secrets

_____ playing practical jokes on company

_____ riding the roller coaster the most times in a row

_____ breaking the most windows with baseballs

AUTOMOTIVE AFFIRMATION

In silence, read over the list of automotive items below as you think about the contribution of each person to your group. Write each person's name next to one item. Then, have one person at a time listen while the others share what they picked for them.

_____ BATTERY: A dependable "die-hard"—provides the "juice" for everything to happen.

_____ SPARK PLUG: Gets things started. Makes sure there is "fire," even on cold mornings.

_____ OIL: "The razor's edge" to protect against engine wear-out, provide longer mileage, and reduce friction for fast-moving parts.

_____ SHOCK ABSORBER: Cushions heavy bumps. Makes for an easy, comfortable ride.

_____ RADIO: The "music machine," making the trip fun and enjoyable. Adds a little "rock 'n' roll" for a good time.

_____ MUFFLER: Reduces the engine's roar to a cat's "purr," even at high speeds over rough terrain.

_____ CUP HOLDER: The servant, always meeting a need.

_____ SUB WOOFER: The strong voice in the crowd. When they talk, people listen.

_____ TRANSMISSION: Converts the energy into motion, enables the engine to slip from one speed to another without stripping the gears.

_____ GASOLINE: Liquid fuel that is consumed, giving away its own life for the energy to keep things moving.

_____ WINDSHIELD: Keeps the vision clear, protects from debris and flying objects.

_____ SEAT BELT / AIR BAG: Restrains or protects others when there is a possibility of them getting hurt.

BROADWAY JOBS

Read over the list of workers that are needed to put on a Broadway show. Choose a job for each person in your group. You can use a person's name only once and you have to use everybody's name once—so think it through before you jot down their names. Then, ask one person to listen while the others share where they have put this person's name. Then, ask the next person to listen and repeat this procedure around your group.

_____ PRODUCER: Typical Hollywood business tycoon; extravagant, big-budget, big-production magnate.

_____ DIRECTOR: Creative, imaginative brains who coordinates the production and draws the best out of others.

_____ HEROINE: Beautiful, captivating, everybody's heart throb; defenseless when men are around, but nobody's fool.

_____ HERO: Tough, macho, champion of the underdog, knight in shining armor, defender of truth.

_____ COMEDIAN: Childlike, happy-go-lucky, outrageously funny, keeps everyone laughing.

_____ CHARACTER PERSON: Rugged individualist, outrageously different, colorful, adds spice to any surrounding.

_____ FALL GUY: Easy-going, nonchalant character who wins the hearts of everyone by being the "foil" of the heavy characters.

_____ TECHNICAL DIRECTOR: The genius for "sound and lights"; creates the perfect atmosphere.

_____ COMPOSER OF LYRICS: Communicates in music what everybody understands; heavy into feelings, moods, outbursts of energy.

_____ PUBLICITY AGENT: Advertising and public relations expert; knows all the angles, good at one-liners, a flair for "hot" news.

_____ VILLAIN: The "bad guy" who really is the heavy for the plot, forces others to think, challenges traditional values; out to destroy anything artificial or hypocritical.

_____ AUTHOR: Shy, aloof; very much in touch with feelings, sensitive to people, puts into words what others only feel.

_____ STAGEHAND: Supportive, behind-the-scenes person who makes things run smoothly; patient and tolerant.

YOU AND ME, PARTNER

Think of the people in your group as you read over the list of activities below. If you had to choose someone from your group to be your partner, who would you choose to do these activities with? Jot down each person's name beside the activity. You can use each person's name only once and you have to use everyone's name once—so think it through before you jot down their names. Then, let one person listen to what the others chose for them. Then, move to the next person, etc., around your group.

WHO WOULD YOU CHOOSE FOR THE FOLLOWING?

_____ ENDURANCE DANCE CONTEST partner

_____ BOBSLED RACE partner for the Olympics

_____ MONDAY NIGHT FOOTBALL ANNOUNCER teammate

_____ TRAPEZE ACT partner

_____ MY UNDERSTUDY for my debut in a Broadway musical

_____ BEST MAN or MAID OF HONOR at my wedding

_____ SECRET UNDERCOVER AGENT copartner

_____ BODYGUARD for me when I strike it rich

_____ MOUNTAIN CLIMBING partner in climbing Mt. Everest

_____ ASTRONAUT to fly the space shuttle while I walk in space

_____ SAND CASTLE TOURNAMENT building partner

_____ PIT CREW foreman for entry in Indianapolis 500

_____ AUTHOR of my biography

_____ SURGEON to operate on me for a life-threatening cancer

_____ NEW BUSINESS START-UP partner

_____ TAG-TEAM partner for a professional wrestling match

_____ HEAVY-DUTY PRAYER partner

MUSICAL INSTRUMENTS

Below are a list of musical instruments. Read over the list and pick one that best describes how you feel about each person in this group. When everyone is through jotting down everyone else's name, ask one person to listen while the others tell this person where they have put their name. When you are through with the first person, ask another person to listen and repeat the affirmation until everyone has been affirmed.

_____ ANGELIC HARP: Soft, gentle, melodious, wooing with heavenly sounds.

_____ OLD-FASHIONED WASHBOARD: Nonconforming, childlike and fun.

_____ PLAYER PIANO: Mischievous, raucous, honky-tonk—delightfully carefree.

_____ KETTLEDRUM: Strong, vibrant, commanding when needed but usually in the background.

_____ PASSIONATE CASTANET: Full of Spanish fervor; intense and always upbeat.

_____ STRADIVARIUS VIOLIN: Priceless, exquisite, soul-piercing—with the touch of the master.

_____ FLUTTERING FLUTE: Tender, lighthearted, wide-ranging and clear as crystal.

_____ SCOTTISH BAGPIPES: Forthright, distinctive and unmistakable.

_____ SQUARE DANCE FIDDLE: Folksy, down-to-earth, toe-tapping—sprightly and full of energy.

_____ ENCHANTING OBOE: Haunting, charming, disarming—even the cobra is harmless with this sound.

_____ MELLOW CELLO: Deep, sonorous, compassionate—adding body and depth to the orchestra.

_____ PIPE ORGAN: Grand, magnificent, rich—versatile and commanding.

_____ HERALDING TRUMPET: Stirring, lively, invigorating—signaling attention and attack.

_____ CLASSICAL GUITAR: Contemplative, profound, thoughtful *and* thought-provoking.

_____ ONE-MAN BAND: Able to do many things well, all at once.

_____ COMB AND TISSUE PAPER: Makeshift, original, uncomplicated—homespun and creative.

_____ SWINGING TROMBONE: Warm, rich—great in solo or background support.

AFFIRMATION GUESSING GAME

Write your name on a slip of paper, fold it and put it in a hat. Let everyone in the group select a name from the hat, but don't tell anyone who you picked. (If you pick your own name, call for a reshuffle.) Select an animal, car and boat that best describes the person you picked. Share this with the group and see if anyone can guess who you are describing. If you have time left over, let each person share the animal they would choose to describe themselves.

 Playful Porpoise: Agile, intelligent, lively—the life of the party.

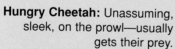 **Puppy Dog:** Soft, furry, fun-loving, playful, irresistible—disarmingly childlike.

 **New Ultra Trans Am:** With side pipes, spider markings, fancy seat covers and enough horses under the hood to pull a tank.

 Tireless Turtle: Slow and steady, persistent plodder—willing to stick their neck out.

 Lordly Peacock: Colorful, spectacular—with a rain-bow of plumage.

Wells Fargo Stagecoach: With updated Monroe shocks and a strong undercarriage, designed for rip-snortin' rough ridin' out west.

 Cuddly Teddy Bear: Lovable, warm, playful—brings out the "heart" in all of us.

 Gentle Lamb: Sweet, beautiful spirit—soothing to be with.

'29 Model A Ford: With rumble seat and genuine leather uphol-stery, built to last and just as fun as the day it came from the factory.

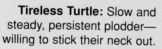 **Wise Old Owl:** Quiet, thoughtful—with the appearance of being in deep contemplation.

 Honey Bee: Energetic, quick and tireless worker.

 '56 Belair Hardtop Chevy: With side pipes, high jacks and a mahogany steering wheel—the radio tuned to a '50s station and a foxtail on the antenna.

 Hungry Cheetah: Unassuming, sleek, on the prowl—usually gets their prey.

 Peaceful Dove: Serene, calm in the midst of heavy storms.

'41 Red MG Ragtop: With bucket headlights and a stick shift, Scotch-plaid quilt and a hint of bagpipes in the air.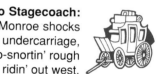

 Mother Hen: Warm, sensitive, protective—always on the lookout for the well-being of others.

 Graceful Swan: Majestic, smooth-sailing, unruffled—always in command.

 '82 Dune Buggy: With sky-blue sparkle paint; balloon tires, roll bar and bucket seats.

New Harley-Davidson: With extended forks, double seat and custom sport bar.

Porsche Turbo Carrera: With air foils, spoilers and racing slicks—tuned to perfection and ready for the Le Mans.

'74 Original Customized Van: With swivel seats, floor-to-ceiling carpet, 40–channel CB and a water bed.

Circus Car: With horns blaring, firecrackers exploding and Roman candles going off, and a musical calliope turning out a medley of fun songs.

'62 Pink T-Bird: With fur steering wheel, leopard-skin upholstery, tape deck and digital clock.

Sugar Plum Fairy, Make-Believe Carriage: With silvery wheels and diamond-studded trim, and a trunk of exotic magical items from far-off lands.

Aristocratic Queen Elizabeth II: Dignified, luxurious—extravagantly equipped but tasteful.

Rubber Dingy: With makeshift paddle; compact, transportable, inflatable—fun to be in.

Mythical Treasure Ship: Carrying hidden treasure and exotic spices, full of mystery and surprises and a little mischief.

Yankee Clipper: Even-keeled, smooth-sailing, majestic queen—sails unfurled to catch the wind, gliding through deep waters with effortless composure.

Cruising Yacht: Sleek, posh, totally equipped for luxurious travel and deep-sea sport.

Venetian Gondola: With love seat in the back and a mustached oarsman to guide through the romantic canals.

Toy Sailboat: With paper sail—original, handmade, creative, childlike, authentic.

Mississippi River Ferry Boat: Elegant, perfectly appointed, with minstrel music and the smell of perfume.

Aircraft Carrier: Sophisticated, complex—equipped with the latest in technological advances.

High-speed Motorboat: Awesome power but low profile—versatile and fun.

Tenacious Tugboat: Conscientious, workhorse of the docks—capable of pulling heavy loads and guiding big ships.

Old-Fashioned Rowboat: Uncomplicated, but sturdy—made for fishing in quiet ponds with cane poles.

FROG TEMPERAMENTS

Every person is a prince or princess! Below are four different types of temperaments as Hippocrates, the Greek philosopher, analyzed people about 400 B.C. Read over the description of each frog carefully. Then jot down the names of the people in your group next to the frogs; and under each name, write the particular temperament or temperaments you see. For instance, for John you might jot down: 60% super salesman and 40% super leader, because you see John as an extrovert with a lot of leadership skills.

When everyone has finished, one person listens while the others share how they see him or her. Then have that person share which temperament they feel they have.

Repeat the process for each person.

SUPER SALESMAN (sanguine)

This frog is warm, friendly, outgoing, energetic, optimistic and fun to be around. Could sell a refrigerator to an Eskimo. Also makes a good preacher, actor, after-dinner speaker and Dale Carnegie promoter. This frog is the life of the party, a "now" person, happy-go-lucky—at least on the surface. They usually cover up any feelings of inadequacy or insecurity. Better at short dashes than long-distance runs. Voted "most likely to succeed" in high school, but not always does.

To kiss this frog (affirm this person), give them a chance to take off their mask. To feel accepted for who they are, not for their jokes. To get in touch with his or her feelings ... and "spiritual resources." Ask them to share their dreams ... and don't let them give up when the going gets tough.

SUPER LEADER (choleric)

This frog is the strong, self-willed driver that makes the free enterprise system work. An organizer, practical, capable—extremely talk-oriented. Comes across as sure, self-confident and determined. This frog has given the world its generals, crusaders and politicians. Can be cruel, sarcastic and intolerant of others—or the selfless, dedicated champion of the downtrodden. Usually successful at what they undertake—but sometimes wear themselves out in the process.

To kiss this frog, let them know that they are important for their own sake, not for their accomplishments. Help them discover the secret of inner peace of "being" not "doing." Help them celebrate the "now"—to love and be loved, to touch and be touched.

SUPER IDEALIST (melancholic)

This frog is imaginative, creative, sensitive and artistic—a real lover of beauty, solitude and perfection. Usually quiet, gentle and withdrawn. Experiences extreme emotional highs and lows; either effervescent and exuberant or moody, irritable and depressed. This frog has given the world most of its artists, composers, writers, thinkers, inventors and theoreticians. Intensely loyal to friends and deeply hurt when friendships turn sour.

To kiss this frog, help them to affirm their great gifts and strengths. To accept ups and downs without dwelling on them. To claim the spiritual stability of an ever-constant God. To celebrate their God-given capacity to feel deeply.

SUPER PERSON (phlegmatic)

This frog is easy-going, likable, dependable—ever-cautious, conservative and practical. The original "nice" person. Never gets upset or excited, never rocks the boat, avoids conflict at all costs—even at the expense of their own rights. This frog has produced diplomats, civil servants, social workers, teachers and spouses of strong-willed leaders! Invaluable as a peacemaker. Extremely loyal, goes the "extra mile" without complaint. Can be stepped on by others to the extent that their own self-esteem is diminished.

To kiss this frog, encourage them to take a chance, to take a stand on issues and the initiative on projects. Give them a lot of positive feedback and reinforcement when they step out. Call them to face up to their own responsibility for their life and their spiritual potential as a person.

THE GIVING GAME

Get together in groups of about 4. This game is a beautiful way to express your love and appreciation for one another. Follow the three steps below.

1. Ask everyone to sit in silence and ask themselves this question, "If I could give something of myself to each person in this group ... that expresses my feelings right now for them, what would I want to give each person that they could keep for the rest of their lives?" (This is for keeps.)

2. Still in silence for five to six minutes, take out your purse or wallet ... or things in your pockets ... and try to find symbols or tokens of the real thing you would like to give this person. For instance:

   ❏ a fishing license—to remember the time we went fishing together ... or want to go in the future

   ❏ a picture of my family—to remember the times we have shared together

   ❏ a ticket stub to a concert—to remember the music that we enjoy in Christ

   ❏ a Band-Aid—for the "little hurts" that come along in life

   Remember, you need ONE gift (a different gift) for each person—a token or symbol of the real gift.

3. Ask one person to sit in silence while the others go around and explain their gift and hand it to this person. The person who receives the gift is to say, "Thanks." Nothing more.

Repeat this procedure until everyone in your group has been given their gifts. In the giving and receiving of gifts, you are able to say two things: (1) What I have appreciated most about you, and (2) What I want you to keep as a token of our friendship—for the rest of your life.

WILD PREDICTIONS

Try to match the people in your group to the crazy forecasts below. (Don't take it too seriously; it's meant to be fun!) Which of the following would you choose for each of the members of your group? After you have read through the list and jotted down people's names in silence, ask one person to read the first item and everyone call out the name of the person they selected. Then move on to the next item, etc.

THE PERSON IN OUR GROUP MOST LIKELY TO ...

_____ be the used-car salesperson of the year

_____ replace Regis Philbin on *Regis and Kathie Lee*

_____ replace Vanna White on *Wheel of Fortune*

_____ rollerblade across the country

_____ open a charm school for Harley-Davidson bikers

_____ discover a new use for underarm deodorant

_____ run a dating service for lonely singles

_____ rise to the top in the CIA

_____ appear on the cover of *Muscle & Fitness Magazine*

_____ win the Iditarod dogsled race in Alaska

_____ join the French Foreign Legion

_____ make a fortune on pay toilet rentals

_____ be selected the choreographer for Dallas Cowboys cheerleaders

_____ write a best-selling novel based on their love life

_____ get listed in the *Guiness Book of World Records* for marathon dancing

_____ win the blue ribbon at the state fair for best Rocky Mountain oyster recipe

_____ bungee jump off the Golden Gate Bridge

_____ be the first woman to win the Indianapolis 500

_____ become the most famous pet psychologist in Beverly Hills

_____ win the *MAD Magazine* award for worst jokes

INTERACTIVE EXERCISES

FOR SMALL GROUPS

KICK-OFF SENTENCES

One of the quickest and easiest ways to get a conversation started is to give a group a list of half-finished sentences to complete. The best sentences to use are ones that are nonthreatening and yet give people a chance to share some interesting facts and insights about themselves.

MY FAVORITES
Get together with one or two other people and take turns finishing the following sentences.

1. My favorite time of day is ...

2. My favorite room in the house is ...

3. My favorite holiday of the year is ...

4. My favorite kind of literature is ...

5. My favorite color is ...

6. My favorite style of music is ...

7. My favorite season of the year is ...

8. My favorite sports team is ...

9. My favorite TV show is ...

10. My favorite pastime is ...

MY OUTLOOK ON LIFE
Get together with one or two other people from your group and complete the half-finished sentences below to share your outlook on life. When you are through, let your partners do the same.

1. If I'm bored at a party, I will usually ...

2. At halftime in a basketball game when my team is way behind, I'm likely to ...

3. My mood right now is ...

4. When I get really excited, I usually ...

5. When I'm really down, I usually ...

6. People who know me best will tell you I am ...

7. The best thing happening right now is ...

8. My biggest concern right now is ...

MY FANTASY WORLD
Get together with one or two other people from your group and answer the questions below. When you are through, let your partners do the same.

1. If you could be a famous person, who would you choose to be?

2. If you could have a dream car given to you, what would you choose?

3. If you could join a circus, what would you like to be?

4. If you had unlimited cash to blow on one glorious vacation, where would you go, and what would you do?

5. If you could live at any time in history, what period would you like to live in?

6. If you could live anywhere in the world, where would you like to live?

DOWN MEMORY LANE

Get together with one or two others from your group and take a walk down memory lane. One of you begin by completing the first sentence, then take turns going through the list.

1. My favorite TV program when I was in grade school was ...

2. My best subject in grade school was ...

3. My first pet was ...

4. The chore I hated to do was ...

5. My first big trip or vacation was ...

6. The adult who took time to play with me was ...

7. My favorite thing to do on a summer day was ...

8. The fun thing we often did as a family when I was in grade school was ...

9. The person who helped me with my homework was ...

10. The first thing I remember wanting to be when I grew up was ...

11. My hero at age 7 was ...

12. My favorite food or dessert was ...

13. The best Christmas present I received was ...

MY DAILY ROUTINE

Everybody gets 24 hours a day. It's how you use those hours that counts. Get together with one or two others and explain your daily routine by finishing the sentences below. Then, reverse the roles and let your partner explain their daily routine.

1. I usually get up around ...

2. I usually start the day by ...

3. For breakfast I usually have ...

4. My most creative time of the day is ...

5. I get home from school or work around ...

6. To unwind I usually ...

7. My biggest meal is generally at ...

8. My favorite thing to do in the evening is ...

9. On the average, I watch about _____ hour(s) of TV.

10. I wish I could spend more time each day ...

11. I usually go to bed around ...

12. It takes me about _____ minutes to fall asleep.

MULTIPLE-CHOICE OPTIONS

HOW DO YOU FEEL ABOUT ...
If you had to rank each activity WOW ... SO-SO ... or HO-HUM, how would you do it? Get together with one or two other people and go over the list together.

		WOW	SO-SO	HO-HUM
1.	Spending a day with the president of the United States	___	___	___
2.	Winning a Nobel Peace Prize	___	___	___
3.	Having $1,000 to spend on clothes	___	___	___
4.	Receiving a week-of-golf vacation	___	___	___
5.	Owning the latest hot car	___	___	___
6.	Having a continual supply of junk food at my disposal	___	___	___
7.	Getting the lead in a movie	___	___	___
8.	Making the Olympic team	___	___	___
9.	Being the lead singer in a popular music group	___	___	___
10.	Getting two seats on the 50-yard line at the Super Bowl	___	___	___

ROBINSON CRUSOE
Imagine that you are going to be Robinson Crusoe for a year and live on a deserted tropical island. Besides adequate food and clothing, you can choose five of the following items to take with you. Which will you choose? Share your answers in groups of 4.

- golf clubs
- lots of novels
- a CD player and lots of CDs
- a fishing rod
- a solar-powered curling iron
- exercise equipment
- a cellular phone
- a rifle
- a bed
- a Bible
- a surfboard
- a battery-powered TV and satellite dish
- a pet
- a first-aid kit
- a deck of cards
- other: _____

PRECIOUS TIME

God has given us a precious gift: the time to live. Maybe that's why now is called "the present." Complete the following three sentences about precious time—sharing your answers with your group.

MY IDEA OF A GREAT TIME IS ...

- ❏ a quiet evening at home
- ❏ a hot bath after a long day
- ❏ a delicious meal
- ❏ a brisk walk on a fall afternoon
- ❏ a day shopping with friends
- ❏ hard work that pays off
- ❏ watching an exciting sports event
- ❏ playing my favorite game or sport
- ❏ watching a good movie
- ❏ reading a good book
- ❏ a night out
- ❏ fishing or hiking
- ❏ going to a party
- ❏ going to a great concert

WHAT MAKES A BAD DAY FOR ME IS ...

- ❏ crummy weather
- ❏ mood swings
- ❏ boring work or classes
- ❏ conflict with others
- ❏ being alone on a weekend
- ❏ Mondays
- ❏ paying bills
- ❏ heavy traffic
- ❏ my team losing
- ❏ lousy financial news

IF I KNEW I HAD ONLY THREE MONTHS TO LIVE, I WOULD SPEND MY TIME ...

- ❏ doing exactly what I'm doing now
- ❏ seeing the world
- ❏ partying
- ❏ writing my memoirs
- ❏ finishing my "big project"
- ❏ spending all my money
- ❏ giving everything away
- ❏ being very angry
- ❏ loving everyone more
- ❏ climbing Mt. Everest
- ❏ being with friends and family
- ❏ doing all I can for God

MY BEST AND WORST SIDE

Everyone in the group should pick from the following list three ways to finish the sentence, "If you want to see my best side ... ." Then when everyone is finished sharing, each person should pick three ways to finish the sentence, "If you want to see my worst side ..."—using the same list.

- ❏ play country music on the radio
- ❏ play rock music on the radio
- ❏ tell me what you really think
- ❏ take me to a health food store
- ❏ ask my mom to show old photos
- ❏ give me a week with just my kids
- ❏ buy me tickets to a football game
- ❏ take me camping in the mountains
- ❏ watch me when the pressure is on
- ❏ stick around while I try to fix something mechanical
- ❏ ride along while I drive in heavy traffic
- ❏ buy me tickets to the opera
- ❏ play a competitive game with me
- ❏ laugh at what I say
- ❏ call me by my nickname
- ❏ serve me liver and onions

TV QUIZ SHOW

Your group has been chosen to be participants on the latest TV quiz show! This is your chance to reveal some interesting characteristics about yourself and win some "funny money" by predicting what the others in the group are likely to choose. Like a TV quiz show, someone from the group picks a category and reads the four questions—pausing to let the others in the group guess before revealing the answer. When the first person is finished, everyone adds up the money they won by guessing right. Go around the group and have each person take a category. The person with the most money at the end wins.

For $1: In music, I am closer to:
❏ Bach   ❏ Beatles

For $2: In furniture, I prefer:
❏ Early American
❏ French Provincial
❏ Scandinavian—contemporary
❏ Hodgepodge—little of everything

For $3: My choice of reading material is:
❏ science fiction   ❏ sports
❏ mystery   ❏ romance

For $4: If I had $1,000 to splurge, I would buy:
❏ one original painting
❏ two numbered prints
❏ three reproductions and an easy chair
❏ four cheap imitations, easy chair and color TV

For $1: For travel, I prefer:
❏ excitement   ❏ enrichment

For $2: On a vacation, my lifestyle is:
❏ go-go all the time
❏ slow and easy
❏ party every night and sleep in

For $3: In packing for a trip, I include:
❏ toothbrush and change of underwear
❏ light bag and good book
❏ small suitcase and nice outfit
❏ all but the kitchen sink

For $4: If I had money to blow, I would choose:
❏ one glorious night in a luxury hotel
❏ a weekend in a nice hotel
❏ a full week in a cheap motel
❏ two weeks camping in the boondocks

For $1: My car is likely to be:
❏ spotless   ❏ messy

For $2: The part of my car that I keep in the best condition is the:
❏ interior
❏ exterior
❏ engine

For $3: I am more likely to buy a:
❏ luxury car—10 mpg
❏ sports car—20 mpg
❏ economy car—30 mpg
❏ tiny car—40 mpg

For $4: If I had my choice of antique cars, I would choose a:
❏ 1955 pink T-Bird
❏ 1937 silver Rolls Royce
❏ 1952 red MG convertible
❏ 1929 Model A Ford with rumble seat

For $1: I'm more likely to shop at:
❏ Sears   ❏ Saks Fifth Avenue

For $2: I feel more comfortable wearing:
❏ formal clothes
❏ casual clothes
❏ sport clothes
❏ grubbies

For $3: In buying clothes, I look for:
❏ fashion/style
❏ price
❏ name brand
❏ quality

For $4: In buying clothes, I usually:
❏ shop all day for a bargain
❏ choose one store, but try on everything
❏ buy the first thing I try on
❏ buy without trying it on

Food

For $1: I prefer to eat at a:
- ❑ fast-food restaurant
- ❑ fancy restaurant

For $2: On the menu, I look for something:
- ❑ familiar
- ❑ different
- ❑ way-out

For $3: When eating chicken, my preference is a:
- ❑ drumstick
- ❑ wing
- ❑ breast
- ❑ gizzard

For $4: I draw the line when it comes to eating:
- ❑ frog legs
- ❑ snails
- ❑ raw oysters
- ❑ Rocky Mountain oysters

Work

For $1: I prefer to work at a job that is:
- ❑ too big to handle
- ❑ too small to be challenging

For $2: The job I find most unpleasant is:
- ❑ cleaning the house
- ❑ working in the yard
- ❑ balancing the checkbook

For $3: In choosing a job, I look for:
- ❑ salary
- ❑ security
- ❑ fulfillment
- ❑ working conditions

For $4: If I had to choose between these jobs, I would choose:
- ❑ pickle inspector at processing plant
- ❑ complaint officer at department store
- ❑ bedpan changer at hospital
- ❑ personnel manager in charge of firing

Habits

For $1: I am more likely to squeeze the toothpaste:
- ❑ in the middle ❑ from the end

For $2: If I am lost, I will probably:
- ❑ stop and ask directions
- ❑ check the map
- ❑ find the way by driving around

For $3: I read the newspaper starting with the:
- ❑ front page
- ❑ funnies
- ❑ sports
- ❑ entertainment section

For $4: When I undress at night, I put my clothes:
- ❑ on a hanger in the closet
- ❑ folded neatly over a chair
- ❑ into a hamper or clothes basket
- ❑ on the floor

Shows

For $1: I am more likely to:
- ❑ go see a first-run movie
- ❑ rent a video at home

For $2: On TV, my first choice is:
- ❑ news
- ❑ sports
- ❑ sitcoms

For $3: If a show gets scary, I will usually:
- ❑ go to the restroom
- ❑ close my eyes
- ❑ clutch a friend
- ❑ love it

For $4: In movies, I prefer:
- ❑ romantic comedies
- ❑ serious drama
- ❑ action films
- ❑ Disney animations

I DREAM OF GENIE

If you could have three wishes, which three would you choose from the list below? Get together with one or two others and explain your choices.

- ❒ WIN THE LOTTERY: never have to work
- ❒ ROMANCE: an active and exciting love life
- ❒ SECURE JOB: lifetime guarantee with benefits
- ❒ STRESS-FREE LIFE: no pain, no struggle, no tension
- ❒ POPULARITY: everybody knocking at my door to spend time with me
- ❒ CLOSE FAMILY: no hassles, lots of love and support
- ❒ GOOD HEALTH: long life, full of vigor and vitality
- ❒ ONE DEEP, ABIDING FRIENDSHIP: someone who will always be there
- ❒ SUCCESS: fame and recognition in my chosen field
- ❒ STRONG, SPIRITUAL FAITH: a deep, satisfying relationship with God

MY LAST WILL AND TESTAMENT

Get together with one or two other people from your group and discuss the funeral arrangements below, choosing from the multiple-choice options.

HOW WOULD YOU CHOOSE TO DIE?
- ❒ prolong life as long as possible with support systems
- ❒ die naturally in a hospital, with pain relievers if needed
- ❒ die at home without medical care, but with family

WHAT FUNERAL WOULD YOU CHOOSE?
- ❒ big funeral with lots of flowers
- ❒ small funeral, money to charity
- ❒ no funeral, just family at grave

WHAT WOULD YOU WANT ON YOUR TOMBSTONE?
- ❒ words from my favorite Scripture, poem, song, etc.
- ❒ something about my life
- ❒ just my date of birth and death

HOW WOULD YOU MOST LIKE TO BE REMEMBERED?
- ❒ someone who cared for people
- ❒ someone who loved God
- ❒ someone who lived life to the fullest

HOW WOULD YOU WANT YOUR BODY TREATED?
- ❒ cremated
- ❒ given to science / organ donation
- ❒ buried intact

WHERE WOULD YOU LIKE YOUR MONEY TO GO?
- ❒ to my children
- ❒ to a charity
- ❒ to a memorial in my honor

SELF-DISCLOSURE SPECTRUMS

MR. / MISS AMERICA

Get together with one or two from your group and discuss the exercise below. For each category, put an **"X"** somewhere in between the two extremes to indicate how you see yourself. For instance, on ATHLETICISM you might put the **"X"** in the middle because you are in between the two extremes.

ATHLETICISM
Michael Jordan _____Rodney Dangerfield

MANNERS
Queen Elizabeth _____Ace Ventura

FITNESS
Sylvester Stallone _____Garfield

TACT
Oprah _____Beavis and Butt-head

SENSITIVITY
Mister Rogers _____Roseanne

FASHION
Princess Diana _____Madonna

NEATNESS
Frasier Crane _____*Peanuts'* Pigpen

SEX APPEAL
Tom Cruise / Cindy Crawford _____Kermit the Frog / Miss Piggy

MUSICAL ABILITY
Gloria Estefan _____Edith Bunker

CHARM
James Bond _____The Three Stooges

COOKING ABILITY
Betty Crocker _____Microwave dinner

I AM MORE LIKE ...

How would you describe yourself? Are you more like a trapeze artist ... or a circus clown? Finish the sentence below by filling in the blanks. In groups of 2, take turns going down the list.

I AM MORE LIKE A _____ THAN A _____

trapeze artist . . . . circus clown
sprinter . . . . distance runner
Porsche . . . . Jeep
microscope . . . . telescope
pitcher . . . . catcher
stand-up comic . . . . news reporter
glassy lake . . . . white-water rapids
candle . . . . lightbulb
amusement park . . . . library
coach . . . . player
dill pickle . . . . candy bar
dictionary . . . . mystery novel
in the game . . . . on the sideline
tortoise . . . . hare
teddy bear . . . . hungry tiger
choir member . . . . soloist
big city . . . . small town
pioneer . . . . settler
clinging vine . . . . touch-me-not flower
sunrise . . . . sunset

MY TEMPERAMENT

How do you see yourself in the eight categories below? In each category circle one of the two statements—the one that best represents the way you are. Share your answers with your group.

ON SHOWING MY FEELINGS:
Big boys / girls don't cry. _____ I love you, man!

ON INTENSITY:
Chill out. _____ Just do it.

ON BEING GENTLE AND KIND:
Nice guys finish last. _____ You say "Jump"; I say "How high?"

ON SPIRITUAL DESIRE:
Don't go overboard. _____ Full speed ahead.

ON CARING FOR OTHER PEOPLE:
Not my problem. _____ He ain't heavy; he's my brother.

ON BEING OPEN AND HONEST:
Mind your own business. _____ Lay it on the line.

ON HANDLING CONFLICT:
Peace at any price. _____ I don't get mad; I get even.

ON PERSPECTIVE:
The glass is half full. _____ The glass is half empty.

LAY IT ON THE LINE

Where do you stand on these issues? Pick a point on each line. For instance, on FEMINISM you might put yourself in the middle, because you are equal distance between the two positions on feminism. Go through the categories, with each person sharing their answer.

ON FEMINISM: A woman's place is in the home._____A woman's place is in the House ... of Representatives.

ON LAW AND ORDER: Lock the "losers" up. _____Educate and rehabilitate these victims of society.

ON ABORTION: People should have a choice. _____Fetuses have rights too.

ON CONDOMS: Kids have got to learn to protect themselves. _____They encourage promiscuity.

ON PORNOGRAPHY: It's a first amendment right._____We can't let such "freedom" destroy society.

ON SMOKING: It's my right. _____Your right to smoke stops at my nose.

MUSIC IN MY LIFE

Go around and let everyone explain this past week—somewhere between the two extremes—in each area of their life. If you do not know the songs, just go with the titles.

IN MY WORK THIS PAST WEEK, IT HAS BEEN ...
Some days the windshield,
somedays the bug _____ Everything is beautiful

ABOUT MYSELF, I'M FEELING ...
Nobody loves me but my mama,
and she might be lying, too _____ Jesus loves me

ABOUT THE FUTURE, I'M FEELING ...
There's a light at the end of the tunnel;   Call me a
I hope it's not a train _____ cock-eyed optimist

LIFESTYLE CHECKUP

How healthy is your lifestyle? Mark with an *"X"* on the lines below where you would rate yourself for each of the areas. Then get together with one to three others and take turns sharing the results of your checkup.

DIET / NUTRITION:
health food _____ junk food

EXERCISE / PHYSICAL ACTIVITY:
marathon runner _____ couch potato

SLEEPING HABITS:
"Good morning, Lord!" _____ "O Lord, it's morning!"

TOBACCO:
Mr. Clean _____ Joe Camel

ALCOHOL:
teetotaler _____ party animal

STRESS / HYPERACTIVITY:
Goofy _____ Tazmanian Devil

MENTAL ALERTNESS:
Road Runner _____ Wile E. Coyote

OVERALL FITNESS:
Arnold Schwarzenegger _____ Danny DeVito

RISKY BUSINESS

There are people in the world who go for all the gusto they can. Others simply try to keep their waters as calm as possible. Where are you on the risk scale? Place an **"X"** on the following lines. Get in groups of about 4 and share your responses with each other.

go skydiving _____ go bowling

spend my inheritance _____ put the money in the bank

take a lap around the track with an Indy driver _____ sit in the stands

try new foods _____ eat the same thing

go to a party where I don't know anybody _____ stay at home

say what I think _____ keep my opinions to myself

explore the city _____ stay close to home

watch a suspense thriller _____ watch a Disney animation

take an African safari _____ vacation on my front porch

FRIENDSHIP SURVEY

Get together with one or two others and discuss your preferences in choosing friends. On the first category—PERSONALITY—put an **"X"** on the line somewhere in between the two extremes and explain why. Then, let your partners explain where they marked themselves and why. Move to each category, through the list.

PERSONALITY: similar to mine _____ different from mine

COMMUNICATION: motormouth _____ quiet as a mouse

TEMPERAMENT: laid-back _____ intense

COMPATIBILITY: like doing the same things _____ not afraid to disagree and go their own way

LOYALTY: go along with me through thick and thin _____ challenge me when I need it

SELF-ESTEEM: put themselves down all the time _____ brag about themselves all the time

RELATIONSHIP TO FAMILY: speak highly of their family _____ always complaining about their family

MORAL STANDARDS: wild and free _____ stick to the rules

RELATIONSHIP TO A CHURCH: couldn't care less _____ very committed

ATTITUDE ABOUT LIFE: optimistic _____ pessimistic

INTERVIEWS

ASSESSING THE FUTURE

Get together with one or two others and take turns interviewing each other about the future.

1. Which phrase would best describe your philosophy about facing the future?
   - ❑ "I don't want to grow up!"
   - ❑ "Back to the future!"
   - ❑ "You can't go home again."
   - ❑ "One day at a time, sweet Jesus."
   - ❑ "Climb every mountain" (from *The Sound of Music*)
   - ❑ "He who isn't busy being born is busy dying."
   - ❑ "The future belongs to those who plan for it."
   - ❑ "I don't know what the future holds, but I know who holds the future."
   - ❑ "Every day in every way, things are getting better."
   - ❑ "The future's so bright, I've got to wear shades!"

2. What would you like to be doing 10 years from now?

3. What is one thing you expect to have in the future which you do not have now?

THE OLD NEIGHBORHOOD

Get together with one or two other people and interview each other about your "old neighborhood." If you have moved a lot, talk about the neighborhood where you spent the most time, or the one which was your favorite. On the other hand, you may still be living in your "old neighborhood."

1. Where was your "old neighborhood"?

2. Which of the following was your old neighborhood like?
   - ❑ *Sesame Street*—urban and multicultural
   - ❑ *Family Matters*—distinctively ethnic
   - ❑ *Home Improvement*—suburban housing with a common cultural background
   - ❑ *Dr. Quinn, Medicine Woman*—spread out but close-knit

3. Share your responses to as many of the following questions as you have time for:
   - ❑ Where did the kids gather in your neighborhood?
   - ❑ What were your favorite things to do together?
   - ❑ What were the special places—the best places to climb trees, skateboard or rollerblade, hide from adults, etc.?
   - ❑ Where were the "danger spots"—the yards with mean dogs, the "grumpy old Mr. Wilson" who didn't like kids, the "haunted" houses or boarded-up buildings?
   - ❑ Who was the Dennis the Menace who always got into trouble or got you into trouble?
   - ❑ Who were some kids you remember having really distinctive things about them—the "Weird Harolds" and "Fat Alberts"?

MY FAMILY SUPPER TABLE

Get together with one or two people and share some important facts about your life at age 7. Focus on your supper table—the place where you ate your nightly meal. Let your partner interview you like a talk show host— *This Is Your Life*. Then, reverse the roles and interview your partner.

1. When you were 7 years old, where were you living?

2. What was the shape of the table where you ate your evening meal? Round? Square? Rectangle?

3. How often did you eat together as a family? All the time? Most of the time? Half the time? Seldom? Almost never?

4. Where did you sit? Who else was at the table and where did they sit?

5. Who did most of the talking? About what usually?

6. How would you describe the typical atmosphere at the table? Relaxed? Tense? Quiet? Exciting? Peaceful? Crazy? Dull? Rushed?

7. Did anyone say the blessing? If so, who?

8. Who reached out to you and always included you in the conversation?

9. What is your favorite or best memory of your childhood supper table?

LIVES OF THE RICH AND FAMOUS

Get together with one or two others and interview each other for a feature story on the TV program, *Lives of the Rich and Famous*. Let your partner read the questions and you answer. Then, reverse the roles and you interview your partner.

1. What is your nickname? What do your friends call you?

2. Who was your first "crush"?

3. How have your ideas about love and romance changed?

4. What do you do for kicks?

5. Where do you go when you want to be alone?

6. If you got into the *Guinness Book of World Records*, what would it be for?

7. What do you consider your greatest accomplishment?

8. What is one thing you've tried that you never want to do again?

9. What has been your biggest disappointment or regret?

10. What future challenge or opportunity excites you the most?

LESSONS IN CONFLICT

Get together with one or two other people and take turns interviewing each other about the conflict in your lives.

1. Looking back, what was the funniest thing you did as a teenager that got you in trouble with your parents?

2. What important thing did you learn in conflicts with your parents?
   - ❏ Always apologize (even if you're right!).
   - ❏ Father (and mother) knows best.
   - ❏ It's best to talk it out.
   - ❏ Even parents can be wrong sometimes.
   - ❏ What your parents don't know won't hurt them (or you either!).
   - ❏ Listening to each other clears up many conflicts.
   - ❏ It's better to face a conflict and get it over with than to try to hide or ignore it.
   - ❏ other:_____

3. In your normal style of handling conflict, which are you more like?
   - ❏ an ostrich—I hide my head in the sand until the conflict goes away.
   - ❏ a house dog—I timidly slouch away, then chew up the couch when no one's looking.
   - ❏ a hawk—I fly above it all and pick my targets.
   - ❏ a fox—I use my brains to win.
   - ❏ a dolphin—I can fight if necessary, but would rather swim away.

PERSONAL INVENTORIES

MEDICAL HISTORY

Here are some "highly scientific," but not so rare "diseases." As someone reads the descriptions one at a time, stand up if that's part of *your* "medical history"!

INTERNET-ITIS—staring at a monitor for hours while typing messages to people you've never met

MONOTONE-EOSIS—A sure sign of this disease is when people move away from you like you have the plague when you sing *The Star Spangled Banner.*

CHOCO-HOLISM—snarling when people suggest you share your "chocolate decadence" dessert

MALL-ITIS—a strong compulsion to spend many hours (and many dollars!) at the mall

ESPN DEFICIENCY SYNDROME—going into convulsions when you haven't heard the sports scores in too long a time

EXERCISE-SPASTITIS—a spasm that keeps you from exercising, even when you get the urge

CHANNELSURF-EOSIS—cramps in your index finger from having to push the remote control buttons so much—often makes you bed or couch-ridden

FISHERMANEYE-OPIA—makes what you catch appear about a foot longer

INVOLUNTARY LEADFOOT REFLEX—a physiological phenomenon that results in "keeping the pedal to the metal" while driving

LIFE SIGNS

Get together in groups of about 4 and spend some time thinking about your lives in terms of traffic signs. Have each person share their response to each question.

1. If you were to select a traffic sign to tell how you've been seeking to live your life, what sign would it be?
    - ❐ "Merge"—because I've been trying to get along with everyone
    - ❐ "Slow"—because I've been seeking to slow down and experience more of life
    - ❐ "Keep Right"—because I'm trying to keep my life on the right track
    - ❐ "No U-Turn"—because I'm resisting the urge to go back to the past
    - ❐ "One Way"—because I'm seeking to be more decisive in my life
    - ❐ "Yield"—because I'm seeking to yield my life to God
    - ❐ "Children Playing"—because I'm trying to let out the "child" in me
    - ❐ "Under Construction"—because I'm changing so much

2. What sign are you displaying in your relationship with others?
    - ❐ "No Trespassing!"—because I keep people at a distance
    - ❐ "Help Wanted"—because I'm reaching out for support
    - ❐ "One Way"—because I'm not always tolerant of differences
    - ❐ "Open 24 Hours"—because I'm always available to others
    - ❐ "Keep Right"—because I encourage others to do what is right
    - ❐ "No Vacancy"—because there's no room in my life for anyone else right now

3. If God were to give you a "traffic ticket" right now for how you are living your life, what would it be for?
    - ❐ "Speeding"—not slowing down enough to really live
    - ❐ "Failing to Yield"—trying to do things my own way
    - ❐ "Blocking Traffic"—I feel I've gotten in the way of others who are doing more.
    - ❐ "Illegal U-Turn"—I have been trying to live in the past.
    - ❐ "Driving the Wrong Way on a One-Way Street"—I need to turn my life around.

THINGS THAT DRIVE YOU CRAZY

Here's a list of things that drive a lot of people crazy. Do they drive you crazy, too? After checking the appropriate response, form groups of about 4 and share your choices with the group.

	YES	NO	SOMETIMES
bathtub rings that aren't yours	❑	❑	❑
waiting at stoplights	❑	❑	❑
people who constantly channel-surf	❑	❑	❑
dripping faucet	❑	❑	❑
someone talking during a movie	❑	❑	❑
losing one sock	❑	❑	❑
not enough toilet paper	❑	❑	❑
someone who is always late	❑	❑	❑
someone who sings in the car	❑	❑	❑
boring speakers or teachers	❑	❑	❑
a motormouth	❑	❑	❑
preempting of a television program	❑	❑	❑
getting cut off in traffic	❑	❑	❑
getting put on hold on the phone	❑	❑	❑
people who take up two parking spaces	❑	❑	❑
an itch you can't reach	❑	❑	❑
screeching chalk on a chalkboard	❑	❑	❑
an annoying song that gets stuck in your head	❑	❑	❑
people who crack their knuckles	❑	❑	❑
people who crack their gum	❑	❑	❑
people who chew with their mouths open	❑	❑	❑
backseat drivers	❑	❑	❑
telephone solicitors	❑	❑	❑
someone leaving the toilet seat up	❑	❑	❑

SCOUTING REPORT

Get together with one or two others and work together on the scouting report below. In each category check your one or two best points. See if your partners agree with you ... and let them add one more that you did not mention. Then do the next person's list.

MENTAL	EMOTIONAL	SPIRITUAL
____ intelligence	____ warmth	____ compassion
____ creativity	____ sensitivity	____ joyfulness
____ good judgment	____ consistency	____ serenity
____ self-confidence	____ enthusiasm	____ dedication
____ common sense	____ patience	____ gentleness
____ determination	____ self-control	____ generosity
____ sense of humor	____ cheerfulness	____ humility
____ perception	____ dependability	____ discipline
____ comprehension	____ loyalty	____ faith
____ good memory	____ peacefulness	____ courage

121

WHO INFLUENCES YOU?

Get together with one or two others and discuss who has influenced you most in making decisions in your life. In each category, check two columns—either parents / siblings; spouse / boyfriend / girlfriend; friends; teachers; church / youth group or popular culture.

WHO HAS INFLUENCED ...	parents / siblings	spouse / boyfriend / girlfriend	friends	teachers	church / youth group	popular culture
How I spend my time						
How I spend my money						
How I dress						
What I feed my mind						
Where I draw the line						
What I believe						
What I want out of life						
How I see myself						
How I handle fear, failure and guilt						

DO-IT-YOURSELF STRESS TEST

Take a moment and determine your stress level right now, based on a chart developed by Thomas Holmes and Richard Rahe. If you score more than 150 points for events in the last year, you are probably under a lot of stress right now. Share your score (and as many details as you feel comfortable) with the group.

EVENT	STRESS POINTS
Death of a spouse	100
Divorce	73
Marital separation	65
Jail term	63
Death of a close family member	63
Personal injury or illness	53
Marriage	50
Loss of job	47
Marital reconciliation	45
Retirement	45
Health problem in family	44
Pregnancy	40
Sex difficulties	39
Gain of a new family member	39
Business readjustment	39
Change in financial state	38
Death of a close friend	37
Change in line of work	36
Increased arguments with spouse	35
Large mortgage taken out	31
Foreclosure of mortgage or loan	30
Change in work responsibilities	29
Son or daughter leaving home	29
Trouble with in-laws	29
Major personal achievement	28
Spouse starting or stopping work	26
Change in living conditions	25
Revision of personal habits	24
Trouble with boss	23
Change in work hours	20
Change in residence	20
Change in school	20
Change in recreation	19
Change in church activities	19
Change in social activities	19

TOTAL SCORE _____

MY RISK QUOTIENT

Pair off with one or two other people and discuss your "risk quotient." The test below is a fun way to figure out how much of a risk-taker you really are. First complete the questionnaire. Then figure out your score and share your results with each other.

1. In playing Monopoly, I usually:
   a. play it safe / hide money under the table
   b. stay cool and hold back a little
   c. go for broke—gambling everything

2. In choosing a job, I would prefer:
   a. a boring job with security
   b. an interesting job with some security
   c. start my own company with no security

3. On a menu, I usually pick:
   a. something familiar that I know I like
   b. something that's a little different
   c. something way-out that I've never tried

4. At a party, I usually:
   a. stick with my friends
   b. reach out to one stranger
   c. see how many new people I can meet

5. In starting a relationship, I usually:
   a. let the other person do the talking
   b. meet the other person halfway
   c. take the initiative

6. I would prefer my life to have:
   a. no risks and lots of safety
   b. some risks and some safety
   c. lots of risks and little safety

Scoring: Give yourself 1 point for every "a," 2 points for every "b," and 3 points for every "c." Then circle the total on the line below to get your risk quotient.

PLAY IT SAFE   **TAKE A CHANCE**

6   7   8   9   10   11   12   13   14   15   16   17   18

123

POWER PEOPLE

Some people in your life have a powerful effect on you. Different kinds of "power people" are listed below. Fill in the name of at least three of the "power people" in your life. Then share your answers with your group.

_____ LISTENER: the person who is always there to hear what I have to say without trying to change me

_____ CHALLENGER: that special person who has a way of bringing out the best in me, even when I am complacent

_____ CONFRONTER: a person who loves me enough to tell me things I might not want to hear

_____ ENCOURAGER: someone who helps me look on the bright side of things

_____ PRAYER PARTNER: someone I trust enough to come with me when I go to God in prayer

_____ ROLE MODEL: the kind of person I want to be like in my actions, character and reputation

_____ MENTOR: that special person who has been willing to take me under their wing and guide me on my life's journey

_____ INSPIRER: that wonderful person who can elevate my spirit and remind me that God has everything under control

_____ CONSOLER: the person who can calm me down when life gets out of control

_____ PLAYMATE: someone who I can always count on to do something fun and bring out the child in me

_____ DREAMER: that special person who will listen to and appreciate my dreams

RANKINGS

RANKING CAREERS

To recognize our calling in life, it helps to eliminate some lines of work we would *not* like to do. Look over the list below and choose the three WORST options for a future career. Share your choices with your group.

____ crowd-control officer at a rock concert

____ organizer of paperwork for Congress

____ scriptwriter for Barney and Baby Bop

____ public relations manager for Madonna

____ public relations manager for Dennis Rodman

____ researcher studying the spawning habits of Alaskan salmon

____ bodyguard for Rush Limbaugh on a speaking tour of feminist groups

____ toy assembly person for a local toy store over the holidays

____ middle or high school principal

____ nurse's aide at a home for retired Sumo wrestlers

____ consistency expert for a chewing gum manufacturer

____ official physician for the National Association of Hypochondriacs

____ chief animal-control officer at Jurassic Park

____ pump operator for a portable toilet company

FUN MONEY

Imagine that a rich aunt or uncle just gave you $1,000. Decide how much you would spend in each of the following categories. Get together in groups of about 4 and compare your results.

_____ clothes

_____ sports equipment / lessons

_____ eating out

_____ household items

_____ vacation

_____ savings

_____ concerts, movies, theater, etc.

_____ my hobby

_____ computer stuff

_____ gifts for others

_____ sporting events

_____ music or stereo equipment

_____ reading material

_____ church

CHOOSING FRIENDS

Get together with one to three others and look over the list of qualities that you look for in a friend. See if you can agree on the top five.

___ similar lifestyle	___ plenty of time for me	___ laid-back
___ honesty	___ plenty of money	___ loyalty
___ nice smile	___ intelligence	___ common interests
___ generosity	___ dependability	___ straight morals
___ spiritual depth	___ outgoing personality	___ shares personally
___ commitment	___ spontaneous	___ similar background
___ good looks	___ great sense of humor	___ speaks his or her mind
___ good listener	___ popularity	___ fun to be with

FINAL JEOPARDY

Imagine you've entered the final round of *Jeopardy!* with $4,000. Your opponents have $4,500 and $5,000. How much of your $4,000 would you risk if the final category would be each of the following? Write down an amount on each line. Then take turns sharing your answers with the group.

_____ understanding the opposite sex

_____ current rock groups

_____ Federal Income Tax forms

_____ auto mechanics

_____ popular video games

_____ names in the Old Testament

_____ current movies

_____ spelling

_____ famous football players

_____ United States history

_____ world geography

_____ current fashion fads

IRRESISTIBLE BARGAINS

Many of us look for bargains. In groups of 4 or more, go around and let each person answer the first question. Then go around on the second question.

1. Which of the following bargains would you have the greatest trouble resisting? Rank your top two.
   - ❐ 30% off sale on fine gourmet chocolates
   - ❐ one month of a premium cable channel free for signing up for another month
   - ❐ "second entree free" coupon at a romantic restaurant
   - ❐ free airline ticket in exchange for looking at time-share property
   - ❐ 2-for-1 sale in the clothing department of your favorite department store
   - ❐ box seats at general admission prices for your favorite sports team
   - ❐ fine piece of antique furniture going for two-thirds listed value at an auction
   - ❐ chance to get tickets for live performance of your favorite singer or band for half-price
   - ❐ free membership to an athletic club or gym for a month

2. Rank where you would fall on the following continuum. "When it comes to bargains, I am generally ..."

1	2	3	4	5
cynical	suspicious	cautious	receptive	ready and eager!

HOME REMEDY FOR A FEVER

Nearly everyone has a special prescription for treating a fever or cold. But what about your spiritual and emotional ailments? Go around the group on the first question. Then go around on the next question.

1. If your inner emotional state during this past week could be measured with a thermometer, what would have been your temperature?
    ❏ 98.6 degrees—normal, healthy, full of vitality
    ❏ 97.5 degrees—turning cold in the midst of stress and demands
    ❏ 99.9 degrees—Probably no one noticed, but I've been a little out of sorts.
    ❏ 102 degrees—Things have definitely been heating up inside of me.
    ❏ 106 degrees—The stress is burning my brain, everything is hazy, and I'm not sure how I made it this far!

2. In the midst of what is happening inside of you, what has been your favorite "fever reducer" this past week?
    ❏ encouragement from my spouse or significant other
    ❏ a friend or friends who have listened
    ❏ my prayer and devotional time
    ❏ support from this group
    ❏ my extended family
    ❏ playing some of my favorite music
    ❏ time alone
    ❏ watching TV and losing myself in the miseries of others
    ❏ other:_____

BIBLICAL INVENTORIES

HOW'S YOUR LOVE LIFE?

The best-known passage in the Bible about love is 1 Corinthians 13—the "love chapter." The personal inventory below is taken from this passage. Get into groups of about 4. Turn to 1 Corinthians 13:4–7 and have someone read the verses out loud. Then, let one person read the first phrase. Go around the group and have everyone pick a number between 1 and 10. Have someone else read the next phrase, etc. until you've completed the inventory.

Love is patient: I don't take out my frustrations on those I love. I am calm under pressure and careful with my tongue.

FAILURE 1 2 3 4 5 6 7 8 9 10 SUCCESS

Love is kind: I go out of my way to say nice words, and do thoughtful things for others.

FAILURE 1 2 3 4 5 6 7 8 9 10 SUCCESS

Love does not envy: I am not envious of others' gifts and abilities or of what they have. Neither am I jealous with my time toward those who need me.

FAILURE 1 2 3 4 5 6 7 8 9 10 SUCCESS

Love does not boast: I don't consider my role any more important than those I love—or talk like "I know better."

FAILURE 1 2 3 4 5 6 7 8 9 10 SUCCESS

Love is not proud: I don't think of myself as better than those I love; or better at sports ... or singing ... or handling money, etc.

FAILURE 1 2 3 4 5 6 7 8 9 10 SUCCESS

Love is not rude: I don't make cutting or crude remarks when I don't get my way—or become silent and withdrawn.

FAILURE 1 2 3 4 5 6 7 8 9 10 SUCCESS

Love is not self-seeking: I don't put myself first. I try to give those I love spiritual and emotional support.

FAILURE 1 2 3 4 5 6 7 8 9 10 SUCCESS

Love is not easily angered: I don't let little things bother me, especially with those I love. I have a muffler on my mouth.

FAILURE 1 2 3 4 5 6 7 8 9 10 SUCCESS

Love keeps no record of wrongs: I don't keep score of the number of times those I love have said something or done something that upset me, and I don't bring it up when we have conflict.

FAILURE 1 2 3 4 5 6 7 8 9 10 SUCCESS

Love does not delight in evil: There is a difference between acceptance and approval. I accept those I love, but I do not have to approve of everything they do.

FAILURE 1 2 3 4 5 6 7 8 9 10 SUCCESS

Love rejoices with the truth: With a compassionate spirit, I will say what needs to be said to someone, even if it might be difficult. I seek the truth in my own life and encourage others to do the same.

FAILURE 1 2 3 4 5 6 7 8 9 10 SUCCESS

Love always protects: I am always there for those I love—even when they upset me—seeking to comfort and care as Christ would.

FAILURE 1 2 3 4 5 6 7 8 9 10 SUCCESS

Love always trusts: I believe in those I love and I believe in God. And I am willing to let God do the shaping and molding.

FAILURE 1 2 3 4 5 6 7 8 9 10 SUCCESS

Love always hopes: I am good at expecting the best and thinking the best about those I love. I always give those I love the benefit of the doubt.

FAILURE 1 2 3 4 5 6 7 8 9 10 SUCCESS

Love always perseveres: I am committed to those I love and I am prepared to see that commitment through to the end.

FAILURE 1 2 3 4 5 6 7 8 9 10 SUCCESS

THE ARMOR OF GOD

Scripture doesn't promise Christians an easy life. In Ephesians 6, the apostle Paul calls the Christian life a struggle and compares the spiritual equipment of a Christian to a Roman soldier fully dressed for battle.

Get into groups of about 4 to take the personal inventory below. Turn to Ephesians 6:10–18 and have someone read the Scripture out loud. Then, let one person read the first piece of equipment and its application. Go around the group and have everyone give a number from 1 (very low) to 10 (very high), and explain why you gave yourself this number. Have someone else read the next piece of equipment and application, etc., until you've completed the inventory.

BELT OF TRUTH

I am prepared to stake my life on the fact that Jesus Christ is the Son of God. I have thought through what I believe, and I am willing to take a stand.

1   2   3   4   5   6   7   8   9   10

BREASTPLATE OF RIGHTEOUSNESS

I am prepared to put my life where my mouth is—in clean and right living—with genuine integrity—as Christ did. I am serious about being God's man or God's woman.

1   2   3   4   5   6   7   8   9   10

FEET FITTED WITH THE READINESS THAT COMES FROM THE GOSPEL OF PEACE

I am willing to publicly affirm my faith in Christ—at school, work or wherever. I find it easy to talk about my personal faith.

1   2   3   4   5   6   7   8   9   10

SHIELD OF FAITH

I am prepared to step out with Christ—to risk my life, my fortune and my future for him whatever the cost or consequences. And through faith, I am taking a stand against the "evil one."

1   2   3   4   5   6   7   8   9   10

HELMET OF SALVATION

I know that I am part of the family of God because of Jesus Christ. I have a strong inner peace because I am at peace with God.

1   2   3   4   5   6   7   8   9   10

SWORD OF THE SPIRIT, WHICH IS THE WORD OF GOD

I actively seek to know more about God and his will for my life through an ongoing study of his guidebook, the Bible. I discipline myself to reflect on it daily.

1   2   3   4   5   6   7   8   9   10

PRAYER

I set aside time regularly to talk with God and to let him speak to me. I consciously try to submit every decision in my life to God.

1   2   3   4   5   6   7   8   9   10

A HIGH STANDARD

In writing to the early Christians in Rome, the apostle Paul gave them a big challenge—to stand tall for Christ. Gather in groups of about 4 to take the personal inventory below.

Turn to Romans 12:9–21 and have someone read the Scripture out loud. Then, let one person read the first phrase and its paraphrase. Go around the group and have everyone give a number from 1 (very low) to 10 (very high) to indicate how they measure themselves in that area. Have someone else read the next phrase, etc., until you've completed the inventory.

Love must be sincere. I am able to really give myself to others, not in some phony way, but with real meaning.

1   2   3   4   5   6   7   8   9   10

Hate what is evil; cling to what is good. I am learning to stand up for my convictions; to say no to something I know is wrong and yes to God.

1   2   3   4   5   6   7   8   9   10

Be devoted to one another in brotherly love. Honor one another above yourselves. I am learning how to reach out and hug my Christian brothers and sisters warmly—for the right reasons. And I put their needs above my own.

1   2   3   4   5   6   7   8   9   10

Never be lacking in zeal. I have a deep desire to pitch in at home, school, church and work without having to be asked.

1   2   3   4   5   6   7   8   9   10

Keep your spiritual fervor, serving the Lord. I am eager and enthusiastic to do anything I can for Christ because my heart is full of gratitude for what he has done for me.

1   2   3   4   5   6   7   8   9   10

Be joyful in hope. I am experiencing a new freedom that overflows in praise because I know God is in control.

1   2   3   4   5   6   7   8   9   10

Patient in affliction. Problems don't always get me down. I can take the heat. Under pressure I can stay cool.

1   2   3   4   5   6   7   8   9   10

Faithful in prayer. I have learned to turn over every need to Christ and to share every decision I have to make with him. I have learned to "wait on God" and let him work things out.

1   2   3   4   5   6   7   8   9   10

Share with God's people who are in need. Practice hospitality. I have learned that my possessions, my time, my whole being belongs to God—to be shared with those in need.

1   2   3   4   5   6   7   8   9   10

Bless those who persecute you. I have learned to respond with kindness to those who put me down—and to pray on their behalf. I am no longer defensive about my life.

1   2   3   4   5   6   7   8   9   10

Rejoice with those who rejoice; mourn with those who mourn. I celebrate life when others are rejoicing, and grieve openly when others are hurting. I am not afraid to show my feelings.

1   2   3   4   5   6   7   8   9   10

BE-ATTITUDES

Some people cannot see the good things in their lives because they have only been told the bad things: "You are dumb ... clumsy ... no good, etc." In the Scripture known as the Beatitudes, Jesus referred to eight character traits. In the first part of this inventory, you will have a chance to evaluate your progress on each of these traits. In the second half of the activity, your group will add their insights about you.

Go around on the first trait—POOR IN SPIRIT—and let everyone call out a number between 1 and 4 to indicate how they see themselves: 1—VERY LOW, and 4—VERY HIGH. When you have finished with the first trait, go around again on the second trait, etc. ... through all eight traits.

POOR IN SPIRIT: I can feel accepted by God when I feel most unacceptable to myself. I am a person of worth and value even though I don't have it all together.

LOW   1   2   3   4   HIGH

MOURN: I can show my feelings and let others know when I'm hurting. I can be around others when they are hurting without feeling embarrassment. I can weep like Jesus did.

LOW   1   2   3   4   HIGH

MEEK: I don't have to act like a hero or look like a beauty queen. I can just be myself—the person that God made me.

LOW   1   2   3   4   HIGH

SPIRITUAL HUNGER: I am more excited about God's will for my life than my own success, popularity or good time. I am excited about knowing God.

LOW   1   2   3   4   HIGH

MERCIFUL: I can feel the pain of someone who is hurting ... and care for them as God's representative. I really hurt when my friends hurt.

LOW   1   2   3   4   HIGH

PURE IN HEART: I can be open and honest with God and others. I don't have to put on a false mask or pretend to be something that I am not.

LOW   1   2   3   4   HIGH

PEACEMAKER: I work at keeping communication channels open and resolving conflicts—particularly with my family and friends who I love the most.

LOW   1   2   3   4   HIGH

PERSECUTION: I can take criticism without reacting defensively or feeling self-pity. I can take the heat and stand alone if I have to.

LOW   1   2   3   4   HIGH

When you are finished evaluating yourself, let the others in your group tell you some positive things about you that they have observed. Have one person listen silently while the others choose one of the Beatitudes that they see in that person. Go around and affirm each member of the group in this way.

CASE STUDIES

Here are case studies designed especially for youth groups. Get together in groups of about 4. Have one person read the case study out loud; then discuss each question as a group.

VIOLENCE

Jake is 15 and an only child. He spends a lot of time at the video arcade playing the martial arts combat and shoot'em up games with friends. His dad has been long gone since the divorce several years ago; and his mom is gone a lot with her career. Although a bright student, Jake is bored with school and is not really sure he wants to grow up and be "successful" like his parents. Jake begins to hang out late at night with some guys from school, as they cruise around town looking for excitement. They begin doing a little shoplifting, vandalism, graffiti, and sneaking into the porno flicks downtown. Pretty soon that becomes boring too. One night they see a girl from school who hangs with the "in" crowd walking to her car in a secluded lot. One of the guys says, "Hey, let's have some fun with the babe." They start by playing keep-away with her purse until the young woman starts fighting back. A couple of the guys begin to retaliate, mocking her attempts to defend herself. Before it's over some of the guys are taking turns beating and raping her. Jake watches, trying to be cool while inside he knows this is wrong; but fear of rejection, ridicule and physical harm keep him silent. These guys are not just poor, underprivileged kids who grew up in violent and abusive neighborhoods; some are above average students and enjoy the "good" life.

Discussion Questions:

1. Why did Jake get involved with this group of guys?
   - ❏ He was into shoplifting.
   - ❏ He was bored.
   - ❏ He wanted to feel accepted.
   - ❏ He wanted to belong to a tough gang and hurt someone.
   - ❏ other:_____

2. What or who is to blame for Jake's involvement in the group and the things the guys did? Explain.
   - ❏ Jake
   - ❏ Jake's youth group
   - ❏ Jake's parents
   - ❏ the guys in the group
   - ❏ other:_____

3. What effect do you think the video games and other forms of entertainment had on Jake's actions and attitudes? Explain.
   - ❏ little effect
   - ❏ some effect
   - ❏ big effect

4. If you were a part of the jury who tried these guys for what they did to the girl, what do you think should happen to them, especially Jake?

DEPRESSION AND SUICIDE

Bill was the president of the sophomore class, captain of the junior varsity football team and an honor student. Bill was the most popular kid in his class, but one night he put the barrel of a shotgun in his mouth and pulled the trigger. Looking back, his friends say they might have been able to do something if they had known what to look for. He was the youngest in a family of very gifted and successful children. And the family had high expectations for him—which he said he could not live up to.

His older sister was killed the year before in an automobile accident. His friends thought it was just the grieving process when he spoke about "going to see his sister soon." And his favorite comment when he was disappointed or frustrated in a dating relationship was, "I'm going to kill myself."

Discussion Questions:

1. If you had been a close friend of Bill's and you heard him speaking this way, what would you do?
   - ❏ probably ignore it
   - ❏ assume he was only joking
   - ❏ ask him what he was really saying
   - ❏ tell a counselor about it
   - ❏ see to it that he gets help at the risk of offending him

2. If you thought Bill should get help but feared you were going to "break his confidence," what would you do?
   - ❏ tell someone without telling Bill
   - ❏ tell Bill first that I was going to tell someone
   - ❏ get Bill together with his parents and tell them
   - ❏ I don't know what I would do.

3. If Bill was in your youth group, what would you do?
   - ❏ open up about the situation to the whole group
   - ❏ tell the youth leader
   - ❏ tell Bill first that I was going to tell the youth leader
   - ❏ just be a friend to Bill
   - ❏ I don't know.

SEX (case study for girls)

Mary wasn't a Christian in junior high when she got involved with guys. She had a rich fantasy life and enjoyed visualizing herself in sexual experiences with guys. She was quiet at school, but fun to be with, and made it easy or challenging for guys to touch her. She could play hard to get, or give guys the come on, depending on her mood and desires. She knew how to dress to attract their attention, yet still be accepted by the girls. She had lost count of the guys she had made it with, and had no intention of giving any of that up.

When she gave her life to Christ, she figured that it was the attitude about Christ, not all the do's and don'ts, that was important, that "love" was the most important principle, and that she could witness in the back seat of a car as easily as anywhere else.

But to her surprise she found all of that changing. It was not an instant miracle, but it was totally the process of God working on her and in her mind and heart. Changes began to take place from the inside out. One action, one attitude, one thought at a time ... over many months.

SEX (case study for guys)

In Sam's life, lust was not always a problem. It took hold a little at a time. When he was 7 years old, he had his first encounter with sex. Out of curiosity he and a young girl touched and explored each other. Lusts were aroused in him at that early age.

Sam began to think about this experience. He focused his mind on these thoughts and desires. The more he thought about the opposite sex, the stronger his feelings became. In junior high he began looking at "girlie" maga-

zines. He read pornographic stories about sexual conquests. As the thoughts and actions ran unchecked, lustful habit patterns began to form in his life. Sexual fantasy and pornography became a way of life and he couldn't seem to help himself. These reinforced the lustful pattern of thinking. When he saw cute girls, he visualized them like the girls in the magazine. He began to focus on parts of their bodies instead of seeing them as whole people. As time went on, the bondage became stronger. He talked about girls differently, and kept looking forward to when he himself would be the conqueror.

Sam could never get moral victory over lust until he understood why he was lusting. His youth director at church helped him understand that he did not lust primarily for the sexual pleasure it brought him, but because he was getting temporary acceptance and satisfaction from these thoughts and habits.

Discussion Questions:

1. How do you feel about Mary or Sam?

2. If you were Mary or Sam's friend, how would you treat them?

3. How do you think Mary and Sam should deal with the feelings of failure and guilt for the stuff they have done?

4. What could you share from your own experience that might help Mary or Sam?

5. Do these case studies lead you to some questions or concerns? Is there someone you could share them with?

SERIOUS AFFIRMATION

VALUED VALUES

Below is a list of qualities based on positive values. In silence, think about the members of your group and jot down their names next to the value that describes them best. Ask one person to listen while the others explain which value they selected for that individual. Then go to the next person and do the same until everyone is affirmed.

_____ PURE IN HEART: Your life is marked with integrity before God and other people.

_____ PEACEMAKER: You have a gift from God to help people overcome their differences.

_____ TRANSPARENT: You can be yourself without any pretenses and let the light of Christ shine through you.

_____ FAITHFUL: You are faithful to uphold God's morality even under pressure.

_____ MERCIFUL / COMPASSIONATE: You have the ability to feel what others feel—to be happy or to hurt with them.

_____ MEEK / GENTLE: You can be outwardly tender because you are inwardly strong.

_____ SPIRITUALLY HUNGRY: I admire the longing in your heart for a growing, genuine relationship with God.

_____ ALWAYS LOVING: You have a Christlike capacity to love others unconditionally—no matter what.

_____ COMMUNITY BUILDER: God uses you as a bond to bring people together in unity.

_____ HUMBLE: I admire the quiet way you demonstrate what humility is all about.

_____ GENEROUS: You give freely, not for attention or praise—but for the simple joy of giving.

_____ CONTENTED: You know your worth is based on who you are rather than on what you have.

_____ JOYFUL: Regardless of the circumstances, you have a smile on your face and a positive outlook about life.

_____ PATIENT: You never seem to be in a hurry or to get irritated by others.

YOU REMIND ME OF JESUS

Every Christian reflects the character of Jesus in some way. As your group has gotten to know each other, you can begin to see how each person demonstrates Christ in their very own personality. Go around the circle and have each person listen while others take turns telling that person what they notice in him or her that reminds them of Jesus. You may also want to tell them why you selected what you did.

YOU REMIND ME OF ...

_____ JESUS THE HEALER: You seem to be able to touch someone's life with your compassion and help make them whole.

_____ JESUS THE SERVANT: There's nothing that you wouldn't do for someone.

_____ JESUS THE PREACHER: You share your faith in a way that challenges and inspires people.

_____ JESUS THE LEADER: As Jesus had a plan for the disciples, you are able to lead others in a way that honors God.

_____ JESUS THE REBEL: By doing the unexpected, you remind me of Jesus' way of revealing God in unique, surprising ways.

_____ JESUS THE RECONCILER: Like Jesus, you have the ability to be a peacemaker between others.

_____ JESUS THE TEACHER: You have a gift for bringing light and understanding to God's Word.

_____ JESUS THE CRITIC: You have the courage to say what needs to be said, even if it isn't always popular.

_____ JESUS THE SACRIFICE: Like Jesus, you seem to be willing to sacrifice anything to glorify God.

THANK YOU

Below is a list of animals. Read over the list and pick one that best describes how you feel about this group. When everyone has made their choice, take turns sharing your answers as a way of saying "thank you" to the group.

WILD EAGLE: You have helped me discover my spiritual wings and helped me soar like an eagle—spiritually.

HAPPY HIPPOPOTAMUS: You have helped me surface and bask in the warm sunshine of God's love.

LANKY LEOPARD: You have helped me look closely at myself and see some spots, and you still accept me the way I am.

SAFARI ELEPHANT: You have helped me get started on the exciting adventure of the Christian life.

COLORFUL PEACOCK: You have helped me see the new person that Christ has made me—something beautiful and special.

PLAYFUL PORPOISE: You have helped me laugh at some of my problems and realize that I am not alone.

OSTRICH IN LOVE: You have helped me get my head out of the sand, enjoy life and have fun.

TOWERING GIRAFFE: You have helped me hold my head up and feel confident about my faith.

ROARING LION: You have helped me stand up for what I believe and speak out for my faith.

DANCING BEAR: You have helped me celebrate life and show my friends that the Christian life can be fun.

ALL-WEATHER DUCK: You have helped me appreciate the storms that I am going through—and to sing in the rain.

MY GOURMET GROUP

Here is a chance to pass out some much-deserved praise for the people who have made your group something special. Put down the name of each group member next to the delicacy that person has added to your group. Then let one person listen while the others explain where they put this person's name. Repeat this process for each person in the group.

_____ CAVIAR: That special touch of class and aristocratic taste; makes the rest of us feel like royalty.

_____ ARTICHOKE HEARTS: Tender, delicate, disarmingly vulnerable; whets the appetite for heartfelt sharing.

_____ IMPORTED CHEESE: Distinctive, tangy, mellow with age; with a special flavor all its own, that brings depth to any meal.

_____ VINEGAR AND OIL: Tart, witty, dry; a rare combination of healing ointment and pungent spice to add "bite" to the salad.

_____ FRENCH PASTRY: Tempting, irresistible, "creme de la creme" dessert; the connoisseur's delight for topping off a meal.

_____ PHEASANT UNDER GLASS: Wild, untamed, totally unique; a rare dish for very special people who appreciate original fare.

_____ CARAFE OF WINE: Sparkling, effervescent, exuberant, and joyful; outrageously free and liberating to the rest of us.

_____ ESCARGOT AND OYSTERS: Priceless treasures of the sea once out of their shells; succulent, delicate and irreplaceable.

_____ FRESH FRUIT: Vine-ripened, energy-filled, absolutely fresh, invigorating—the perfect treat after a heavy meal.

_____ CANDELABRA: Soft light, jeweled excellence; the special atmosphere for splendor and romance.

_____ PRIME RIB: Stable, brawny, macho, the generous mainstay of any menu; juicy, mouth-watering, "perfect cut" for good nourishment.

_____ MEDITERRANEAN DANCING: Tempestuous, untamed, spontaneous, high-stepping entertainment to cheer the soul.

_____ ITALIAN ICE CREAMS: Colorful, flavorful, delightfully childlike, nonfattening; the unexpected surprise in our group.

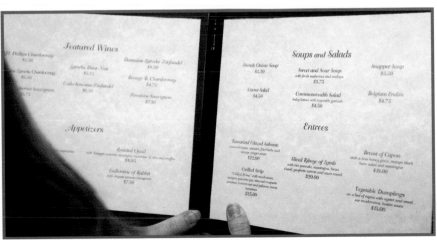

GROUP SHARING BIBLE STUDIES

GUIDED QUESTIONNAIRES ON ...

Identity

MY UNIQUENESS

Introduction

You will be looking at one of the most exciting stories in the Bible—the story of the "little guy" up a tree who Jesus picked out of the crowd because he was special and didn't know it. This man, though a Jew, was a tax collector for the ruling Romans. In those days, tax collectors were hated even more than they are today—because they were known for cheating and were considered traitors.

We recommend that you move into groups of 4 because it is easier to discuss things when you are in a smaller group—and you can finish the discussion in 30 minutes.

Now, listen to the Bible story. Then, quickly move into groups of 4 and discuss the questionnaire.

1. If you were going to make a movie about this Bible story, who would you choose to play the part of Zacchaeus—the little guy/tax collector up a tree?
   - ❏ Danny DeVito
   - ❏ Tim Allen
   - ❏ Martin Short
   - ❏ Jay Leno
   - ❏ Robin Williams
   - ❏ Jim Carey
   - ❏ Jerry Seinfeld

2. If you had been Zacchaeus when Jesus stopped under his tree and told him to "come down immediately," how would you feel?
   - ❏ scared spitless
   - ❏ special
   - ❏ embarrassed
   - ❏ suspicious
   - ❏ surprised that he knew my name

ZACCHAEUS THE TAX COLLECTOR

19 Jesus entered Jericho and was passing through. [2] A man was there by the name of Zacchaeus; he was a chief tax collector and was wealthy. [3] He wanted to see who Jesus was, but being a short man he could not, because of the crowd. [4] So he ran ahead and climbed a sycamore-fig tree to see him, since Jesus was coming that way.

[5] When Jesus reached the spot, he looked up and said to him, "Zacchaeus, come down immediately. I must stay at your house today." [6] So he came down at once and welcomed him gladly.

[7] All the people saw this and began to mutter, "He has gone to be the guest of a 'sinner.' "

[8] But Zacchaeus stood up and said to the Lord, "Look, Lord! Here and now I give half of my possessions to the poor, and if I have cheated anybody out of anything, I will pay back four times the amount."

[9] Jesus said to him, "Today salvation has come to this house, because this man, too, is a son of Abraham. [10] For the Son of Man came to seek and to save what was lost."

Luke 19:1–10

---

3. If you had been Zacchaeus at the end of the story, how would you feel?
   - ❏ clean inside
   - ❏ included in God's family
   - ❏ brand new
   - ❏ loved
   - ❏ broke

4. Jesus saw the positive qualities in Zacchaeus. Who really affirmed you when you were a kid and felt like a "little guy up a tree"?
   - ❏ my mother
   - ❏ my father
   - ❏ my brother or sister
   - ❏ another family member
   - ❏ a close friend
   - ❏ a teacher or coach
   - ❏ a special person at church
   - ❏ other: _____

5. How do the various people in your life see you now? Choose one or two of the following, and give two adjectives. For instance, "MY PARENTS see me as ... immature and rebellious."

- MY PARENTS/SPOUSE see me as ... (two adjectives)

- MY TEACHERS/SUPERVISORS see me as ...

- MY CLOSE FRIENDS see me as ...

- PEOPLE WHO DON'T KNOW ME VERY WELL see me as ...

6. In all honesty, how do you see yourself right now? Put an "**X**" on the lines below.

| I put myself down. (I'm no good and never will be.) | _____ | I build myself up. (I am created in the image of God.) |

| self-defeating attitude (I don't want to try because I know I'll fail.) | _____ | self-confident attitude (I can do everything through Christ.) |

7. Where do you put yourself "down"?
   - ❏ knowledge—"I'm not as smart as ..."
   - ❏ looks—"I'm not as good-looking as ..."
   - ❏ willpower—"I'm not as strong as ..."
   - ❏ success—"I'm not as successful as ..."
   - ❏ personality—"I'm not as well-liked as ..."
   - ❏ physical fitness—"I'm not in as good of shape as ..."
   - ❏ abilities—"I'm not as talented as ..."

8. How do you feel about sharing personal things in your life with others?
   - ❏ uncomfortable–I don't talk about these things.
   - ❏ scared–I don't know if I want to talk about these things.
   - ❏ fine–No problem, our group trusts each other.
   - ❏ thrilled–I love this stuff!
   - ❏ I'm not sure.

9. On a scale of 1 (TERRIBLE) to 10 (GREAT), how would you describe the last week? How can this group pray for you?

MY PERSONALITY

Introduction

It is hard to believe that you can have two totally different personalities in the same family, but this seems to be the case in the Bible story you will be studying. The scene is the home of sisters Martha and Mary (and their brother Lazarus, whom Jesus would later raise from the dead). It seems that Jesus spent time in their home frequently.

After someone has read the Scripture passage, get into groups of 4 and discuss the questionnaire. Remember, there are no right or wrong answers—just your opinion—so you don't have to be afraid to share.

1. Judging by the way the two sisters acted in this story, which would you say was the older sister?
   ❐ Mary   ❐ Martha

2. If you had been Martha, how would you have responded to Jesus' remark?
   ❐ gone to my room and pouted
   ❐ thought to myself: "He doesn't have to live with my sister."
   ❐ flown off the handle
   ❐ accepted the correction, sat down with Mary, and let the supper burn

3. If you could choose one of these types of people for these situations, who would you choose? Finish the sentences by inserting either Mary ... or Martha.
   • For a close friend, I would choose ...
   • For someone to work for, I would choose ...
   • For someone to work for me, I would choose ...
   • For someone to look after my estate, I would choose ...
   • For my small group leader or youth leader, I would choose ...

4. Comparing your personality to the two people in this story, which of them are you more like?
   ❐ Martha—responsible and uptight
   ❐ Mary—carefree and laid-back

5. Who do people say you take after in your personality—your father or your mother? Which one do you think you take after?

> ### AT THE HOME OF MARTHA AND MARY
> *[38]As Jesus and his disciples were on their way, he came to a village where a woman named Martha opened her home to him. [39]She had a sister called Mary, who sat at the Lord's feet listening to what he said. [40]But Martha was distracted by all the preparations that had to be made. She came to him and asked, "Lord, don't you care that my sister has left me to do the work by myself? Tell her to help me!"*
>
> *[41]"Martha, Martha," the Lord answered, "you are worried and upset about many things, [42]but only one thing is needed. Mary has chosen what is better, and it will not be taken away from her."*
>
> *Luke 10:38–42*

6. Of the four classic personality types below, which type do you resemble? Read over all four types, and choose two that describe you: (a) Your dominant type, (b) Your secondary type.

Finish the sentence: *I am mostly the* _____ *type and a little bit of the* _____ *type.*

SANGUINE: People centered. Warm. Outgoing. Sociable. A good salesperson. Loves parties and shopping—just about anything that has to do with people.

CHOLERIC: Task centered. Strong-willed. Natural born leader. Loves challenges. Responsible. Good at making things happen. Likes to win. Takes chances.

MELANCHOLIC: Feelings centered. Sensitive. Introspective. Creative. Artistic. Lover of peace and quiet. Good dreamer. Writer. Expresses self in poetry.

PHLEGMATIC: Team centered. Dependable. Consistent. Organized. Good at getting things done. Methodical. Loves a neat room, a clean car, and running around with people who are the opposite.

7. If you could change something about your personality, what would it be?

8. If Jesus dropped in on you, what would he point out that distracts *you* from the most important things in life?

9. How could others in your group or church help you in this?
   - ❐ by helping me understand what is going on inside of me
   - ❐ by leaving me alone
   - ❐ by telling me it's okay to be me
   - ❐ by sharing some of their own struggles
   - ❐ by challenging me to be all that I can be
   - ❐ other:_____

10. Jesus said Martha was "worried and upset about many things." What are you worried or upset about right now?

11. How can this group remember you in prayer this week?

MY VALUES

Introduction

This is the story of a young ruler who came to Jesus to ask what he co[u]ld do to receive eternal life. He must have come from a rich family becau[se] he had "great wealth" at an early age. Jesus "threw him a curve" a[nd] asked him to sell everything and give the money to the poor.

The questionnaire below is going to ask you some hard questio[ns]. Get into groups of 4 and have someone read the Scripture out loud.

1. If the rich young man in this Bible story lived today, how would [he] dress?
   - ❏ sharp and conservative
   - ❏ in the latest far-out fashions
   - ❏ in jeans and a T-shirt

2. If this person came to your church, how would he be treated?
   - ❏ We would probably be impressed.
   - ❏ Our treasurer would be thrilled.
   - ❏ We would accept him as a person and not care at all about money.
   - ❏ We would expect more out of him because of his money.

3. How do you feel about the rich young ruler?
   - ❏ sorry for him—He couldn't help it that he was rich.
   - ❏ disappointed in him—He walked away from God.
   - ❏ upset—Jesus should not have been so hard on him.
   - ❏ frustrated—Does this mean I have to give up everything I ha[ve] too?

4. What would you do if Jesus asked you to sell everything you had a[nd] give the proceeds to the poor?
   - ❏ have my hearing checked
   - ❏ compute my net worth and think about it
   - ❏ hold a garage sale this Saturday
   - ❏ increase my giving to the church
   - ❏ sadly walk away

> ### THE RICH RULER
>
> [18] *A certain ruler asked him, "Good teacher, what must I do to inherit eternal life?"*
>
> [19] *"Why do you call me good?" Jesus answered. "No one is good—except God alone.* [20] *You know the commandments: 'Do not commit adultery, do not murder, do not steal, do not give false testimony, honor your father and mother.' "*
>
> [21] *"All these I have kept since I was a boy," he said.*
>
> [22] *When Jesus heard this, he said to him, "You still lack one thing. Sell everything you have and give to the poor, and you will have treasure in heaven. Then come, follow me."*
>
> [23] *When he heard this, he became very sad, because he was a man of great wealth.* [24] *Jesus looked at him and said, "How hard it is for the rich to enter the kingdom of God!* [25] *Indeed, it is easier for a camel to go through the eye of a needle than for a rich man to enter the kingdom of God."*
>
> [26] *Those who heard this asked, "Who then can be saved?"*
>
> [27] *Jesus replied, "What is impossible with men is possible with God."*
>
> *Luke 18:18–27*

5. Being totally honest, what are your top three priorities in life now?
   - ❏ a good time
   - ❏ good friendships
   - ❏ a good marriage / family
   - ❏ making lots of money
   - ❏ greater intimacy with God
   - ❏ having nice things
   - ❏ financial independence / security
   - ❏ being true to myself
   - ❏ developing my spiritual gifts
   - ❏ making a contribution to the world
   - ❏ other:_____

6. Right now, who influences you most on your values?
   - ❏ my peers
   - ❏ my pastor / church
   - ❏ my parents / grandparents
   - ❏ my spouse / boyfriend / girlfriend
   - ❏ the media / TV

7. How much has your commitment to Jesus Christ and his way of life influenced your values?
   - ❏ a lot
   - ❏ a little
   - ❏ not as much as I would like
   - ❏ not at all

8. Jesus knew that the young ruler's riches were a barrier between him and God. If Jesus were to evaluate your life, what would he say holds you back from being totally committed to God?
   - ❏ wealth
   - ❏ apathy
   - ❏ habit or temptations
   - ❏ doubts about issues of faith
   - ❏ fear of being labeled a fanatic
   - ❏ other:_____

9. What do you need to do to store up "treasure in heaven"?
   - ❏ Cut back on my lifestyle.
   - ❏ Invest more time in loving people and less in loving things.
   - ❏ Overhaul my priorities.
   - ❏ Talk to more people about Christ.
   - ❏ Spend more time at church.
   - ❏ Keep doing what I'm already doing.
   - ❏ other:_____

10. How would you like the group to pray for you?

Identity

MY ABILITIES

Jesus Feeds the Five Thousand

Introduction

Can one person make a difference in this world? A lot of us would say "no." In this Bible study, you will have a chance to see what Jesus did with a little ... from a few people ... to make a difference. And you will have a chance to discuss where your own gifts and abilities could make a difference.

Keep in mind that this story occurred when the disciples were on a vacation with Jesus. They had just returned from an exhausting job and Jesus invited them to take a break. As you listen to the story, try to put yourself in their situation. Then, move into groups of 4 and discuss the questionnaire.

1. "Come with me by yourselves to a quiet place and get some rest." If you were one of the disciples, what would you expect?
   - ❏ a quiet little vacation
   - ❏ fun and recreation
   - ❏ time to be with Jesus
   - ❏ anything but people

2. Surprise! There are 5,000 men, plus women and children, waiting on the shore. Now how do you feel?
   - ❏ delighted
   - ❏ overwhelmed
   - ❏ compassionate
   - ❏ angry
   - ❏ whipped
   - ❏ frustrated

3. What is guaranteed to ruin a vacation for you?
   - ❏ standing in long lines
   - ❏ losing my suitcase
   - ❏ mosquitoes / jellyfish / ants
   - ❏ seven straight days of rain
   - ❏ car trouble
   - ❏ other:_____

JESUS FEEDS THE FIVE THOUSAND

[30] The apostles gathered around Jesus and reported to him all they had done and taught. [31] Then, because so many people were coming and going that they did not even have a chance to eat, he said to them, "Come with me by yourselves to a quiet place and get some rest."

[32] So they went away by themselves in a boat to a solitary place. [33] But many who saw them leaving recognized them and ran on foot from all the towns and got there ahead of them. [34] When Jesus landed and saw a large crowd, he had compassion on them, because they were like sheep without a shepherd. So he began teaching them many things.

[35] By this time it was late in the day, so his disciples came to him. "This is a remote place," they said, "and it's already very late. [36] Send the people away so they can go to the surrounding countryside and villages and buy themselves something to eat."

[37] But he answered, "You give them something to eat."

They said to him, "That would take eight months of a man's wages! Are we to go and spend that much on bread and give it to them to eat?"

[38] "How many loaves do you have?" he asked. "Go and see."

When they found out, they said, "Five—and two fish."

[39] Then Jesus directed them to have all the people sit down in groups on the green grass. [40] So they sat down in groups of hundreds and fifties. [41] Taking the five loaves and the two fish and looking up to heaven, he gave thanks and broke the loaves. Then he gave them to his disciples to set before the people. He also divided the two fish among them all. [42] They all ate and were satisfied, [43] and the disciples picked up twelve basketfuls of broken pieces of bread and fish. [44] The number of the men who had eaten was five thousand.

Mark 6:30–44

4. "You give them something to eat." Had you been with Jesus during this story, and he asked you to do work after he promised you rest, what would have been your reaction?
   - ❑ "Okay, but you owe me one!"
   - ❑ "Whatever you say, Lord!"
   - ❑ "Hey, I'm outta here!"
   - ❑ "But you PROMISED!"

5. How much of your potential are you giving to God right now?
   - ❑ sorry you asked
   - ❑ maybe 5%
   - ❑ I would say 50%.
   - ❑ I'm giving it all I've got.

6. If you could put your gifts to work in something that you are good at, what would you like to do? (Choose two or three from the list below.)
   - ❑ working with children
   - ❑ listening / caring
   - ❑ helping behind the scenes
   - ❑ playing an instrument
   - ❑ working with older people
   - ❑ peacemaking / reconciling
   - ❑ organizing / administering
   - ❑ being sensitive to others
   - ❑ sharing my faith
   - ❑ motivating / leading
   - ❑ crusading for a cause
   - ❑ cooking / homemaking
   - ❑ teaching the Bible
   - ❑ writing
   - ❑ getting others involved
   - ❑ coaching / teaching
   - ❑ raising money
   - ❑ making people laugh
   - ❑ acting / singing
   - ❑ cheering others on
   - ❑ problem solving
   - ❑ other:_____

7. If you knew you could not fail, what would be one thing you would like to do with your life in the near future?
   - ❑ go on a service or mission trip
   - ❑ do something for the homeless
   - ❑ reach out to some "problem" kids in my school or community
   - ❑ get involved in an inner-city church or ministry
   - ❑ lead a support or recovery group
   - ❑ tutor disadvantaged kids
   - ❑ help out at a hospital or nursing home
   - ❑ other:_____

8. What is keeping you from doing this?
   - ❑ money
   - ❑ feeling inadequate
   - ❑ time
   - ❑ I don't know enough.
   - ❑ I'm really not that committed.

9. How could this group help you get started?
   - ❑ Don't push me—I was only dreaming!
   - ❑ Help me think it through.
   - ❑ Join me.
   - ❑ Encourage me.
   - ❑ Pray for me.

10. If Jesus had you sit down right where you are while he miraculously met your most immediate need, what would he do for you?

MY FUTURE

Introduction

Everybody identifies with Peter. He was always outspoken and doing things that he shouldn't. But he also was someone who was willing to take risks—sometimes crazy risks. This Bible story is one of those times.

Now, move into groups of 4 and have someone read the Scripture passage out loud. Then, discuss the questionnaire.

1. Imagine you were a journalist and met the disciples on the other side of the lake after this incident. What would you do next?
   - ❐ sell the story to *The National Enquirer*
   - ❐ develop a segment for *Unsolved Mysteries* on television
   - ❐ ignore it so that nobody would think I was crazy
   - ❐ gather testimony and write about it for a network news show

2. If you had been in the boat when the disciples saw someone walking on the water, what would you have said?
   - ❐ "I'm seeing things!"
   - ❐ "Where's Jesus?!"
   - ❐ "Let me out of here!"
   - ❐ "Do you see what I see?"
   - ❐ "I think I ate too many anchovies!"
   - ❐ I would have been speechless.

3. If you could put in a good word for Peter here in this story, what would you say?
   - ❐ He meant well.
   - ❐ He learned a lot from this experience.
   - ❐ He at least was willing to ask.

4. How are you at "stepping out of the boat" and taking risks?
   - ❐ just plain scared
   - ❐ I'll try anything once.
   - ❐ daring
   - ❐ I'm good at going second.
   - ❐ cautious—I put my big toe in first.

JESUS WALKS ON THE WATER

²²Immediately Jesus made the disciples get into the boat and go on ahead of him to the other side, while he dismissed the crowd. ²³After he had dismissed them, he went up on a mountainside by himself to pray. When evening came, he was there alone, ²⁴but the boat was already a considerable distance from land, buffeted by the waves because the wind was against it.

²⁵During the fourth watch of the night Jesus went out to them, walking on the lake. ²⁶When the disciples saw him walking on the lake, they were terrified. "It's a ghost," they said, and cried out in fear.

²⁷But Jesus immediately said to them: "Take courage! It is I. Don't be afraid."

²⁸"Lord, if it's you," Peter replied, "tell me to come to you on the water."

²⁹"Come," he said.

Then Peter got down out of the boat, walked on the water and came toward Jesus. ³⁰But when he saw the wind, he was afraid and, beginning to sink, cried out, "Lord, save me!"

³¹Immediately Jesus reached out his hand and caught him. "You of little faith," he said, "why did you doubt?"

³²And when they climbed into the boat, the wind died down. ³³Then those who were in the boat worshiped him, saying, "Truly you are the Son of God."

Matthew 14:22–33

6. Before you can do this, what is standing in the way?
   - ❏ fear of failure
   - ❏ my negative thoughts
   - ❏ inconsistency
   - ❏ intellectual doubts
   - ❏ fear of standing alone
   - ❏ unhealthy relationships
   - ❏ sense of inadequacy
   - ❏ impulse to rush into things before counting the cost
   - ❏ other:_____

7. What would be the best way for God to help in the situation?
   - ❏ be very gentle with me
   - ❏ give me a good kick in the pants
   - ❏ assure me it's okay to fail
   - ❏ surround me with supportive people
   - ❏ get out of the boat with me

8. What dreams do you have for the future? What risks are involved?

9. What are you facing in your life right now that you need to hear Jesus say, "Don't be afraid"?

10. How can this group help you in prayer this week?

5. Where do you feel God is inviting you to get out of the boat now?
   - ❏ in my relationships—dealing with a problem
   - ❏ in my future planning—doing something I've been afraid to try
   - ❏ in my inner life—facing a hang-up
   - ❏ in my spiritual walk—putting God first

FRIENDSHIPS

Introduction

You will be looking at the story of David and Jonathan, one of the best stories in the Bible on friendships. Jonathan was the son of King Saul. King Saul became jealous of David after David killed Goliath, and plotted to kill David. Jonathan found out about it and his friendship with David was put to the test.

Now, listen to the Bible story. Then, quickly move into groups of 4 and discuss the questionnaire.

1. As you think about the story of David and Jonathan, what immediately comes to mind?
    - ❐ This is beautiful.
    - ❐ This is corny.
    - ❐ This sounds like a Hollywood plot.
    - ❐ I wish I had a friend like that.

2. If you had been Jonathan, and knew your father was threatening to kill your best friend, what would you have thought?
    - ❐ There must be something wrong with my dad.
    - ❐ There must be something wrong with my friend.
    - ❐ There must be something wrong with me.
    - ❐ I would feel terribly torn.

3. If you realized that your father was doing this to save the throne for you, how would you have felt?
    - ❐ unworthy
    - ❐ torn
    - ❐ appreciative
    - ❐ disgusted
    - ❐ I would stay out of it.

4. Who was your best friend when you were a kid? What one experience did you have together that you especially remember?

5. As you think back, what was it about this person that brought the two of you together?

- ❑ doing fun things together
- ❑ liking the same things
- ❑ sharing personal things
- ❑ getting in trouble together
- ❑ keeping each other's confidence
- ❑ letting each other have space
- ❑ being there for each other when one of us was hurting
- ❑ going to church together / praying together

6. When it comes to making friends, what do you do? Finish the sentence by picking ONE in each category: "I usually ..."

make friends quickly . . . . slowly

change friends constantly . . . . never

break off friendships easily. . . . . painfully

choose friends wisely. . . . . unwisely

7. What qualities do you look for when you choose a friend? (Choose the top three.)

- ❑ similar lifestyle
- ❑ generosity
- ❑ easy to talk to
- ❑ loyalty
- ❑ ethnic background
- ❑ speaks his or her mind
- ❑ honesty
- ❑ spiritual depth
- ❑ common interests
- ❑ good sense of humor
- ❑ other:_____

8. What is your biggest barrier to having closer friendships?

- ❑ acting like I don't need them
- ❑ being jealous
- ❑ hiding my feelings
- ❑ having been hurt in the past
- ❑ focusing on things rather than people
- ❑ other:_____

---

³And Jonathan made a covenant with David because he loved him as himself. ⁴Jonathan took off the robe he was wearing and gave it to David, along with his tunic, and even his sword, his bow and his belt.

1 Samuel 18:3–4

19 *Saul told his son Jonathan and all the attendants to kill David. But Jonathan was very fond of David ²and warned him, "My father Saul is looking for a chance to kill you. Be on your guard tomorrow morning; go into hiding and stay there. ³I will go out and stand with my father in the field where you are. I'll speak to him about you and will tell you what I find out."*

⁴Jonathan spoke well of David to Saul his father and said to him, "Let not the king do wrong to his servant David; he has not wronged you, and what he has done has benefited you greatly. ⁵He took his life in his hands when he killed the Philistine. The LORD won a great victory for all Israel, and you saw it and were glad. Why then would you do wrong to an innocent man like David by killing him for no reason?"

1 Samuel 19:1–5

⁴¹After the boy had gone, David got up from the south side of the stone and bowed down before Jonathan three times, with his face to the ground. Then they kissed each other and wept together—but David wept the most.

⁴²Jonathan said to David, "Go in peace, for we have sworn friendship with each other in the name of the LORD, saying, 'The LORD is witness between you and me, and between your descendants and my descendants forever.'" Then David left, and Jonathan went back to the town.

1 Samuel 20:41–42

9. How hard is it for you to trust this group with the heavy stuff in your life? What could help?

10. How can your friends in this group pray for you right now?

BEING REAL

Introduction

It's hard to love someone you do not know. And it is hard to get to know someone who wears a mask. In this Bible passage, you will meet two people who pray in different ways. As you read, remember that the Pharisee was a very religious person and the tax collector was probably the most hated person in the community.

Move into groups of 4. Then, have someone read the parable aloud and start on the questionnaire.

1. How do you feel about the Pharisee in this story?
    ❐ I feel sorry for him.
    ❐ I feel a little angry.
    ❐ I feel like punching him in the nose.
    ❐ I have the same attitude that he does.

2. How do you feel about the tax collector?
    ❐ At least he's honest.
    ❐ I can relate to this guy.
    ❐ After cheating people, he has some nerve!
    ❐ I think he was being just as much of a phony as the Pharisee.

3. How much of your own problems could you share with each of these people? Put an **"X"** on the line to indicate your response—somewhere in between the two extremes.

    WITH THE PHARISEE, I COULD SHARE:
    Everything _____ Nothing

    WITH THE TAX COLLECTOR, I COULD SHARE:
    Everything _____ Nothing

> **THE PARABLE OF THE PHARISEE AND THE TAX COLLECTOR**
>
> *⁹To some who were confident of their own righteousness and looked down on everybody else, Jesus told this parable: ¹⁰"Two men went up to the temple to pray, one a Pharisee and the other a tax collector. ¹¹The Pharisee stood up and prayed about himself: 'God, I thank you that I am not like other men—robbers, evildoers, adulterers—or even like this tax collector. ¹²I fast twice a week and give a tenth of all I get.'*
>
> *¹³"But the tax collector stood at a distance. He would not even look up to heaven, but beat his breast and said, 'God, have mercy on me, a sinner.'*
>
> *¹⁴"I tell you that this man, rather than the other, went home justified before God. For everyone who exalts himself will be humbled, and he who humbles himself will be exalted."*
>
> *Luke 18:9–14*

4. For the person with whom you could share the most, why do you feel this way?
    ❐ He is more spiritual.
    ❐ He is more honest.
    ❐ He is more like me.
    ❐ He is more like the person I want to be.
    ❐ He is more likely to understand me.

5. If the tax collector in the parable came to your group or church, how would he be received?
    ❐ with open arms
    ❐ with suspicion
    ❐ with disgust
    ❐ like one of us

6. If the Pharisee in the parable showed up at your group or church, how would he be received?

- ❐ with open arms
- ❐ with a few snickers
- ❐ with sympathy
- ❐ with raised eyebrows
- ❐ with cold stares

7. How much of the Pharisee and the tax collector do you see in yourself? Put a percentage for each—and the two must add up to 100%.

I see myself as _____% Pharisee
and _____% tax collector.

8. Why do you think so many people confess their sins in bars rather than in churches?

9. With whom do you "get real" and share your problems?

- ❐ my spouse
- ❐ my parent(s)
- ❐ another family member
- ❐ a close friend
- ❐ my pastor or small group leader
- ❐ my boyfriend or girlfriend
- ❐ this group
- ❐ no one
- ❐ other:_____

10. How do you feel about sharing personal matters in your life with this group?

- ❐ uncomfortable—I don't talk about these things.
- ❐ scared—I don't know if I want to talk about these things.
- ❐ okay—I can handle it.
- ❐ thrilled—I love this stuff!
- ❐ I'm not sure.

11. How would you like this group to remember you in prayer this week?

TRUE FRIENDS

Introduction

In this Bible study, you will meet four friends who were so concerned about the well-being of their friend that they literally "tore up the roof" for this person. After hearing the Bible story, you will have a chance to share your own feelings about "going the distance" for friends.

Now, move into groups of 4 and listen to the story. Then, discuss the following questionnaire.

1. If CNN reported on this incident, what would be their lead line?
   ❒ A faith healer makes a paralytic walk.
   ❒ Four friends raise the roof to help a friend.
   ❒ A preacher upsets religious leaders.
   ❒ Police are looking for vandals in a house break-in.

2. If you were one of the paralytic's four friends and saw the crowd where Jesus was, what would you do?
   ❒ suggest we come back later
   ❒ politely wait in line
   ❒ make a hole in the roof
   ❒ go along with the hole in the roof, but make it clear it wasn't my idea

3. How would you feel if you were the paralytic when your friends decided to help you "drop in on Jesus"?
   ❒ reluctant—"You will embarrass me."
   ❒ scared—"You're going to drop me!"
   ❒ grateful—"Thanks for your concern."
   ❒ apprehensive—"They are going to throw us out!"
   ❒ mixed feelings—"I don't think this is going to work, but I will trust you guys."

4. What impresses you most about the four friends?
   ❒ their faith   ❒ their boldness
   ❒ their ingenuity and creativity ❒ their determination
   ❒ their concern for their friend

JESUS HEALS A PARALYTIC

2 *A few days later, when Jesus again entered Capernaum, the people heard that he had come home. ²So many gathered that there was no room left, not even outside the door, and he preached the word to them. ³Some men came, bringing to him a paralytic, carried by four of them. ⁴Since they could not get him to Jesus because of the crowd, they made an opening in the roof above Jesus and, after digging through it, lowered the mat the paralyzed man was lying on. ⁵When Jesus saw their faith, he said to the paralytic, "Son, your sins are forgiven."*

⁶Now some teachers of the law were sitting there, thinking to themselves, ⁷"Why does this fellow talk like that? He's blasphem-ing! Who can forgive sins but God alone?"

⁸Immediately Jesus knew in his spirit that this was what they were thinking in their hearts, and he said to them, "Why are you thinking these things? ⁹Which is easier: to say to the paralytic, 'Your sins are forgiven,' or to say, 'Get up, take your mat and walk'? ¹⁰But that you may know that the Son of Man has author-ity on earth to forgive sins . . . ." He said to the paralytic, ¹¹"I tell you, get up, take your mat and go home." ¹²He got up, took his mat and walked out in full view of them all. This amazed everyone and they praised God, saying, "We have never seen anything like this!"

Mark 2:1–12

7. What event in your life brought you closest to God?
- ❏ when some friends really supported me
- ❏ when Jesus healed me when I was hurting
- ❏ when someone I was close to got really sick or died
- ❏ when I attended a camp or special worship experience
- ❏ when I committed my life to Christ
- ❏ when I felt God's forgiveness
- ❏ No event has brought me that feeling.
- ❏ other:_____

8. How do you need to change to receive more support from friends?
- ❏ be more open
- ❏ be a better listener
- ❏ stop trying to be so self-sufficient
- ❏ be more supportive myself
- ❏ find some new or different friends
- ❏ be more patient
- ❏ other:_____

9. Who were the friends in your life who cared enough to bring you to Jesus?

5. What is the closest you have come to having a supportive community who cared for you when you were hurting?

6. It is 12 o'clock at night. You are in trouble. You need some friends to come over and be with you. Four friends that would:
- listen as you talk about the crisis you are going through ...
- be with you as late as necessary ...
- keep your problem confidential ...
- pray for you ...
- and support you through this crisis.

WHAT FRIENDS WOULD YOU CALL? Give four first names.

10. If you had friends who would take you to Jesus for healing today, what kind of healing would you ask for?
- ❏ physical
- ❏ spiritual
- ❏ emotional
- ❏ relational

11. Pray about what was just shared. Then close your meeting by affirming one another. Have each person listen silently while others share what qualities that person has that make him or her a good friend.

PEER PRESSURE

Introduction

The story of the woman caught in the act of adultery is a good example of peer pressure. The Pharisees put a lot of pressure on Jesus to go along with the crowd and condemn this woman.

Listen to the story carefully. Try to put yourself in the shoes of Jesus. See how he dealt with the dilemma that he faced. Then, get together in groups of 4 and discuss the questionnaire.

1. Who do you feel most sorry for in this story?
    - ❏ the woman—for being publicly humiliated
    - ❏ Jesus—for being pressured by the crowd
    - ❏ the religious leaders—for stooping this low

2. If you had been Jesus when the woman caught in the act of adultery was brought before him, how would you have felt?
    - ❏ embarrassed
    - ❏ angry at the Pharisees
    - ❏ ashamed of the woman
    - ❏ torn between mixed feelings
    - ❏ intimidated by the Pharisees
    - ❏ mad for being put on the spot
    - ❏ sorry for the woman

3. Who do you admire for the way they don't cave in to the pressure of the crowd?

4. When it comes to going against the crowd, who are the hardest people for you to stand up against?
    - ❏ supervisors / authority figures
    - ❏ friends at school or work
    - ❏ friends at church
    - ❏ spouse / boyfriend / girlfriend
    - ❏ parents / family members
    - ❏ other:_____

THE WOMAN CAUGHT IN ADULTERY

8 But Jesus went to the Mount of Olives. ²At dawn he appeared again in the temple courts, where all the people gathered around him, and he sat down to teach them. ³The teachers of the law and the Pharisees brought in a woman caught in adultery. They made her stand before the group ⁴and said to Jesus, "Teacher, this woman was caught in the act of adultery. ⁵In the Law Moses commanded us to stone such women. Now what do you say?" ⁶They were using this question as a trap, in order to have a basis for accusing him.

But Jesus bent down and started to write on the ground with his finger. ⁷When they kept on questioning him, he straightened up and said to them, "If any one of you is without sin, let him be the first to throw a stone at her." ⁸Again he stooped down and wrote on the ground.

⁹At this, those who heard began to go away one at a time, the older ones first, until only Jesus was left, with the woman still standing there. ¹⁰Jesus straightened up and asked her, "Woman, where are they? Has no one condemned you?"

¹¹"No one, sir," she said.

"Then neither do I condemn you," Jesus declared, "Go now and leave your life of sin."

John 8:1–11

5. How tough is it to face the following pressures from the crowd? Rate yourself from 1 to 10 in each category. Then, share with the group your easiest and your hardest.

ABUSING DRUGS OR ALCOHOL

Easy   1   2   3   4   5   6   7   8   9   10   **Hard**

CHEATING ON TESTS OR TAXES

Easy   1   2   3   4   5   6   7   8   9   10   **Hard**

LYING TO COVER UP WRONGDOING

Easy   1   2   3   4   5   6   7   8   9   10   **Hard**

KEEPING UP WITH FRIENDS IN MATERIAL THINGS

Easy   1   2   3   4   5   6   7   8   9   10   **Hard**

CURSING / PROFANITY / DIRTY JOKES

Easy   1   2   3   4   5   6   7   8   9   10   Hard

RAUNCHY MOVIES, MAGAZINES, ETC.

Easy   1   2   3   4   5   6   7   8   9   10   Hard

NOT STANDING UP FOR YOUR FAITH

Easy   1   2   3   4   5   6   7   8   9   10   Hard

6. What have you found helpful in dealing with peer pressure?
   ❑ attend church regularly
   ❑ study the Bible and pray
   ❑ stay away from the wrong crowd
   ❑ just say no
   ❑ let others know where I stand on issues and why

7. What grade would you give your group or church on how well you support each other and stand together against peer pressure?
   ❑ I would give us an A+.   ❑ Well, I'd give us a C-.
   ❑ I'd give us a B+ for effort.   ❑ I'm sorry you asked.

8. If the woman who was caught in adultery came to your group or church, how would she feel?
   ❑ weird   ❑ tried and convicted
   ❑ uncomfortable at first   ❑ right at home

9. What do you do when you blow it?
   ❑ crawl into a hole   ❑ try to be extra good
   ❑ confess it to God and move on ❑ shrug it off
   ❑ confess it to another person

10. How does the way Jesus treated this woman help you face your sins?

11. How can the group pray for you?

FAMILY EXPECTATIONS

Introduction

Your family probably has certain expectations of you. But what if they went to Jesus and asked him to make you his prime minister? In the Bible story, you will have a chance to see what happened in a situation like this and to talk about some of your own "stories."

Now, listen to the Bible story. Then, move into groups of 4 to share your responses.

1. If you were one of these two brothers, how would you have felt about your mother's request at the beginning of this story?
    ❒ embarrassed
    ❒ honored
    ❒ angry

2. How would you have felt at the end of the story?
    ❒ humiliated   ❒ mad at my mother
    ❒ grateful for the lesson I learned   ❒ disappointed in Jesus
    ❒ afraid the other disciples would hold a grudge against me

3. These brothers turned out to be significant leaders in the church. How much credit do you give their mother for this?
    ❒ a whole lot   ❒ a little   ❒ none

4. What did your parents expect you to do when you were young?
    ❒ play a musical instrument   ❒ compete in sports
    ❒ make good grades   ❒ "be seen and not heard"
    ❒ do lots of chores   ❒ other:_____

5. Which of the following comes closest to the truth concerning your family's expectations for you?
    ❒ My family expects very little—I wonder if they even care.
    ❒ My family expects too much—I can never live up to their expectations.
    ❒ My family's expectations are high enough to challenge me, but not too high to discourage me.
    ❒ My family has helped me to set my own expectations.

A MOTHER'S REQUEST

²⁰Then the mother of Zebedee's sons came to Jesus with her sons and, kneeling down, asked a favor of him.

²¹"What is it you want?" he asked.

She said, "Grant that one of these two sons of mine may sit at your right and the other at your left in your kingdom."

²²"You don't know what you are asking," Jesus said to them. "Can you drink the cup I am going to drink?"

"We can," they answered.

²³Jesus said to them, "You will indeed drink from my cup, but to sit at my right or left is not for me to grant. These places belong to those for whom they have been prepared by my Father."

²⁴When the ten heard about this, they were indignant with the two brothers. ²⁵Jesus called them together and said, "You know that the rulers of the Gentiles lord it over them, and their high officials exercise authority over them. ²⁶Not so with you. Instead, whoever wants to become great among you must be your servant, ²⁷and whoever wants to be first must be your slave—²⁸just as the Son of Man did not come to be served, but to serve, and to give his life as a ransom for many."

Matthew 20:20–28

6. Are you living up to your family's expectations?
   - ❏ Are you kidding?!
   - ❏ I'm trying.
   - ❏ I quit trying.
   - ❏ Yes.
   - ❏ I think I am exceeding their expectations for me.

7. How do (or will) you let your children know your expectations for them?
   - ❏ I (will) let my kids set their own rules.
   - ❏ I (will) sit down with my kids and explain things.
   - ❏ I (will) spend extra time with my kids.
   - ❏ I (will) teach my kids by example.
   - ❏ other:_____

8. When you have a difference with a family member over expectations, what have you found helpful?
   - ❏ I take the opportunity to sit down and talk.
   - ❏ I tell them what they want to hear and forget it.
   - ❏ I try to see where they are coming from.
   - ❏ I try to help us come up with a compromise together.
   - ❏ I put expectations in writing to prevent such problems.
   - ❏ other:_____

9. What issues cause the greatest conflict between you and other family members? (Choose the top three.)

   ____ household duties   ____ discipline
   ____ work schedules   ____ drugs / alcohol
   ____ leisure time / activities   ____ manners
   ____ going to church   ____ language
   ____ clothes / hairstyle   ____ respect
   ____ other relatives / in-laws ____ money
   ____ future plans   ____ music preferences
   ____ friends   ____ favoritism
   ____ school / grades   ____ curfew

10. For the three issues you just identified, who do you think causes the problem? For each issue, put one of these symbols:

    M = Me (It's my problem or I cause it.)

    F = Family Member (It's their problem or they cause it.)

    O = Other (Someone or something else causes the problem.)

11. How can this group help you in prayer this week?

TOUGH LOVE

Introduction

This Bible story is about a disabled person who waited hopefully at a pool that had a reputation of healing the first person who got in when the water was stirred. Jesus stopped to talk to this man and asked him a very interesting question: "Do you want to get well?"

Listen to this story as it is read. Then, move into groups of 4 and discuss the questionnaire.

1. How would you feel if you had been disabled for 38 years like the man in this story?
   - ❏ helpless and dependent
   - ❏ bitter and angry
   - ❏ discouraged and depressed
   - ❏ accepting of my condition

2. How would you have felt when Jesus asked you, "Do you want to get well?"
   - ❏ insulted   ❏ cared for
   - ❏ challenged   ❏ mocked
   - ❏ hopeful   ❏ cynical

3. Where is the "watering hole" for the dropouts in your school or community?

4. If Jesus asked these people, "Do you want to get well?" what would they say?
   - ❏ "I want to get well, but my friends won't help me."
   - ❏ "My parents have ruined my life."
   - ❏ "I have a learning disability."
   - ❏ "I was abused as a child."
   - ❏ "I can't break my addiction."
   - ❏ "My gang would kill me if I left."
   - ❏ "I'm not sick!"

THE HEALING AT THE POOL

5 Some time later, Jesus went up to Jerusalem for a feast of the Jews. ²Now there is in Jerusalem near the Sheep Gate a pool, which in Aramaic is called Bethesda and which is surrounded by five covered colonnades. ³Here a great number of disabled people used to lie—the blind, the lame, the paralyzed. ⁵One who was there had been an invalid for thirty-eight years. ⁶When Jesus saw him lying there and learned that he had been in this condition for a long time, he asked him, "Do you want to get well?"

⁷"Sir," the invalid replied, "I have no one to help me into the pool when the water is stirred. While I am trying to get in, someone else goes down ahead of me."

⁸Then Jesus said to him, "Get up! Pick up your mat and walk." ⁹At once the man was cured; he picked up his mat and walked.

The day on which this took place was a Sabbath, ¹⁰and so the Jews said to the man who had been healed, "It is the Sabbath; the law forbids you to carry your mat."

¹¹But he replied, "The man who made me well said to me, 'Pick up your mat and walk.' "

¹²So they asked him, "Who is this fellow who told you to pick it up and walk?"

¹³The man who was healed had no idea who it was, for Jesus had slipped away into the crowd that was there.

¹⁴Later Jesus found him at the temple and said to him, "See, you are well again. Stop sinning or something worse may happen to you." ¹⁵The man went away and told the Jews that it was Jesus who had made him well.

John 5:1–15

---

5. Who has shown you "tough love"?
- ❏ my father
- ❏ my mother
- ❏ my brother / sister
- ❏ another family member
- ❏ a pastor / group leader
- ❏ a teacher
- ❏ a coach
- ❏ a friend
- ❏ a counselor
- ❏ a group like this

6. How well do you accept tough love? How well do you show tough love to others?

7. What is the closest Jesus has come to saying to you, "Get up! Pick up your mat and walk"?
- ❏ when I turned my life over to him
- ❏ when I experienced his healing
- ❏ when I had a self-pity problem
- ❏ when I was overly dependent on others
- ❏ when I lost my will to get better
- ❏ other:_____

8. If Jesus were to stop by the "watering hole" where you hang out, what would he probably ask you?
- ❏ "Do you want to get well?"
- ❏ "What are you doing with your life?"
- ❏ "Are you satisfied with what you are doing?"
- ❏ "Are you looking for the real thing?"
- ❏ "When will you quit complaining and be content?"

9. When you go through something that leaves you feeling like a cripple, what have you found helpful?
- ❏ time alone with God
- ❏ talking things over with a friend
- ❏ getting back into a spiritual discipline
- ❏ being in a group or church like this
- ❏ listening to music
- ❏ getting a good night's sleep
- ❏ admitting I have blown it and getting on with life

10. What connection between your physical and spiritual health have you noticed? When do you find yourself getting physically sick over problems in other areas of your life?

11. What ailments—physical, spiritual or otherwise—does Jesus need to treat in your life?

Caring

DOWN AND DIRTY

Introduction

Where would you look in the Bible for a model of true caring? This story occurs during a special meal Jesus ate with his disciples on the night before his death. It was customary for people's dusty, sandaled feet to be washed, usually by the lowest ranking servant, before a meal was served.

JESUS WASHES HIS DISCIPLES' FEET

13 *It was just before the Passover Feast. Jesus knew that the time had come for him to leave this world and go to the Father. Having loved his own who were in the world, he now showed them the full extent of his love.*

²The evening meal was being served, and the devil had already prompted Judas Iscariot, son of Simon, to betray Jesus. ³Jesus knew that the Father had put all things under his power, and that he had come from God and was returning to God; ⁴so he got up from the meal, took off his outer clothing, and wrapped a towel around his waist. ⁵After that, he poured water into a basin and began to wash his disciples' feet, drying them with the towel that was wrapped around him. ...

¹²When he had finished washing their feet, he put on his clothes and returned to his place. "Do you understand what I have done for you?" he asked them. ¹³"You call me 'Teacher' and 'Lord,' and rightly so, for that is what I am. ¹⁴Now that I, your Lord and Teacher, have washed your feet, you also should wash one another's feet. ¹⁵I have set you an example that you should do as I have done for you."

John 13:1–5, 12–15

Listen to the story. Imagine yourself sitting there as the tension mounts. Watch Jesus as he gets up ... takes off his garment ... wraps a towel around his waist ... and begins to wash ... your feet. Then, move into groups of 4 and discuss the questionnaire.

1. What is your first impression of this story about footwashing?
   - ❏ This is confusing.
   - ❏ This is gross.
   - ❏ This is embarrassing.
   - ❏ This is moving.
   - ❏ This is irrelevant for our culture.
   - ❏ This is a model for any culture.

2. What would you have done if you had been there and Jesus started to wash your feet?
   - ❏ left the room
   - ❏ refused to let him
   - ❏ broken down and cried
   - ❏ felt honored by his caring act
   - ❏ just sat there—feeling guilty
   - ❏ jumped up and tried to wash *his* feet

3. When you were in the seventh grade, what kind of servant-tasks were you expected to do around the house?
   - ❏ make my bed
   - ❏ clean my room
   - ❏ take out the trash
   - ❏ wash the dishes
   - ❏ look after my sibling(s)
   - ❏ do yard work
   - ❏ help with cooking
   - ❏ do laundry
   - ❏ dust and vacuum
   - ❏ all of the above
   - ❏ none of the above

Shirt Off My Back ®

4. How did you feel about doing those tasks? What ingenious ways did you come up with to avoid them?

5. What's the lowliest or most disgusting chore you have to do at home or work now? How's your attitude toward it?

6. Who is one person in your life who has demonstrated what it means to "wash feet"? What did that person do for you?

7. What is the closest you have come to being part of a Christian community where you genuinely cared for one another and showed it?
   - ❏ a music or drama group
   - ❏ a youth group / small group
   - ❏ a mission trip I went on
   - ❏ a church
   - ❏ the "gang" I used to run around with
   - ❏ a group of people I got to know at a retreat or camp
   - ❏ I'm not sure I have experienced this.
   - ❏ a sports team
   - ❏ my family
   - ❏ other:_____

8. If your pastor went around and washed feet—including your feet—how would you feel?
   - ❏ embarrassed
   - ❏ nervous
   - ❏ really touched
   - ❏ confused

9. If Jesus came to you and wanted to care for you in a personal way right now, what would he probably do?
   - ❏ I can't imagine.
   - ❏ He would probably wash my feet.
   - ❏ He might give me a hug.
   - ❏ He would take me to a ball game—to get away from it all.
   - ❏ He would be a friend and let me talk about my problems.
   - ❏ He would take away my problems.
   - ❏ other:_____

10. What's holding you back from living a life of service like Jesus demonstrated and taught?
   - ❏ I'm afraid I'll be taken advantage of.
   - ❏ I don't have time.
   - ❏ I guess I'm too selfish.
   - ❏ I haven't had many good role models.
   - ❏ Nothing really—I'm doing my best.

11. What one thing will you do at home, work, school or church this week to follow Jesus' example of caring through serving?

12. How can the group pray for you?

Caring
A Parable of Forgiveness
FRIENDLY FIRE

Introduction

Even among the closest of friends, sometimes we hurt each other. In this Bible story, the apostle Peter asks Jesus what to do when you get hurt by a friend. He was probably talking about relationships within the close circle of friends who were followers of Christ.

Have someone read the story. Then, divide into groups of 4 and discuss the questionnaire. Remember, there are no right answers ... so feel free to share.

1. If you were Peter, what would have been your thoughts after Jesus answered your question?
   - ❏ I don't understand.
   - ❏ This is serious stuff.
   - ❏ This is going to be hard for me to do.
   - ❏ I'm anxious to give this a try.
   - ❏ I'm sorry I asked.

2. What was one of the worst things your brother or sister ever did to you?

3. To whom do you have to say "I'm sorry" the most?
   - ❏ my spouse / boyfriend / girlfriend
   - ❏ my parent(s)
   - ❏ my children
   - ❏ my brother / sister
   - ❏ another family member
   - ❏ a friend
   - ❏ my boss
   - ❏ a coworker
   - ❏ other:_____

> **THE PARABLE OF THE UNMERCIFUL SERVANT**
> ²¹*Then Peter came to Jesus and asked, "Lord, how many times shall I forgive my brother when he sins against me? Up to seven times?"*
> ²²*Jesus answered, "I tell you, not seven times, but seventy-seven times.*
> ²³*"Therefore, the kingdom of heaven is like a king who wanted to settle accounts with his servants. ²⁴As he began the settlement, a man who owed him ten thousand talents was brought to him. ²⁵Since he was not able to pay, the master ordered that he and his wife and his children and all that he had be sold to repay the debt.*
> ²⁶*"The servant fell on his knees before him. 'Be patient with me,' he begged, 'and I will pay back everything.' ²⁷The servant's master took pity on him, canceled the debt and let him go.*
> ²⁸*"But when that servant went out, he found one of his fellow servants who owed him a hundred denarii. He grabbed him and began to choke him. 'Pay back what you owe me!' he demanded.*
> ²⁹*"His fellow servant fell to his knees and begged him, 'Be patient with me, and I will pay you back.'*
> ³⁰*"But he refused. Instead, he went off and had the man thrown into prison until he could pay the debt. ³¹When the other servants saw what had happened, they were greatly distressed and went and told their master everything that had happened.*
> ³²*"Then the master called the servant in. 'You wicked servant,' he said, 'I canceled all that debt of yours because you begged me to. ³³Shouldn't you have had mercy on your fellow servant just as I had on you?' ³⁴In anger his master turned him over to the jailers to be tortured, until he should pay back all he owed.*
> ³⁵*"This is how my heavenly Father will treat each of you unless you forgive your brother from your heart."*
> *Matthew 18:21–35*

4. Do you tend to be more like the master who forgave (v. 27) or the servant who wouldn't forgive (v. 30)?

6. When you get hurt in relationships, what do you usually do?
   ❏ have it out with the person
   ❏ sulk for three days
   ❏ withdraw into myself
   ❏ cry on someone's shoulder
   ❏ try to look at it from the other person's point of view
   ❏ watch reruns all night
   ❏ complain to God
   ❏ other:_____

7. What have you found helpful in dealing with conflict?
   ❏ writing out my feelings
   ❏ breaking off the relationship
   ❏ being up front with the person
   ❏ doing something nice for the person
   ❏ ignoring it and hoping it goes away
   ❏ appreciating God's forgiveness of me
   ❏ asking someone else to help deal with it
   ❏ seeing the other person as hurting himself or herself

8. What is hardest for you?
   ❏ forgiving again and again
   ❏ not punishing those who hurt me
   ❏ forgiving from my heart—I can say the words but I don't feel them.
   ❏ wondering how I can forgive without encouraging irresponsibility

5. Word gets back to you that something you shared in confidence with your youth group or small group last week is "all over town." What do you do?
   ❏ stop going to the group
   ❏ confront the group and tell them how this hurt me
   ❏ never share anything again at the meetings
   ❏ go to the leaders and ask them to handle it
   ❏ go to the person I think said it and confront him or her
   ❏ accept this as part of life and try to get on with it

9. Is there someone you need to forgive? If so, what is keeping you from forgiving them?

10. How would you like the group to pray for you?

Caring

SHARING YOUR FAITH

Introduction

How do you share your faith? What is witnessing? Witnessing is one beggar telling another beggar where to find food. This is an old definition, but it illustrates the Bible story that you are going to study.

This story takes place shortly after Jesus ascended to heaven and the Holy Spirit was poured out on the believers on the Day of Pentecost. At the gate to the temple in Jerusalem, a beggar approaches the apostles Peter and John for a handout. Listen to the story. Try to imagine yourself in this situation. Then move into groups of 4 and discuss the questionnaire.

1. Had you been a reporter for *The Jerusalem Herald* and you were to write an article on this event, which of the following headlines would you have been most likely to have given it?
   - ❏ "Beggar Gets More Than He Asks For"
   - ❏ "Faith Healers Amaze Temple Crowd"
   - ❏ "Cripple Walks for First Time in His Life"
   - ❏ "Welfare Rolls Reduced by One"

2. How do you feel when you see someone begging on the street?
   - ❏ compassionate　　　　　❏ embarrassed
   - ❏ I have really mixed feelings.　❏ disgusted

3. If you were Peter, what would you have done when the beggar asked you for money?
   - ❏ the same thing Peter did
   - ❏ quickly walked by
   - ❏ asked John for a dime

PETER HEALS THE CRIPPLED BEGGAR

3 One day Peter and John were going up to the temple at the time of prayer—at three in the afternoon. ²Now a man crippled from birth was being carried to the temple gate called Beautiful, where he was put every day to beg from those going into the temple courts. ³When he saw Peter and John about to enter, he asked them for money. ⁴Peter looked straight at him, as did John. Then Peter said, "Look at us!" ⁵So the man gave them his attention, expecting to get something from them.

⁶Then Peter said, "Silver or gold I do not have, but what I have I give you. In the name of Jesus Christ of Nazareth, walk." ⁷Taking him by the right hand, he helped him up, and instantly the man's feet and ankles became strong. ⁸He jumped to his feet and began to walk. Then he went with them into the temple courts, walking and jumping, and praising God. ⁹When all the people saw him walking and praising God, ¹⁰they recognized him as the same man who used to sit begging at the temple gate called Beautiful, and they were filled with wonder and amazement at what had happened to him.

¹¹While the beggar held on to Peter and John, all the people were astonished and came running to them in the place called Solomon's Colonnade. ¹²When Peter saw this, he said to them: "Men of Israel, why does this surprise you? Why do you stare at us as if by our own power or godliness we had made this man walk? ¹³The God of Abraham, Isaac and Jacob, the God of our fathers, has glorified his servant Jesus. You handed him over to be killed, and you disowned him before Pilate, though he had decided to let him go. ¹⁴You disowned the Holy and Righteous One and asked that a murderer be released to you. ¹⁵You killed the author of life, but God raised him from the dead. We are witnesses of this. ¹⁶By faith in the name of Jesus, this man whom you see and know was made strong. It is Jesus' name and the faith that comes through him that has given this complete healing to him, as you can all see."

Acts 3:1–16

6. Who do you admire, particularly in your school or workplace, for the way they share their faith?

7. If someone asked you, "Why do you go to church?" how would you answer?

8. What have you found to be the best way for you to share your faith?
   - ❏ just being a friend
   - ❏ giving the facts of the Gospel
   - ❏ telling my own story of how I met Jesus
   - ❏ living my life as a good example
   - ❏ inviting a person to go to church or another event
   - ❏ other:_____

9. What is your favorite excuse for *not* sharing the Good News of Christ?
   - ❏ claiming I don't know enough
   - ❏ saying I don't have time
   - ❏ being too concerned with my own life
   - ❏ thinking others can do it
   - ❏ just ignoring it
   - ❏ other:_____

4. When you have reached out to Jesus in the past, what motivated you to do so?
   - ❏ fear—of the judgment day
   - ❏ guilt—my conscience
   - ❏ heritage—the faith of my family
   - ❏ despair—I was burned out.
   - ❏ logic—I was convinced.
   - ❏ other:_____

5. Peter and John shared what they had with this beggar. What do you have that you can share with others?
   - ❏ maybe my lunch—that's about it
   - ❏ my ability to listen to their problems
   - ❏ my empathy with people who are hurting
   - ❏ my knowledge of the Bible
   - ❏ my faith in God and how it has helped me
   - ❏ my smiles and hugs
   - ❏ other:_____

10. Who is someone that you would like to share the Good News of Christ with?

11. What area of your life is "crippled" and in need of Christ's healing?

I APPRECIATE YOU

Introduction

This Scripture is taken from a longer passage about the kingdom of God. Jesus had been teaching his disciples about when the kingdom would come and who would be invited. He ends with this passage about "the sheep and the goats." Listen to the passage. Then move into groups of 4 and discuss the questionnaire.

1. What little prize from the past have you kept because it was special to you?

2. Thinking about this parable Jesus told, how would you feel if you were placed in the group of sheep?
    - ❏ surprised
    - ❏ overjoyed
    - ❏ unworthy
    - ❏ grateful
    - ❏ relieved

3. How would you feel if you were placed in the group of goats?
    - ❏ surprised
    - ❏ terrified
    - ❏ angry
    - ❏ guilty

4. What person has always been there for you when you needed them?
    - ❏ my mother
    - ❏ my father
    - ❏ both of my parents
    - ❏ my brother / sister
    - ❏ a grandparent
    - ❏ another family member
    - ❏ a close friend
    - ❏ a neighbor
    - ❏ no one
    - ❏ other:_____

5. What kind of people do you have the most compassion for?
    - ❏ homeless
    - ❏ starving
    - ❏ lonely
    - ❏ refugees
    - ❏ sick or disabled
    - ❏ elderly
    - ❏ prisoners
    - ❏ other:_____

THE SHEEP AND THE GOATS

³¹ *"When the Son of Man comes in his glory, and all the angels with him, he will sit on his throne in heavenly glory.* ³² *All the nations will be gathered before him, and he will separate the people one from another as a shepherd separates the sheep from the goats.* ³³ *He will put the sheep on his right and the goats on his left.*

³⁴ *"Then the King will say to those on his right, 'Come, you who are blessed by my Father; take your inheritance, the kingdom prepared for you since the creation of the world.* ³⁵ *For I was hungry and you gave me something to eat, I was thirsty and you gave me something to drink, I was a stranger and you invited me in,* ³⁶ *I needed clothes and you clothed me, I was sick and you looked after me, I was in prison and you came to visit me.'*

³⁷ *"Then the righteous will answer him, 'Lord, when did we see you hungry and feed you, or thirsty and give you something to drink?* ³⁸ *When did we see you a stranger and invite you in, or needing clothes and clothe you?* ³⁹ *When did we see you sick or in prison and go to visit you?'*

⁴⁰ *"The King will reply, 'I tell you the truth, whatever you did for one of the least of these brothers of mine, you did for me.'*

⁴¹ *"Then he will say to those on his left, 'Depart from me, you who are cursed, into the eternal fire prepared for the devil and his angels.* ⁴² *For I was hungry and you gave me nothing to eat, I was thirsty and you gave me nothing to drink,* ⁴³ *I was a stranger and you did not invite me in, I needed clothes and you did not clothe me, I was sick and in prison and you did not look after me.'*

⁴⁴ *"They also will answer, 'Lord, when did we see you hungry or thirsty or a stranger or needing clothes or sick or in prison, and did not help you?'*

⁴⁵ *"He will reply, 'I tell you the truth, whatever you did not do for one of the least of these, you did not do for me.'*

⁴⁶ *"Then they will go away to eternal punishment, but the righteous to eternal life."*

Matthew 25:31–46

6. When was the last time you did something for someone hungry, alone, poor, sick or imprisoned?

7. If Jesus were to come today and evaluate your life, what would he say about how you have "looked after" him by caring for others?
- ❐ "You're doing great!"
- ❐ "You're doing a lot better than you used to."
- ❐ "You used to do much better."
- ❐ "You're doing the best you can."
- ❐ "You're in big trouble!"

8. How would you rate this group on taking care of each other when someone is hurting or in need?
- ❐ I think we do a pretty good job.
- ❐ We are learning.
- ❐ We have a long way to go.
- ❐ We don't talk about these things.
- ❐ We really don't have any needs.

9. Think of this group as a community of love in which all of you are hurting in some way, and all of you are ministers in some way. Who would you nominate for special recognition for the following gifts of caring? Read the first category and let everyone nominate someone.

_____*I was hungry and you gave me something to eat:* Your sharing of yourself in this group has caused me to grow.

_____*I was thirsty and you gave me something to drink:* Your spiritual life and devotion to God has helped me find spiritual refreshment.

_____*I was a stranger and you invited me in:* Your welcome when I came made me feel at home.

_____*I needed clothes and you clothed me:* Your caring when I felt vulnerable and alone made me feel that somebody understands me.

_____*I was sick and you looked after me:* Your reaching out to me when I was really down caused me to feel better and whole again.

10. What is one need you would like the group to pray about?

PRIORITIES

Introduction

Stop the camera. If a soil inspector came today to inspect the soils in your life, what would they find?

Jesus used this parable to explain why some people show the results of a healthy, balanced spiritual life and some do not. In this Bible study, you will have a chance to check your priorities and see if you can improve them.

Now, listen to the parable. Then, move into groups of 4 to share your responses.

1. As you listened to the description of the four soils in the Scripture, what was your first impression?
   ❐ This sounds like an article from *Better Homes and Gardens*.
   ❐ Oh no, this is going to be a boring Bible study.
   ❐ What is Jesus trying to say?
   ❐ I wonder which soil I am.

2. Who is the "green thumb" in your family? How are you at making things grow?

3. How are you at finishing what you start?

4. In the period of your life when your spiritual life was the most unfruitful, what was the main reason?
   ❐ I had a whole lot of problems.
   ❐ I didn't know about Christ.
   ❐ I knew about Christ, but my priorities were messed up.
   ❐ I lacked a supportive Christian community.
   ❐ I was living life *my* way.

THE PARABLE OF THE SOWER

[4]While a large crowd was gathering and people were coming to Jesus from town after town, he told this parable: [5]"A farmer went out to sow his seed. As he was scattering the seed, some fell along the path; it was trampled on, and the birds of the air ate it up. [6]Some fell on rock, and when it came up, the plants withered because they had no moisture. [7]Other seed fell among thorns, which grew up with it and choked the plants. [8]Still other seed fell on good soil. It came up and yielded a crop, a hundred times more than was sown."

When he said this, he called out, "He who has ears to hear, let him hear." ...

[11]"This is the meaning of the parable: The seed is the word of God. [12]Those along the path are the ones who hear, and then the devil comes and takes away the word from their hearts, so that they may not believe and be saved. [13]Those on the rock are the ones who receive the word with joy when they hear it, but they have no root. They believe for a while, but in the time of testing they fall away. [14]The seed that fell among thorns stands for those who hear, but as they go on their way they are choked by life's worries, riches and pleasures, and they do not mature. [15]But the seed on good soil stands for those with a noble and good heart, who hear the word, retain it, and by persevering produce a crop.

Luke 8:4–8,11–15

---

5. What was the main factor at the time your life produced the best crop?
   ❐ I continually sought God's will.
   ❐ I had my priorities in order.
   ❐ I had few distractions in my life.
   ❐ I had a supportive Christian community.
   ❐ I had a strong devotional life.

LY 85 SHOPPING DAYS LEFT TIL
THE END OF THE WORLD

7. What are the "thorns" and "rocks" in your life which tend to choke out your spiritual growth? (Choose as many as apply.)
   - ❏ pressure from friends or family
   - ❏ influence of TV / movies / music
   - ❏ concern about money
   - ❏ lack of commitment or discipline
   - ❏ a "rocky" home life
   - ❏ suffering that makes it hard to believe in a good God
   - ❏ desire for material things
   - ❏ sexual temptations
   - ❏ parties / alcohol / drugs
   - ❏ worry about the future

8. How would you describe the root system of your spiritual life right now?
   - ❏ pretty shallow
   - ❏ growing
   - ❏ strong and deep
   - ❏ really dry

9. How often do you make hearing and acting on God's Word a priority in your life?
   - ❏ all of the time
   - ❏ most of the time
   - ❏ some of the time
   - ❏ Sorry you asked!

10. What specific "thorn of worry" would you like the group to pray with you about?

6. What do you have in your life now that gives "depth to your soil" and nurtures your growth? (Choose as many as apply, and put a star by the one that is most important to you.)
   - ❏ Christian parents / spouse
   - ❏ other Christian relatives
   - ❏ group Bible study
   - ❏ personal devotions
   - ❏ Christian friends
   - ❏ Christian music
   - ❏ regular worship
   - ❏ some books I've read
   - ❏ church activities
   - ❏ other:_____

POSSESSIONS

> **THE PARABLE OF THE RICH FOOL**
>
> [13]*Someone in the crowd said to him, "Teacher, tell my brother to divide the inheritance with me."*
>
> [14]*Jesus replied, "Man, who appointed me a judge or an arbiter between you?"* [15]*Then he said to them, "Watch out! Be on your guard against all kinds of greed; a man's life does not consist in the abundance of his possessions."*
>
> [16]*And he told them this parable: "The ground of a certain rich man produced a good crop.* [17]*He thought to himself, 'What shall I do? I have no place to store my crops.'*
>
> [18]*"Then he said, 'This is what I'll do. I will tear down my barns and build bigger ones, and there I will store all my grain and my goods.* [19]*And I'll say to myself, "You have plenty of good things laid up for many years. Take life easy; eat, drink and be merry." '*
>
> [20]*"But God said to him, 'You fool! This very night your life will be demanded from you. Then who will get what you have prepared for yourself?'*
>
> [21]*"This is how it will be with anyone who stores up things for himself but is not rich toward God."*
>
> *Luke 12:13–21*

Introduction

The following parable shows us the effects of greed. Jesus calls us to share our resources with others for the sake of God's kingdom. Listen to the parable. Then, move into groups of 4 and discuss the questionnaire.

1. Just for fun, if the Rich Fool in the parable (you can call him George Megabucks) lived in your community, what neighborhood would he live in and what kind of car would he drive?

2. Where would Mr. Megabucks go to church? How regular would he be in attendance?

3. How would you describe George?
   - ❑ clever
   - ❑ secure
   - ❑ a show-off
   - ❑ immature
   - ❑ unhappy
   - ❑ selfish
   - ❑ content
   - ❑ materialistic
   - ❑ screwed up
   - ❑ brilliant
   - ❑ dumb
   - ❑ lucky

4. After dying, how would the local paper describe George in the obituaries?
   - ❑ a tireless worker
   - ❑ a success story
   - ❑ foolish
   - ❑ enterprising

5. If you had been a friend of the rich man in this parable, how would you have acted toward him?
   - ❑ kissed up to him so he would invite me to his parties
   - ❑ snubbed him just to show everyone I don't care about money
   - ❑ treated him like everyone else
   - ❑ witnessed to him about Christ
   - ❑ shown him how to relax and just enjoy life

6. If you suddenly came into money, what would you do with it?
   - ❑ quit school or work—travel the world
   - ❑ share it with friends or family
   - ❑ buy a car or motorcycle
   - ❑ throw a huge party
   - ❑ not let anyone know
   - ❑ give it to the needy
   - ❑ keep doing the things I am doing now
   - ❑ other:_____

7. What do you value most in life? (Rank your top three choices.)

___ my family

___ my friends

___ my assets

___ my good health

___ my work

___ my faith

___ my integrity

___ my memories

___ my time

8. If you should die today, what would the people closest to you say about you in the newspaper? Finish the sentences below with the first thing that comes to mind. If the others in your group want to help you with your answers, let them speak up.

❏ Last night (fill in your name) died suddenly.

❏ He / She will always be remembered at church for their ...

❏ He / She always had time for ...

❏ He / She felt that possessions were ...

❏ He / She treated people like ...

❏ On his / her tombstone, the following words are inscribed:

9. If you were to give a "weather report" on your life recently, what would it be?

❏ dark and stormy

❏ bright and sunny

❏ partly cloudy

❏ dreary and gray

❏ other: _____

10. In light of the "weather" in your life, how would you like the group to pray for you this week?

RESPONSIBILITY

Introduction

In this Bible study, you are going to study the parable of the talents. (A talent was a unit of coins worth more than a thousand dollars.) We will look at a man who didn't use the money he was given. Jesus calls this man wicked and lazy.

The present-day use of "talent" as an ability comes from this parable. As you listen to the parable, think about what Jesus might say to you about taking responsibility for your time, money and abilities.

Now, move into groups of 4 and discuss the questionnaire.

1. What would the *Wall Street Journal* call the way the master in the parable treated his servants?
   - ❏ shrewd
   - ❏ businesslike
   - ❏ fair
   - ❏ unfair

2. Are you more of a saver or a spender?

3. Which of the three servants in this parable can you relate to most easily?
   - ❏ the one who was given five talents—I've been greatly blessed.
   - ❏ the one who was given two talents—I've done okay with what I've had to work with.
   - ❏ the one who was given one talent—I always get the short end!

THE PARABLE OF THE TALENTS

[14]"*Again, it will be like a man going on a journey, who called his servants and entrusted his property to them.* [15]*To one he gave five talents of money, to another two talents, and to another one talent, each according to his ability. Then he went on his journey.* [16]*The man who had received the five talents went at once and put his money to work and gained five more.* [17]*So also, the one with the two talents gained two more.* [18]*But the man who had received the one talent went off, dug a hole in the ground and hid his master's money.*

[19]"*After a long time the master of those servants returned and settled accounts with them.* [20]*The man who had received the five talents brought the other five. 'Master,' he said, 'you entrusted me with five talents. See, I have gained five more.'*

[21]"*His master replied, 'Well done, good and faithful servant! You have been faithful with a few things; I will put you in charge of many things. Come and share your master's happiness!'*

[22]"*The man with the two talents also came. 'Master,' he said, 'you entrusted me with two talents; see, I have gained two more.'*

[23]"*His master replied, 'Well done, good and faithful servant! You have been faithful with a few things; I will put you in charge of many things. Come and share your master's happiness!'*

[24]"*Then the man who had received the one talent came. 'Master,' he said, 'I knew that you are a hard man, harvesting where you have not sown and gathering where you have not scattered seed.* [25]*So I was afraid and went out and hid your talent in the ground. See, here is what belongs to you.'*

[26]"*His master replied, 'You wicked, lazy servant! So you knew that I harvest where I have not sown and gather where I have not scattered seed?* [27]*Well then, you should have put my money on deposit with the bankers, so that when I returned I would have received it back with interest.*

[28]" *'Take the talent from him and give it to the one who has the ten talents.* [29]*For everyone who has will be given more, and he will have an abundance. Whoever does not have, even what he has will be taken from him.* [30]*And throw that worthless servant outside, into the darkness, where there will be weeping and gnashing of teeth.' "*

Matthew 25:14–30

4. How do you feel when you are given a lot of responsibility?
   ❐ nervous—I hope I don't blow it!
   ❐ proud—People believe in me!
   ❐ overwhelmed—I can't handle it!
   ❐ confident—I can handle it!

5. Write three talents you have discovered or which others have said you have. Then assign each talent a number (from the scale below) according to how well you're using that talent right now:

1	2	3	4	5	6	7	8	9	10
burying it									fully invested

   talent #1:_____ usage:_____

   talent #2:_____ usage:_____

   talent #3:_____ usage:_____

6. What motivates you to use your time, resources and abilities for God's kingdom?
   ❐ fear of the Master
   ❐ people's appreciation
   ❐ God's approval
   ❐ a chance for greater responsibility
   ❐ fellowship with the Master
   ❐ rewards in the next life
   ❐ other:_____

7. Which of the following statements best describes how you feel about the way you are "investing" your life?
   ❐ I am quite satisfied.
   ❐ I would like to make some changes.
   ❐ I'm not sure what it means to invest my life.
   ❐ I'm not being very responsible in this area.
   ❐ I feel like I'm on hold.

8. What are your goals for the future? What are you doing now to get you there?

9. What do you need to do to be a more responsible "servant"?
   ❐ have more confidence I can do what is asked of me
   ❐ become more aware of my strengths and abilities
   ❐ take my responsibilities more seriously
   ❐ trust in God to help me
   ❐ get more encouragement from others
   ❐ Responsible?—I just want to have fun!

10. If the Master returned today, how well would he say you have been using what he gave you?

11. Name one thing you can do this week to prepare for Christ's coming. How can the group support you in prayer?

MORALITY

Introduction

Try to imagine the picture of a giant banquet hall where King Herod is sitting at a drunken feast. Herodias, his wife, is sitting next to him. (Herodias left Herod's brother to marry Herod.) Off in prison is John the Baptist, who dared to tell the king that it was wrong to marry his brother's wife. Herod faces a moral dilemma after his stepdaughter (whose name was Salome) performs what was surely a highly sensual dance.

Listen to the story as it develops. Then, move into groups of 4 and discuss the questionnaire below.

1. If tabloids existed back then, what would the headlines be?
   ❐ "Prophet Loses Head Over Girl"
   ❐ "First Lady in Charge at Palace"
   ❐ "Popular Preacher Pays the Price for Exotic Dancer"
   ❐ "Royal Birthday Party Gets Out of Hand"
   ❐ "John the Baptist Returns From the Dead to Haunt Herod"

2. What rating would you give this story?
   ❐ G   ❐ R
   ❐ PG   ❐ X
   ❐ PG-13

3. Of the three people involved in the death of John the Baptist, which one do you feel the greatest anger toward because of their moral corruption?
   ❐ King Herod—because he took his brother's wife and gave the order to kill the person who spoke out against him
   ❐ Herodias—because she deserted her husband and tricked the king into killing John the Baptist out of spite
   ❐ Herodias' daughter—because she let her mother use her "dirty dancing" to have John the Baptist killed

4. John the Baptist dared to tell the king that it was wrong to take his brother's wife. If you were John the Baptist, what would you have done?
   ❐ just what he did
   ❐ kept my mouth shut
   ❐ written an anonymous letter to the editor
   ❐ said my peace and then ran for the hills

JOHN THE BAPTIST BEHEADED

[14]King Herod heard about this, for Jesus' name had become well known. Some were saying, "John the Baptist has been raised from the dead, and that is why miraculous powers are at work in him."

[15]Others said, "He is Elijah."

And still others claimed, "He is a prophet, like one of the prophets of long ago."

[16]But when Herod heard this, he said, "John, the man I beheaded, has been raised from the dead!"

[17]For Herod himself had given orders to have John arrested, and he had him bound and put in prison. He did this because of Herodias, his brother Philip's wife, whom he had married. [18]For John had been saying to Herod, "It is not lawful for you to have your brother's wife." [19]So Herodias nursed a grudge against John and wanted to kill him. But she was not able to, [20]because Herod feared John and protected him, knowing him to be a righteous and holy man. When Herod heard John, he was greatly puzzled; yet he liked to listen to him.

[21]Finally the opportune time came. On his birthday Herod gave a banquet for his high officials and military commanders and the leading men of Galilee. [22]When the daughter of Herodias came in and danced, she pleased Herod and his dinner guests.

The king said to the girl, "Ask me for anything you want, and I'll give it to you." [23]And he promised her with an oath, "Whatever you ask I will give you, up to half my kingdom."

[24]She went out and said to her mother, "What shall I ask for?"

"The head of John the Baptist," she answered.

[25]At once the girl hurried in to the king with the request: "I want you to give me right now the head of John the Baptist on a platter."

[26]The king was greatly distressed, but because of his oaths and his dinner guests, he did not want to refuse her. [27]So he immediately sent an executioner with orders to bring John's head. The man went, beheaded John in the prison, [28]and brought back his head on a platter. He presented it to the girl, and she gave it to her mother. [29]On hearing of this, John's disciples came and took his body and laid it in a tomb.

Mark 6:14–29

5. In your own circles, who do you admire for they way they have stood up for what is right?

6. What is the closest you have come to "losing your head" for something you said or believed in?

7. When you have to make a moral decision, what do you do?
   - ❏ struggle for days
   - ❏ make a snap decision
   - ❏ hope it will go away
   - ❏ go for a long walk
   - ❏ ask for help
   - ❏ see what my friends or family are doing
   - ❏ other:_____

8. Specifically, where do you draw the line when it comes to entertainment with sexual or violent content?

9. How would you rate yourself in standing up for what is right? Finish the sentence below by choosing one in each category:

   IN STANDING UP FOR WHAT I THINK IS RIGHT, I (AM) ...

   Rock of Gibraltar _____Jello pudding

   stick to my convictions _____waver back and forth

   usually follow the crowd_____rely on my own judgment

10. What is your biggest fear in standing up for what you believe?
    - ❏ that I will be laughed at
    - ❏ that I will be alone
    - ❏ that I will lose my friends
    - ❏ that I will look stupid

11. How can the group pray for you, particularly in relation to moral issues?

BOTTOM LINE

> **THE WISE AND FOOLISH BUILDERS**
> [24]*"Therefore everyone who hears these words of mine and puts them into practice is like a wise man who built his house on the rock.* [25]*The rain came down, the streams rose, and the winds blew and beat against that house; yet it did not fall, because it had its foundation on the rock.* [26]*But everyone who hears these words of mine and does not put them into practice is like a foolish man who built his house on sand.* [27]*The rain came down, the streams rose, and the winds blew and beat against that house, and it fell with a great crash."*
>
> *Matthew 7:24–27*

Introduction

This Bible study looks at a parable that Jesus used at the close of the Sermon on the Mount to illustrate two different kinds of people. Listen to the parable carefully, then move into groups of 4 and discuss the questionnaire.

1. If you could build your dream house, where would you build it and what would it be like?

2. What is the worst storm you can remember?

3. Who (other than God) is the "Rock of Gibraltar" in your life? What is it about that person that makes them so stable?

4. In this parable, what exactly is Jesus promising to someone who is willing to live by his words?
    - ❒ that you will never experience storms
    - ❒ that you will experience the same storms as everybody else
    - ❒ that the storms will not destroy your faith
    - ❒ that you will get a new house if your old one collapses

5. If you could compare your life to a house, and every room in your house to a living space in your life, what would a building inspector say?

Let one person in your group read the description of one room below. Then, let everyone in your group call out a number from 1 to 10—1 being SHAKY and 10 being ROCK SOLID. Then, go on to the next room and let everyone call out a number for this room.

LIVING ROOM: I have my life in order; I know what I want to do; my values are well-defined; my moral principles are clear; I am feeling good about myself and my lifestyle right now.

1   2   3   4   5   6   7   8   9   10

RECREATION ROOM: I have a healthy balance in my schedule for leisure; I use my spare time carefully—to restore my mind and spirit as well as my body; I am feeling good about my priorities and the way I use my time.

1   2   3   4   5   6   7   8   9   10

FAMILY ROOM: I have a good relationship with my family; we have learned to talk about our differences; we deal with our conflicts; we build up one another during "stormy" times; I am feeling good about my family and enjoy being with them.

1   2   3   4   5   6   7   8   9   10

LIBRARY: I feed my mind in wholesome, appropriate and balanced ways; I make decisions based on definite values and moral principles, and don't just cave in to the pressures of the world.

1   2   3   4   5   6   7   8   9   10

PHYSICAL FITNESS ROOM: I try to keep in shape and maintain a healthy lifestyle; I can sleep nights and weather the "storms" of life without getting fatigued and depressed.

1   2   3   4   5   6   7   8   9   10

GUEST ROOM: I have a good relationship with my friends; I enjoy being with people without feeling dependent upon them; I can belong to the crowd without accepting or bowing to their values; I can stand against social pressure to conform, yet am sensitive to open the door when someone needs a little warmth.

1   2   3   4   5   6   7   8   9   10

6. Being totally honest, what is the foundation you depend on?
- ❒ my abilities
- ❒ wishful thinking
- ❒ good health
- ❒ my resources
- ❒ my status
- ❒ self-confidence
- ❒ other people
- ❒ faith in Christ

7. If you could compare your spiritual foundation right now to a house, what would it be?
- ❒ shaky
- ❒ brand new
- ❒ slipping
- ❒ solid
- ❒ temporary
- ❒ rebuilding

8. In the last year, would you say your spiritual formation has gotten weaker or stronger?

9. What "storm" are you facing now? How can the group pray for you right now and in the days ahead?

STRESS

Introduction

In this Bible study you will take a look at a story of Jesus and his disciples in a storm—a big storm—that caused a lot of stress.

Now, listen to the Bible story. Then, quickly move into groups of 4 and discuss the questionnaire.

1. If you were a reporter assigned to the Lake of Galilee beat, what headline would you give this event?
   - ❏ "Self-Proclaimed Messiah Proves Himself"
   - ❏ "Religious Leader Gives Followers a Scare"
   - ❏ "Prophet Demonstrates Sleeping Disorder"
   - ❏ "Even Nature Obeys Miracle Worker"

2. If you had been one of the disciples when the boat was about to sink, what would you have done?
   - ❏ jumped overboard
   - ❏ screamed for help
   - ❏ started bailing water
   - ❏ taken command
   - ❏ acted like nothing was wrong
   - ❏ woken up Jesus

3. Who in your family is good at keeping calm in the storms of life? How do they do it?

4. What brings on most of the "storms" in your life?
   - ❏ pressures at work or school
   - ❏ family problems
   - ❏ financial difficulties
   - ❏ hassles with other relationships
   - ❏ health problems
   - ❏ overwhelming demands
   - ❏ insecurity: worry about the future
   - ❏ disappointment: feelings of failure
   - ❏ tragedy: grief and loss
   - ❏ other:_____

JESUS CALMS THE STORM

35 That day when evening came, he said to his disciples, "Let us go over to the other side." 36 Leaving the crowd behind, they took him along, just as he was, in the boat. There were also other boats with him. 37 A furious squall came up, and the waves broke over the boat, so that it was nearly swamped. 38 Jesus was in the stern, sleeping on a cushion. The disciples woke him and said to him, "Teacher, don't you care if we drown?"

39 He got up, rebuked the wind and said to the waves, "Quiet! Be still!" Then the wind died down and it was completely calm.

40 He said to his disciples, "Why are you so afraid? Do you still have no faith?"

41 They were terrified and asked each other, "Who is this? Even the wind and the waves obey him!"

Mark 4:35–41

5. If you could have three wishes, which three would you choose from the list below?
- ❐ win the lottery: never have to work again
- ❐ secure job: lifetime guarantee with benefits
- ❐ stress-free life: no struggles, no tension
- ❐ close family: no hassles, lots of love and support
- ❐ good health: long life full of vigor and vitality
- ❐ one deep, abiding friendship: someone who will be close to me forever
- ❐ happiness: a life full of joy and surprises
- ❐ success: fame and recognition in my chosen field
- ❐ direction: to know what I should do with my life
- ❐ strong faith: a deep, satisfying relationship with God

6. What do you do when storms come up in your life?
- ❐ turn to a person I can trust
- ❐ withdraw into myself
- ❐ turn to God
- ❐ get touchy and irritable
- ❐ take charge of things
- ❐ act like nothing is wrong
- ❐ panic

7. As time goes on, have you seen improvement in the way you handle storms? What difference does your faith in Christ make?

8. The disciples asked Jesus an interesting question—"Don't you care if we drown?" When was the last time you wondered if God cared about you?

9. If you could compare your own life to the storm in this story, where are you right now?
- ❐ floating on smooth waters
- ❐ seeing just a few storm clouds
- ❐ sensing a storm is brewing
- ❐ in the middle of the storm, bailing water like mad
- ❐ sinking fast
- ❐ seeing the storm winds die down and calm return

10. "Quiet! Be still!" If Jesus were to speak these words to you today, what would they mean?
- ❐ Settle down.
- ❐ Shut up and listen.
- ❐ Hang in there.
- ❐ Turn the controls of your life over to God.
- ❐ Relax and let God handle this.
- ❐ Keep the faith.
- ❐ other:_____

11. What stress do you have that you need Jesus to calm? Pray for each other.

Pressures — "Do not worry"

WORRIES

Introduction

"Don't worry—be happy" the song says. If only it were that easy! Jesus had a lot to say about pressures like worry. This Bible study comes from a well-known Scripture about worry. Listen to these words of Jesus as someone reads the passage. Then move into groups of 4 and discuss the questionnaire.

1. If Jesus lived today, how would he dress?
   ❏ in jeans and a T-shirt
   ❏ in a business suit
   ❏ with thrift store donations
   ❏ like a pastor or priest
   ❏ like a fashion model—the latest fad
   ❏ He wouldn't care what he wore.

2. What kind of car do you think Jesus would drive?
   ❏ a fancy Mercedes
   ❏ an old junker
   ❏ a classic Corvette
   ❏ a pickup truck
   ❏ a minivan, to hold his disciples
   ❏ a bus—to bring in the crowds
   ❏ nothing—He would either walk or use public transportation.

3. When Jesus said, "Do not worry about tomorrow," what did he mean?
   ❏ Don't plan ahead.
   ❏ Plan ahead so you don't worry.
   ❏ Worry is a waste of time and energy.
   ❏ Live for today.
   ❏ Trust God with things you can't control.

DO NOT WORRY

24 "No one can serve two masters. Either he will hate the one and love the other, or he will be devoted to the one and despise the other. You cannot serve both God and Money.

25 "Therefore I tell you, do not worry about your life, what you will eat or drink; or about your body, what you will wear. Is not life more important than food, and the body more important than clothes? 26 Look at the birds of the air; they do not sow or reap or store away in barns, and yet your heavenly Father feeds them. Are you not much more valuable than they? 27 Who of you by worrying can add a single hour to his life?

28 "And why do you worry about clothes? See how the lilies of the field grow. They do not labor or spin. 29 Yet I tell you that not even Solomon in all his splendor was dressed like one of these. 30 If that is how God clothes the grass of the field, which is here today and tomorrow is thrown into the fire, will he not much more clothe you, O you of little faith? 31 So do not worry, saying, 'What shall we eat?' or 'What shall we drink?' or 'What shall we wear?' 32 For the pagans run after all these things, and your heavenly Father knows that you need them. 33 But seek first his kingdom and his righteousness, and all these things will be given to you as well. 34 Therefore do not worry about tomorrow, for tomorrow will worry about itself. Each day has enough trouble of its own."

Matthew 6:24–34

---

4. If you really followed the teaching of this passage, how would it change your behavior?
   ❏ I wouldn't be caught up in material things.
   ❏ I would spend more time helping people.
   ❏ I would be less concerned about how I look and dress.
   ❏ I would give more money to the poor.
   ❏ I would make my spiritual life my highest priority.
   ❏ I wouldn't worry so much.
   ❏ I would spend more time with church activities.
   ❏ other:_____

5. What is your favorite way of dealing with your problems? Pick your most and least frequent ways:
    - ❐ deny that I have any
    - ❐ talk to a close friend
    - ❐ worry a lot
    - ❐ eat a lot
    - ❐ ask for help
    - ❐ go for a walk
    - ❐ talk to God about them
    - ❐ get busy and try to forget them
    - ❐ accept problems as part of life
    - ❐ listen to music until I feel better
    - ❐ other:_____

6. If you could describe a good goal for dealing with the most difficult problem you are facing at the moment, what would it be?
    - ❐ learn to laugh more at my troubles
    - ❐ learn to live one day at a time
    - ❐ get out of the situation I'm in
    - ❐ lower the expectations I've placed on myself and others
    - ❐ focus more on God's kingdom and less on mine
    - ❐ simplify my lifestyle
    - ❐ take time to smell the flowers
    - ❐ other:_____

7. On a scale from 1 (low) to 10 (high), what is the stress level in your life at the moment?

8. If your doctor told you that you had to reduce the stress in your life, what would have to change?

9. What is the biggest worry you have about the coming week? How can this group pray for you regarding that concern?

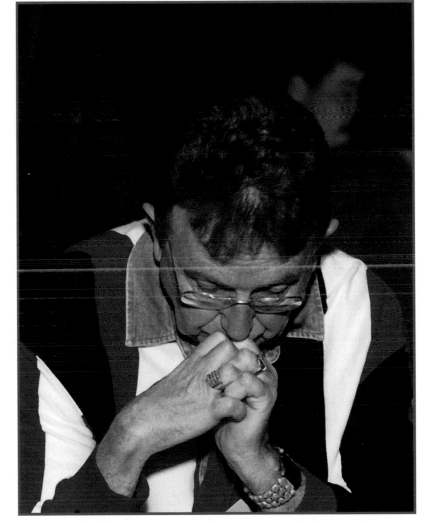

SHATTERED DREAMS

Introduction

In this Bible study, we want you to listen to the experience of two followers of Jesus who may have lost hope and decided to return home.

It is right after the resurrection of Jesus, but these two followers are still sad and confused. Listen in on their conversation as Jesus comes alongside of them and lets them talk about their disappointment and shattered dreams. Then, move quickly into groups of 4 and discuss the questionnaire.

1. If you got some really bad news today, where would you go to get yourself together?

ON THE ROAD TO EMMAUS

13Now that same day two of them were going to a village called Emmaus, about seven miles from Jerusalem. 14They were talking with each other about everything that had happened. 15As they talked and discussed these things with each other, Jesus himself came up and walked along with them; 16but they were kept from recognizing him.

17He asked them, "What are you discussing together as you walk along?"

They stood still, their faces downcast. 18One of them, named Cleopas, asked him, "Are you only a visitor to Jerusalem and do not know the things that have happened there in these days?"

19"What things?" he asked.

"About Jesus of Nazareth," they replied. "He was a prophet, powerful in word and deed before God and all the people. 20The chief priests and our rulers handed him over to be sentenced to death, and they crucified him; 21but we had hoped that he was the one who was going to redeem Israel. And what is more, it is the third day since all this took place. 22In addition, some of our women amazed us. They went to the tomb early this morning 23but didn't find his body. They came and told us that they had seen a vision of angels, who said he was alive. 24Then some of our companions went to the tomb and found it just as the women had said, but him they did not see."

25He said to them, "How foolish you are, and how slow of heart to believe all that the prophets have spoken! 26Did not the Christ have to suffer these things and then enter his glory?" 27And beginning with Moses and all the Prophets, he explained to them what was said in all the Scriptures concerning himself.

28As they approached the village to which they were going, Jesus acted as if he were going farther. 29But they urged him strongly, "Stay with us, for it is nearly evening; the day is almost over." So he went in to stay with them.

30When he was at the table with them, he took bread, gave thanks, broke it and began to give it to them. 31Then their eyes were opened and they recognized him, and he disappeared from their sight. 32They asked each other, "Were not our hearts burning within us while he talked with us on the road and opened the Scriptures to us?"

33They got up and returned at once to Jerusalem. There they found the Eleven and those with them, assembled together 34and saying, "It is true! The Lord has risen and has appeared to Simon." 35Then the two told what had happened on the way, and how Jesus was recognized by them when he broke the bread.

Luke 24:13–35

2. Why didn't the two disciples in this story recognize Jesus when he joined them?
   ❒ They were preoccupied.
   ❒ They were depressed.
   ❒ They couldn't recognize Jesus in his resurrected body.
   ❒ They refused to believe their eyes.
   ❒ God kept them from recognizing him.

3. When did you last experience a broken dream or a broken heart?

4. What is the closest you have come to "throwing in the towel" and giving up on your relationship with God?

5. What was it that brought you back to faith?

6. What did you learn during that time you were away from God?
   ❒ It's lonely out there.
   ❒ God never leaves you alone.
   ❒ It's okay to struggle.
   ❒ Once you've given your heart to God, God is going to be more visible.
   ❒ There is always a way home.

7. What helps you recognize Jesus alongside you when you are down?
   ❒ taking time to be alone with God
   ❒ talking with someone who cares
   ❒ reading Scripture
   ❒ getting away from the situation
   ❒ focusing on worship
   ❒ fellowshipping with others
   ❒ other:_____

8. What does the resurrected Jesus need to change in your life?
   ❒ my spiritual vision
   ❒ my unbelief
   ❒ my discouragement
   ❒ my loneliness
   ❒ my disillusionment
   ❒ other:_____

9. How would you describe your "walk" with Christ right now?
   ❒ up and down   ❒ growing
   ❒ very close   ❒ slipping
   ❒ blah   ❒ other:_____
   ❒ exciting

10. If Jesus showed up at your meeting today, what would he likely say to you personally? To your group?

11. How can the group pray for you?

OLD HABITS

Introduction

This Bible story finds the apostle Peter in jail because of his faith and preaching. As you listen to the story, try to identify with Peter and with his fellow believers as they pray for him. Then think about what this story of Peter's miraculous escape has to say about the things that may hold you captive.

Read the Scripture passage now. Then, move into groups of 4 and discuss the questionnaire.

1. "The night before Herod was to bring him to trial, Peter was sleeping between two soldiers, bound with two chains, and sentries stood guard at the entrance. Suddenly an angel of the Lord appeared and a light shone in the cell. He struck Peter on the side and woke him up. 'Quick, get up!' he said, and the chains fell off Peter's wrists." Imagine you are Peter. What would you have said?

   ❑ "Okay, okay—I'm getting up!"
   ❑ "This must be a dream."
   ❑ "This must be my guardian angel!"
   ❑ "This isn't going to go over very well with the guards."
   ❑ "Praise God! My prayers have been answered!"

PETER'S MIRACULOUS ESCAPE FROM PRISON

12 It was about this time that King Herod arrested some who belonged to the church, intending to persecute them. ²He had James, the brother of John, put to death with the sword. ³When he saw that this pleased the Jews, he proceeded to seize Peter also. This happened during the Feast of Unleavened Bread. ⁴After arresting him, he put him in prison, handing him over to be guarded by four squads of four soldiers each. Herod intended to bring him out for public trial after the Passover.

⁵So Peter was kept in prison, but the church was earnestly praying to God for him.

⁶The night before Herod was to bring him to trial, Peter was sleeping between two soldiers, bound with two chains, and sentries stood guard at the entrance. ⁷Suddenly an angel of the Lord appeared and a light shone in the cell. He struck Peter on the side and woke him up. "Quick, get up!" he said, and the chains fell off Peter's wrists.

⁸Then the angel said to him, "Put on your clothes and sandals." And Peter did so. "Wrap your cloak around you and follow me," the angel told him. ⁹Peter followed him out of the prison, but he had no idea that what the angel was doing was really happening; he thought he was seeing a vision. ¹⁰They passed the first and second guards and came to the iron gate leading to the city. It opened for them by itself, and they went through it. When they had walked the length of one street, suddenly the angel left him.

¹¹Then Peter came to himself and said, "Now I know without a doubt that the Lord sent his angel and rescued me from Herod's clutches and from everything the Jewish people were anticipating."

¹²When this had dawned on him, he went to the house of Mary the mother of John, also called Mark, where many people had gathered and were praying. ¹³Peter knocked at the outer entrance, and a servant girl named Rhoda came to answer the door. ¹⁴When she recognized Peter's voice, she was so overjoyed she ran back without opening it and exclaimed, "Peter is at the door!"

¹⁵"You're out of your mind," they told her. When she kept insisting that it was so, they said, "It must be his angel."

¹⁶But Peter kept on knocking, and when they opened the door and saw him, they were astonished.

Acts 12:1–16

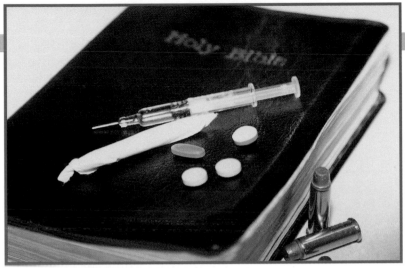

2. Now imagine that you were at the prayer meeting when Rhoda announced (without opening the door) that "Peter is at the door!" What would you have said?
- ❐ "You're out of your mind!"
- ❐ "Well, let him in!"
- ❐ "It must be Peter's guardian angel."
- ❐ "Just as I expected!"
- ❐ "Praise God! My prayers have been answered!"

3. When has God surprised you by intervening in an "imprisoning" situation that you thought was hopeless?

4. In your school or job, what is the most common addiction?
- ❐ alcohol
- ❐ food / weight control
- ❐ exercise
- ❐ spending / gambling
- ❐ anger / violence
- ❐ work / achievement
- ❐ drugs
- ❐ tobacco
- ❐ TV / movies
- ❐ sex / pornography
- ❐ other:_____

5. From your experience, what could you share to help someone who feels they are helplessly addicted?

6. What kinds of things do you find to be most imprisoning?
- ❐ habits / addictions
- ❐ my desire for things
- ❐ a stagnant spiritual life
- ❐ my fears
- ❐ my friends' expectations
- ❐ my parents' / spouse's expectations
- ❐ a health problem / physical limitation
- ❐ bad relationships
- ❐ school / work
- ❐ my impulses
- ❐ other:_____

7. What would most help you to find freedom from these things?
- ❐ an angel coming from heaven to take care of it all
- ❐ friends praying for me, and really believing it can happen
- ❐ my own confidence in God's ability to help me
- ❐ my own desire to change
- ❐ So who wants to change—a prison is a secure place!

8. What can this group do to help you be free?
- ❐ leave me alone
- ❐ pray for me
- ❐ let me know I'm okay
- ❐ hold me accountable
- ❐ call me to see how I'm doing
- ❐ share some of their own struggles
- ❐ help me to understand myself and to change
- ❐ other:_____

9. If you, like Peter, were arrested by a repressive government for being a Christian, what evidence would there be that you are "guilty"? What evidence would there be that you are "innocent"?

10. What is God saying to you through this study? How can the group pray for you?

189

Pressures

A Touching Incident

SHAME AND BLAME

Introduction

As a prostitute, the woman in this Bible story felt a great deal of shame and blame. Yet she longed for God's forgiveness. Listen to the story as it unfolds. Then, move into groups of 4 and discuss the questionnaire.

1. What section would the local newspaper put this story in?
    - ❏ the society page—highlighting that a prostitute crashed the dinner this Pharisee had for Jesus
    - ❏ the gossip column—because of the scandalous way the prostitute acted toward Jesus
    - ❏ the religion page—headlining Jesus' claim that the prostitute's sins were forgiven
    - ❏ the business section—announcing the woman's departure from her profession

2. How would you have felt watching the woman anoint Jesus like she did in verse 38?
    - ❏ embarrassed
    - ❏ moved
    - ❏ confused
    - ❏ disgusted

3. How would your group react if this woman "crashed" your meeting?
    - ❏ We would accept her easily.
    - ❏ We would want to accept her, but it would be awkward.
    - ❏ We wouldn't accept her.
    - ❏ We would want to see some evidence of change.

4. When in your life have you most felt like an outsider who didn't belong?

JESUS ANOINTED BY A SINFUL WOMAN

³⁶Now one of the Pharisees invited Jesus to have dinner with him, so he went to the Pharisee's house and reclined at the table. ³⁷When a woman who had lived a sinful life in that town learned that Jesus was eating at the Pharisee's house, she brought an alabaster jar of perfume, ³⁸and as she stood behind him at his feet weeping, she began to wet his feet with her tears. Then she wiped them with her hair, kissed them and poured perfume on them.

³⁹When the Pharisee who had invited him saw this, he said to himself, "If this man were a prophet, he would know who is touching him and what kind of woman she is—that she is a sinner."

⁴⁰Jesus answered him, "Simon, I have something to tell you."

"Tell me, teacher," he said.

⁴¹"Two men owed money to a certain moneylender. One owed him five hundred denarii, and the other fifty. ⁴²Neither of them had the money to pay him back, so he canceled the debts of both. Now which of them will love him more?"

⁴³Simon replied, "I suppose the one who had the bigger debt canceled."

"You have judged correctly," Jesus said.

⁴⁴Then he turned toward the woman and said to Simon, "Do you see this woman? I came into your house. You did not give me any water for my feet, but she wet my feet with her tears and wiped them with her hair. ⁴⁵You did not give me a kiss, but this woman, from the time I entered, has not stopped kissing my feet. ⁴⁶You did not put oil on my head, but she has poured perfume on my feet. ⁴⁷Therefore, I tell you, her many sins have been forgiven—for she loved much. But he who has been forgiven little loves little."

⁴⁸Then Jesus said to her, "Your sins are forgiven."

⁴⁹The other guests began to say among themselves, "Who is this who even forgives sins?"

⁵⁰Jesus said to the woman, "Your faith has saved you; go in peace."

Luke 7:36–50

5. Who in your life has played the role of Simon, questioning your value? Who has played the role of Jesus, believing in and sticking up for you?

6. Who do you identify with most in this story?
   ❐ the woman—because I feel bad about my past
   ❐ the Pharisee—because I have a tendency to be judgmental
   ❐ Jesus—because hypocritical attitudes make me angry

7. What have you found to be the hardest thing about dealing with sin and failure?
   ❐ admitting it to myself
   ❐ admitting it to someone who can help me
   ❐ receiving God's forgiveness
   ❐ forgiving myself
   ❐ facing the blame of others
   ❐ facing my own feelings of shame
   ❐ making amends
   ❐ other:_____

8. What needs to happen for you to feel the kind of forgiveness this woman felt?
   ❐ I need to take an honest look at my life.
   ❐ I need to get my life straightened out first.
   ❐ I need to find someone to talk to who is as sympathetic as Jesus.
   ❐ I need to stop listening to the "Pharisees" who condemn me.
   ❐ I need to accept the forgiveness which Jesus has already offered.
   ❐ Nothing really, because I'm feeling Christ's forgiveness fully right now.
   ❐ other:_____

9. Where in your life do you need to reach out and "touch" Jesus? Specifically, what do you need to receive from him?
   ❐ forgiveness   ❐ spiritual healing
   ❐ strength   ❐ relational healing
   ❐ emotional healing   ❐ other:_____

10. How can this group help you in prayer this week?

MORAL ANGER

Introduction

"Row, row, row your boat ... Gently down the stream ... Merrily, merrily, merrily, merrily ... Life is but a dream." Well, maybe. Maybe not. Sometimes the current in the stream is going in the wrong direction, and you have to make a choice. In this Bible study, you will look at one of those times in the life of Jesus when he had to make a choice ... and upset a few people.

In biblical times, the people were required to sacrifice animals in the temple. If you were very poor, your sacrifice could be a dove which you could buy at the temple. Merchants had turned this into a profit-making business, and because local currency had to be used, travelers were forced to deal with money changers who ripped them off in the exchange. In addition, these chaotic activities took place in the court of the Gentiles, the only part of the temple in which God-fearing non-Jews could worship and pray.

Now, listen to the Bible story. Then, quickly move into groups of 4 and discuss the questionnaire.

1. Who does Jesus remind you of in this story?
   ❑ a bouncer ❑ a fiery prophet
   ❑ a Marine sergeant ❑ a political activist
   ❑ a bull in a china shop

2. How surprising is it to you to see Jesus turning over tables and driving money changers out of the temple?
   ❑ very much
   ❑ a little bit
   ❑ none at all

3. When you see something wrong, are you more likely to act without thinking or think without acting?

JESUS CLEARS THE TEMPLE

[15]*On reaching Jerusalem, Jesus entered the temple area and began driving out those who were buying and selling there. He overturned the tables of the money changers and the benches of those selling doves,* [16]*and would not allow anyone to carry merchandise through the temple courts.* [17]*And as he taught them, he said, "Is it not written:*

> *" 'My house will be called*
> *a house of prayer for all nations'?*

But you have made it 'a den of robbers.' "
[18]*The chief priests and the teachers of the law heard this and began looking for a way to kill him, for they feared him, because the whole crowd was amazed at his teaching.*

Mark 11:15–18

---

4. If Jesus came to clean up your town, where would he start?
   ❑ porno shops ❑ my school or workplace
   ❑ newspaper / TV station ❑ my church
   ❑ drug houses and corners ❑ my home
   ❑ city hall

5. In your school or work, what makes you angry because it is clearly wrong, unethical or immoral?

6. If Jesus came to your school or workplace, what would he do?
   ❑ congratulate the people in charge on their moral values
   ❑ overturn a few tables
   ❑ hang out with the "sinners"
   ❑ start a Bible study
   ❑ become class president or CEO—where he could have influence
   ❑ befriend the lonely and discouraged
   ❑ stay quiet and set a good example
   ❑ He wouldn't come to my school or workplace.

7. In each of the following categories, choose between the two options.

I AM MORE LIKELY TO GET INVOLVED IN ISSUES THAT ...

threaten my own life _____ threaten the life or
or interests   interests of others

involve physical health _____ involve moral health
or well-being   or well-being

my friends are _____ my family is
concerned about   concerned about

8. Which of these issues would you get involved in? Choose the top three.

____ world hunger

____ peace and justice issues

____ banning smoking in public places

____ passing out condoms in schools

____ fighting pornography

____ promoting prayer and Bible reading in school

____ freedom not to wear motorcycle helmets

____ legalizing marijuana for medical uses

____ income tax break for private school tuition

____ fighting discrimination and racism

____ abortion

____ environmental issues

____ keeping child molesters in jail

9. How would you describe yourself on taking a stand that could lead to conflict? Choose a number from 1 to 10 below.

PEACE AT ANY PRICE   1   2   3   4   5   6   7   8   9   10   LET'S HAVE IT OUT

10. How much does your spiritual commitment influence the way you stand on moral issues?
- ❏ a lot
- ❏ some
- ❏ not much
- ❏ I've never thought about it.

11. Where do you need to take a righteous stand? What is keeping you from doing so? How can this group support you in prayer?

RACISM AND PREJUDICE

Introduction

Have you ever felt shut out ... not invited to the party because of ... ? Well, this is what this study is all about. The Bible story is about a revelation made to the apostle Peter when the church was still young. In the orthodox Judaism of the time, food was considered "unclean" (religiously unacceptable) if it was from certain animals. In the same way, certain people were religiously unacceptable to them—in particular Gentiles, people who were foreigners and not raised in their religious traditions. Peter found that in Christ this was going to change.

Just prior to this passage, God had given a God-fearing Gentile by the name of Cornelius a vision. In the vision, an angel of God told this Roman army officer to send for Peter. Listen to the Bible story. Then, move into groups of 4 and discuss the questionnaire.

1. What immediately strikes you in this Bible story?
   - ❏ the attitude of Peter toward Gentiles
   - ❏ the spiritual desire of Cornelius the Gentile
   - ❏ the way God communicated through visions
   - ❏ the willingness of Peter to break the rules

2. If a sheet were to drop from heaven with all the foods on your "avoid" list, what would be on the sheet?
   - ❏ meat
   - ❏ vegetables
   - ❏ high-fat foods
   - ❏ health foods
   - ❏ anything not sold at McDonald's
   - ❏ anchovy pizza
   - ❏ sushi
   - ❏ raw oysters
   - ❏ other:_____

3. Imagine you are Peter. First you are told in a vision to eat meat that Jews are forbidden to eat. Now God tells you to go visit a Gentile, who was also considered impure or unclean. How are you feeling?
   - ❏ cautious
   - ❏ excited
   - ❏ confused
   - ❏ angry
   - ❏ fearful
   - ❏ awkward

4. What kind of person would you have the most trouble going to if God asked you to go to his or her house and give help?
   - ❏ a person of another race
   - ❏ a homosexual
   - ❏ a person who lives in a dirty, smelly house
   - ❏ a person who lives in a wealthy, exclusive neighborhood
   - ❏ an atheist
   - ❏ a person with AIDS
   - ❏ a person who speaks another language
   - ❏ other:_____

PETER'S VISION

⁹*About noon the following day as they were on their journey and approaching the city, Peter went up on the roof to pray.* ¹⁰*He became hungry and wanted something to eat, and while the meal was being prepared, he fell into a trance.* ¹¹*He saw heaven opened and something like a large sheet being let down to earth by its four corners.* ¹²*It contained all kinds of four-footed animals, as well as reptiles of the earth and birds of the air.* ¹³*Then a voice told him, "Get up, Peter. Kill and eat."*

¹⁴*"Surely not, Lord!" Peter replied. "I have never eaten anything impure or unclean."*

¹⁵*The voice spoke to him a second time, "Do not call anything impure that God has made clean."*

¹⁶*This happened three times, and immediately the sheet was taken back to heaven.*

¹⁷*While Peter was wondering about the meaning of the vision, the men sent by Cornelius found out where Simon's house was and stopped at the gate.* ¹⁸*They called out, asking if Simon who was known as Peter was staying there.*

¹⁹*While Peter was still thinking about the vision, the Spirit said to him, "Simon, three men are looking for you.* ²⁰*So get up and go downstairs. Do not hesitate to go with them, for I have sent them."* ...

²⁵*As Peter entered the house, Cornelius met him and fell at his feet in reverence.* ²⁶*But Peter made him get up. "Stand up," he said, "I am only a man myself."*

²⁷*Talking with him, Peter went inside and found a large gathering of people.* ²⁸*He said to them: "You are well aware that it is against our law for a Jew to associate with a Gentile or visit him. But God has shown me that I should not call any man impure or unclean.* ²⁹*So when I was sent for, I came without raising any objection. May I ask why you sent for me?"*

Acts 10:9–20, 25–29

6. What's the most common reason you feel excluded from a group?
   - ❒ race
   - ❒ religion
   - ❒ social status
   - ❒ interests / abilities
   - ❒ cliques
   - ❒ career
   - ❒ other:_____

7. If you were put in charge of reconciliation in your school or community, what would you do?

8. What people wouldn't feel at home in your group or church?
   - ❒ people from the other side of the tracks
   - ❒ people of a different color or ethnic background
   - ❒ people who don't wear our kind of clothes
   - ❒ people who are not very religious
   - ❒ people who are too religious
   - ❒ people who are down-and-out
   - ❒ people who are upper class
   - ❒ other:_____

9. What can your group or church do to help those people feel accepted?

10. If God gave you personally a vision about your attitude toward other people, what would he tell you?

11. Respond to that message in prayer. How else would you like the group to pray for you?

5. Being totally honest, what kind of walls have you permitted between yourself and others?
   - ❒ racial
   - ❒ religious
   - ❒ economic
   - ❒ denominational
   - ❒ moral
   - ❒ political
   - ❒ other:_____

VIOLENCE AND APATHY

Introduction

Violence and apathy are not new. In the time of Jesus in the first century, there was a road that was so notorious for assault and murder that Jesus used it in the parable about the Good Samaritan. (Samaritans were people the Jews despised as half-breeds both physically and spiritually.) Roving gangs would ambush pedestrians on their way to or from Jericho. Often one of the gang would lay down on the side of the road as though they were injured. Then, when a pedestrian stopped to help, the rest of the gang would jump out of the shadows and assault the would-be helper.

Jewish priests and Levites (assistants to the priests) would have been concerned about getting too close to a dead mugging victim. According to the Law of Moses, touching a corpse would have made them "unclean" and unable to perform their religious duties. As you listen to this parable, try to imagine what you would do in this situation. Then, move into groups of 4 and discuss the questionnaire. (In addition—for a case study on violence, designed especially for youth, see page 133.)

1. How would the media respond if something like the story in this parable happened today?
   - ❐ The violence would make big news.
   - ❐ The apathy would make big news.
   - ❐ It would be ignored because stuff like this is so common.

2. Have you ever helped a stranger or been helped by a stranger? What happened?

THE PARABLE OF THE GOOD SAMARITAN

25On one occasion an expert in the law stood up to test Jesus. "Teacher," he asked, "what must I do to inherit eternal life?"

26"What is written in the Law?" he replied. "How do you read it?"

27He answered: " 'Love the Lord your God with all your heart and with all your soul and with all your strength and with all your mind'; and 'Love your neighbor as yourself.' "

28"You have answered correctly," Jesus replied. "Do this and you will live."

29But he wanted to justify himself, so he asked Jesus, "And who is my neighbor?"

30In reply Jesus said: "A man was going down from Jerusalem to Jericho, when he fell into the hands of robbers. They stripped him of his clothes, beat him and went away, leaving him half dead. 31A priest happened to be going down the same road, and when he saw the man, he passed by on the other side. 32So too, a Levite, when he came to the place and saw him, passed by on the other side. 33But a Samaritan, as he traveled, came where the man was; and when he saw him, he took pity on him. 34He went to him and bandaged his wounds, pouring on oil and wine. Then he put the man on his own donkey, took him to an inn and took care of him. 35The next day he took out two silver coins and gave them to the innkeeper. 'Look after him,' he said, 'and when I return, I will reimburse you for any extra expense you may have.'

36"Which of these three do you think was a neighbor to the man who fell into the hands of robbers?"

37The expert in the law replied, "The one who had mercy on him."

Jesus told him, "Go and do likewise."

Luke 10:25–37

---

3. If you were on your way to an important appointment and saw someone who looked beat up (but you didn't know if they were faking it or not), what would you do?
   - ❐ find someone to check it out
   - ❐ pass on by
   - ❐ stop and try to help
   - ❐ call 911

4. After reading this parable, who would you say is your "neighbor"?
   ❐ any person in need
   ❐ those I have a reasonable hope of being able to help
   ❐ those I'm most afraid of helping
   ❐ everyone—even my enemies

5. If Jesus wanted to bring home to your community the same lesson as he did in this story, what place would he use?
   ❐ one of our dangerous inner city streets
   ❐ a convenience store
   ❐ a public park
   ❐ the street in front of the high school
   ❐ the parking lot at the mall
   ❐ We don't have any place like that in our town.
   ❐ Any street will do; they are all unsafe.

6. What is the scariest form of violence in your city?
   ❐ drive-by shootings   ❐ drug or turf wars
   ❐ sex clubs / gang rape   ❐ date rape
   ❐ child abuse   ❐ other:_____
   ❐ vandalism / burning of church property

7. What are you doing about the situation?
   ❐ I just try to stay out of the way.
   ❐ I support the police department.
   ❐ I pray God will keep my family safe.
   ❐ I don't go through certain neighborhoods at night.
   ❐ I try to stand up and be counted.

8. If the Good Samaritan came to your city, what would he do about these problems?
   ❐ He would pass by on the other side.
   ❐ He would get involved in criminal rehabilitation programs.
   ❐ He would get our church to do something for broken families.
   ❐ He would get our schools to offer help for young kids before they turn to violence.
   ❐ He would hire a crisis counselor.
   ❐ other:_____

9. On a scale of 1 (low) to 10 (high), rate yourself on the first part of verse 27: "Love the Lord your God with all your heart and with all your soul and with all your strength and with all your mind."

10. Using the same scale, rate yourself on the second part of verse 27: "Love your neighbor as yourself."

11. How can this group help you in prayer this week?

SEXUAL DESIRES

Introduction

Many people consider David their favorite character in the Bible. He was a musician, a poet, a military genius and the greatest leader the nation of Israel ever produced. As a teenager, he volunteered to fight Goliath for the honor of God and his country, and he defeated the giant.

But he had one weakness, and he let it get the best of him. We are going to pick up the story of David and Bathsheba at the time of the year when the king usually went with his army to battle, but David stayed home and let his general lead the army. Listen to the story and move into groups of 4 to discuss the questionnaire. (Also, for a case study on sex, designed especially for youth, see page 135.)

1. This story happened in the spring. Who was your first "crush" or what was your worst case of "spring fever"?

2. Imagine that this scandal had occurred today between a woman and a major political figure. Which of the following scenarios would you expect?
   - ❐ Everyone would say, "Ho, hum—again?"
   - ❐ Their pictures would be splashed on all the papers.
   - ❐ The politician would categorically deny it.
   - ❐ The woman would be cast as a bimbo and the villainess.
   - ❐ They would both write about it and have competing best-sellers.
   - ❐ It would be one of those scandals that quickly fades from the news.

3. Since God created David with sexual urges, when did his thoughts or actions become sin?
   - ❐ when he didn't go with the army like he should have
   - ❐ when he saw Bathsheba taking a bath
   - ❐ when he sent someone to find out about her
   - ❐ when he sent messengers to get her
   - ❐ when he made love to her

4. How do you imagine Bathsheba felt about this whole affair?
   - ❐ used
   - ❐ flattered
   - ❐ guilty
   - ❐ swept off her feet
   - ❐ forced against her will

5. How do you feel about God's standards for sexual purity? Choose one of the two options in each of the following pairs. God's standards are:

clear	_____	unclear
outdated	_____	relevant
attainable	_____	unattainable
for our good	_____	unnecessary

DAVID AND BATHSHEBA

11 In the spring, at the time when kings go off to war, David sent Joab out with the king's men and the whole Israelite army. They destroyed the Ammonites and besieged Rabbah. But David remained in Jerusalem.

²One evening David got up from his bed and walked around on the roof of the palace. From the roof he saw a woman bathing. The woman was very beautiful, ³and David sent someone to find out about her. The man said, "Isn't this Bathsheba, the daughter of Eliam and the wife of Uriah the Hittite?" ⁴Then David sent messengers to get her. She came to him, and he slept with her. (She had purified herself from her uncleanness.) Then she went back home. ⁵The woman conceived and sent word to David, saying, "I am pregnant."

⁶So David sent this word to Joab: "Send me Uriah the Hittite." And Joab sent him to David. ⁷When Uriah came to him, David asked him how Joab was, how the soldiers were and how the war was going. ⁸Then David said to Uriah, "Go down to your house and wash your feet." So Uriah left the palace, and a gift from the king was sent after him. ⁹But Uriah slept at the entrance to the palace with all his master's servants and did not go down to his house.

¹⁰When David was told, "Uriah did not go home," he asked him, "Haven't you just come from a distance? Why didn't you go home?"

¹¹Uriah said to David, "The ark and Israel and Judah are staying in tents, and my master Joab and my lord's men are camped in the open fields. How could I go to my house to eat and drink and lie with my wife? As surely as you live, I will not do such a thing!"

¹²Then David said to him, "Stay here one more day, and tomorrow I will send you back." So Uriah remained in Jerusalem that day and the next. ¹³At David's invitation, he ate and drank with him, and David made him drunk. But in the evening Uriah went out to sleep on his mat among his master's servants; he did not go home.

¹⁴In the morning David wrote a letter to Joab and sent it with Uriah. ¹⁵In it he wrote, "Put Uriah in the front line where the fighting is fiercest. Then withdraw from him so he will be struck down and die."

¹⁶So while Joab had the city under siege, he put Uriah at a place where he knew the strongest defenders were. ¹⁷When the men of the city came out and fought against Joab, some of the men in David's army fell; moreover, Uriah the Hittite died.

2 Samuel 11:1–17

6. How can a relationship with God influence the way we handle our sexual desires? What advice would you give a friend who is caught up with pornography or sexual immorality?

7. When do you find yourself most vulnerable to temptation?
   - ❏ when I'm bored
   - ❏ when I'm under a lot of stress
   - ❏ when I let my mind dwell on certain things
   - ❏ when I'm away from home
   - ❏ after a spiritual high
   - ❏ other:_____

8. Where do you need to set some boundaries for what you are going to watch, read and see?

9. On a scale of 1 (great) to 10 (terrible), how would you rate your spiritual life right now? How can the group pray for you?

10. How can this group remember you in prayer this week?

CULTS / OCCULT

Introduction

Welcome to the crazy world called modern religion. We've got horoscopes and tarot cards, Ouija boards and crystals, satanic music and horror movies, witchcraft and seances, and a library of science fiction books and videos that introduce you to the dark side of the spiritual world. And we have groups like the Branch Davidians, Moonies, the Children of God and Heaven's Gate who promise you spiritual ecstasy and live-in family if you will only turn over your mind and all of your possessions to them. What a deal!

In this Bible study, you will take on the issue of cults, the occult, counterfeits and New Age religions. The Bible story is familiar. It is the story of the temptation of Jesus by Satan right after he was baptized. In the three temptations, you will discover a lot of the temptations that the cults and counterfeits offer to every seeker after spiritual truth. Listen to the story. Then, move into groups of 4 and discuss the following questionnaire and case studies.

1. Who does the devil remind you of in this story?
   - ❐ a prostitute
   - ❐ a drug pusher
   - ❐ a corrupt politician
   - ❐ a pushy used-car salesman
   - ❐ the emperor in *Star Wars*
   - ❐ someone much more subtle

2. How vulnerable to temptation was Jesus?
   - ❐ He was just as vulnerable as I am.
   - ❐ He was vulnerable, but in a different way.
   - ❐ He really wasn't vulnerable at all.

3. What do you do when you are approached by someone from a cult?

CASE STUDIES

Case Study #1: Jeff

Jeff was an outgoing, fun-loving, handsome guy. At school he was into

---

THE TEMPTATION OF JESUS

4 Then Jesus was led by the Spirit into the desert to be tempted by the devil. ²After fasting forty days and forty nights, he was hungry. ³The tempter came to him and said, "If you are the Son of God, tell these stones to become bread."

⁴Jesus answered, "It is written: 'Man does not live on bread alone, but on every word that comes from the mouth of God.' "

⁵Then the devil took him to the holy city and had him stand on the highest point of the temple. ⁶"If you are the Son of God," he said, "throw yourself down. For it is written:

" 'He will command his angels concerning you,
and they will lift you up in their hands,
so that you will not strike your foot against a stone. ' "

⁷Jesus answered him, "It is also written: 'Do not put the Lord your God to the test.' "

⁸Again, the devil took him to a very high mountain and showed him all the kingdoms of the world and their splendor. ⁹"All this I will give you," he said, "if you will bow down and worship me."

¹⁰Jesus said to him, "Away from me, Satan! For it is written: 'Worship the Lord your God, and serve him only.' "

¹¹Then the devil left him, and angels came and attended him.

Matthew 4:1–11

---

everything. He had lots of friends, was a good student and was fun to be around. But something went wrong. One spring he became interested in magic and some of the mystical things mentioned in his science fiction books. His parents had divorced and he wanted to escape from the pain. When his mother objected to some of the books on horoscopes and the occult he was reading, he got angry and threatened to move out. He retreated to his headphones and his music.

Things are not much better now. His sparkle and charm are gone. He has shut off most of his old friends and withdrawn more into himself. His friends are boring, he thinks school is a drag ... and he seems to spend a lot of time reading about mediums and people who can contact the spirit world. He is fascinated with occult symbols like the scarab, the skull and the Southern Cross.

Case Study #2: Simone

Simone also was an outgoing, fun person to be around. She did certain things well, but school was a struggle for her. So, her mom enrolled her in an after-school program off-campus that was supposed to improve her learning skills and self-esteem toward higher academic achievement. During the sessions, however, she was led into heavy meditation, visualization (meant to alter the way one thinks), and was told she could have a spirit-guide to go with her on the mental journeys. She was told she had unlimited potential if she would just tap into the power within her.

Her grades didn't improve, and she got into heavy drug use as well as promiscuous, even abusive, relationships. By age 18 she signed her name in blood to join a witches coven that practiced white magic (magic for "positive" purposes). While this was not the type of coven involved in animal sacrifices and destructive acts, they did come in contact with the darker types of occult groups. Who knows where Simone would have ended up had she not come in contact with a group of Christians who shared God's truth and love with her.

4. Have you ever run across someone like Jeff or Simone? How did they make you feel? How did they get in the occult?

5. How did you deal with the situation? How can Jesus Christ meet the needs of someone attracted to the occult?

6. Have you had any contact or personal experience with any of the following, and, if so, what was the experience like?

___ tarot cards	___ satanic / horror flicks
___ Ouija boards	___ horoscopes
___ seances	___ mind control
___ Yoga / Eastern meditation	___ spirit-guides
___ satanic music	___ astrology
___ witchcraft	___ crystals
___ occultic literature	___ New Age philosophies
___ Dungeon and Dragons, etc.	___ cults / false religions

7. If the devil had three "shots" at you, which area of your life would he focus on?
- ❏ spiritual temptations
- ❏ physical temptations
- ❏ financial temptations
- ❏ ambition / power
- ❏ my self-identity
- ❏ other:_____

8. How do you deal with temptation?
- ❏ give in to it
- ❏ fight it off
- ❏ beat myself up with guilt
- ❏ just say "no"
- ❏ do something to get my mind off of it
- ❏ ask for God's help
- ❏ talk to someone about it
- ❏ other:_____

9. What has helped you overcome temptation when it comes?
- ❏ Scripture
- ❏ telling someone about it
- ❏ talking myself out of it
- ❏ prayer
- ❏ running away
- ❏ other:_____

10. How can this group pray for you—specifically in the area of temptation?

201

MY SPIRITUAL JOURNEY

Introduction

To answer some of his critics who thought he was running around with the wrong people, Jesus told a story about a wayward son and a father who threw a party for this son when he came home.

As you listen to this familiar story again, try to put yourself in the situation of all three characters: the father, the younger brother, and the older brother. Then, move into groups of 4 and discuss the questionnaire.

1. Where are you in the birth order of your family?
   ❑ oldest
   ❑ youngest
   ❑ in the middle
   ❑ I'm an only child.

2. When was the first time you thought about leaving home? Did you do it?

3. If you had been the father in this Bible story, what would you have said to the younger son when he asked for his inheritance early in order to leave home?
   ❑ "Are you crazy?!"
   ❑ "Why you ungrateful ... !!"
   ❑ "Well, I'm disappointed, but here you are."
   ❑ "No problem, son."

THE PARABLE OF THE LOST SON

[11]Jesus continued: "There was a man who had two sons. [12]The younger one said to his father, 'Father, give me my share of the estate.' So he divided his property between them.

[13]"Not long after that, the younger son got together all he had, set off for a distant country and there squandered his wealth in wild living. [14]After he had spent everything, there was a severe famine in that whole country, and he began to be in need. [15]So he went and hired himself out to a citizen of that country, who sent him to his fields to feed pigs. [16]He longed to fill his stomach with the pods that the pigs were eating, but no one gave him anything.

[17]"When he came to his senses, he said, 'How many of my father's hired men have food to spare, and here I am starving to death! [18]I will set out and go back to my father and say to him: Father, I have sinned against heaven and against you. [19]I am no longer worthy to be called your son; make me like one of your hired men.' [20]So he got up and went to his father.

"But while he was still a long way off, his father saw him and was filled with compassion for him; he ran to his son, threw his arms around him and kissed him.

[21]"The son said to him, 'Father, I have sinned against heaven and against you. I am no longer worthy to be called your son.'

[22]"But the father said to his servants, 'Quick! Bring the best robe and put it on him. Put a ring on his finger and sandals on his feet. [23]Bring the fattened calf and kill it. Let's have a feast and celebrate. [24]For this son of mine was dead and is alive again; he was lost and is found.' So they began to celebrate.

[25]"Meanwhile, the older son was in the field. When he came near the house, he heard music and dancing. [26]So he called one of the servants and asked him what was going on. [27]'Your brother has come,' he replied, 'and your father has killed the fattened calf because he has him back safe and sound.'

[28]"The older brother became angry and refused to go in. So his father went out and pleaded with him. [29]But he answered his father, 'Look! All these years I've been slaving for you and never disobeyed your orders. Yet you never gave me even a young goat so I could celebrate with my friends. [30]But when this son of yours who has squandered your property with prostitutes comes home, you kill the fattened calf for him!

[31]" 'My son,' the father said, 'you are always with me, and everything I have is yours. [32]But we had to celebrate and be glad, because this brother of yours was dead and is alive again; he was lost and is found.' "

Luke 15:11–32

---

4. If you had been the father and had a pretty good idea where your son had gone, would you have gone after him?
   ❒ Yes, you don't want to see your kid get in trouble.
   ❒ Maybe, if I thought I could get him to come home.
   ❒ No, you have to let people make their own mistakes.
   ❒ It all depends.

5. What is the closest you have come to going through a wild period like the young man in this story?

6. Of the two sons, which reminds you the most of your own spiritual story?
   ❒ the son who left home at an early age—and came back
   ❒ the son who did not leave home—but felt left out of his father's party

7. When did you spiritually "leave home" in your relationship with God, and what caused the comeback?

8. If you could compare your spiritual journey to this story, where are you right now?
   ❒ just leaving home
   ❒ in a far country
   ❒ on my way back home

9. How do you sense God calling you to get closer to him? What will you do to respond?

10. How do you feel about sharing your spiritual journey like this with your group? How can the group pray for you?

FORGIVENESS OF SINS

Introduction

This Bible study is about the crucifixion of Jesus Christ, because you can't talk about the forgiveness of sins without giving the explanation—that somebody had to pay the price. And that somebody had to be sinless. And that person was Jesus—"the Lamb of God." Right now, you are going to look at the death of Jesus as a historical record.

Listen to the story of the crucifixion and death of Christ. Then, move into groups of 4 and discuss the questionnaire.

1. If you were the editor of the *Jerusalem Times*, what headline would you pick to describe the events of the death of Christ?
   ❒ "Daytime Darkness Descends"
   ❒ "Crucifixion Stuns City"
   ❒ "Self-Proclaimed Messiah Killed"
   ❒ "Temple Curtain Ruined"

2. If the following people were interviewed for your newspaper coverage of Jesus' crucifixion, whose opinion would you personally share?
   ❒ the followers of Jesus—despairing of all hope
   ❒ those who made fun of Jesus—unable to see the purpose of Jesus' suffering and death
   ❒ the centurion—understanding suddenly who Jesus really was

---

THE CRUCIFIXION AND DEATH OF JESUS

³²*Two other men, both criminals, were also led out with him to be executed.* ³³*When they came to the place called the Skull, there they crucified him, along with the criminals—one on his right, the other on his left.* ³⁴*Jesus said, "Father, forgive them, for they do not know what they are doing." And they divided up his clothes by casting lots.*

³⁵*The people stood watching, and the rulers even sneered at him. They said, "He saved others; let him save himself if he is the Christ of God, the Chosen One."*

³⁶*The soldiers also came up and mocked him. They offered him wine vinegar* ³⁷*and said, "If you are the king of the Jews, save yourself."*

³⁸*There was a written notice above him, which read:* THIS IS THE KING OF THE JEWS.

³⁹*One of the criminals who hung there hurled insults at him: "Aren't you the Christ? Save yourself and us!"*

⁴⁰*But the other criminal rebuked him. "Don't you fear God," he said, "since you are under the same sentence?* ⁴¹*We are punished justly, for we are getting what our deeds deserve. But this man has done nothing wrong."*

⁴²*Then he said, "Jesus, remember me when you come into your kingdom."*

⁴³*Jesus answered him, "I tell you the truth, today you will be with me in paradise."*

⁴⁴*It was now about the sixth hour, and darkness came over the whole land until the ninth hour,* ⁴⁵*for the sun stopped shining. And the curtain of the temple was torn in two.* ⁴⁶*Jesus called out with a loud voice, "Father, into your hands I commit my spirit." When he had said this, he breathed his last.*

⁴⁷*The centurion, seeing what had happened, praised God and said, "Surely this was a righteous man."* ⁴⁸*When all the people who had gathered to witness this sight saw what took place, they beat their breasts and went away.* ⁴⁹*But all those who knew him, including the women who had followed him from Galilee, stood at a distance, watching these things.*

Luke 23:32–49

3. What would be most likely to make *you* proclaim publicly (like the centurion), in the presence of your friends, "Surely this was a righteous man"?
   - ❏ a lot of scary signs, like those that happened that day
   - ❏ feeling forgiven for all the bad things I've done
   - ❏ seeing how badly my friends need Christ
   - ❏ No way I'd *ever* say such a thing!
   - ❏ I say it all the time already.

4. In the midst of such pain and ridicule, how could Jesus say, "Father, forgive them"? How do these words make you feel?

5. How easy is it for you to forgive people who hurt you?

6. When did you come to realize that Jesus died for you and for the forgiveness of your sins?

7. How does it make you feel when you think about what God has done for you through the death of Jesus Christ on the cross?
   - ❏ guilty
   - ❏ interested
   - ❏ relieved
   - ❏ I've heard all of this before.
   - ❏ grateful
   - ❏ uncomfortable
   - ❏ loved
   - ❏ doubtful

8. How would you describe the difference that Christ's death and God's forgiveness has made in the way you live your life?
   - ❏ a little bit
   - ❏ a whole lot
   - ❏ not as much as it should
   - ❏ a lot more than it used to
   - ❏ I'm not sure.

9. Are you closer to Christ now than you were five years ago? If yes, in what way? If no, explain why.

10. If you could invite one person to join your group—someone who really needs Christ—who would you like to invite?

11. How can this group remember you in prayer this week?

TURNING AROUND

Introduction

This Bible story is a familiar one—the conversion of the apostle Paul. Paul (whose name was Saul until he became a Christian) grew up as a very religious person. In fact, in his early life, he led the persecution of Christians and was involved in the stoning of a Christian by the name of Stephen. But God brought this guy to the ground and turned him around.

Listen to the story. Then, move into groups of 4 and discuss the questionnaire.

1. How would the medical profession today explain what happened to Saul (Paul) on the road to Damascus?

   ❐ He was struck by lightning.

   ❐ He had a physical breakdown.

   ❐ He had a mental breakdown.

   ❐ He had a partial stroke that rendered him temporarily blind.

   ❐ He had a psychological crisis due to an overly-religious personality.

   ❐ He suffered from repressed guilt for his role in persecuting people.

2. How would you feel if you were Paul during the three days that he sat in his room in Damascus—blind—trying to figure out what had happened to him?

   ❐ wiped out   ❐ humbled

   ❐ confused   ❐ angry

   ❐ terrified   ❐ repentant

SAUL'S CONVERSION

9 Meanwhile, Saul was still breathing out murderous threats against the Lord's disciples. He went to the high priest ²and asked him for letters to the synagogues in Damascus, so that if he found any there who belonged to the Way, whether men or women, he might take them as prisoners to Jerusalem. ³As he neared Damascus on his journey, suddenly a light from heaven flashed around him. ⁴He fell to the ground and heard a voice say to him, "Saul, Saul, why do you persecute me?"

⁵"Who are you, Lord?" Saul asked.

"I am Jesus, whom you are persecuting," he replied. ⁶"Now get up and go into the city, and you will be told what you must do."

⁷The men traveling with Saul stood there speechless; they heard the sound but did not see anyone. ⁸Saul got up from the ground, but when he opened his eyes he could see nothing. So they led him by the hand into Damascus. ⁹For three days he was blind, and did not eat or drink anything.

¹⁰In Damascus there was a disciple named Ananias. The Lord called to him in a vision, "Ananias!"

"Yes, Lord," he answered.

¹¹The Lord told him, "Go to the house of Judas on Straight Street and ask for a man from Tarsus named Saul, for he is praying. ¹²In a vision he has seen a man named Ananias come and place his hands on him to restore his sight." ...

¹⁷Then Ananias went to the house and entered it. Placing his hands on Saul, he said, "Brother Saul, the Lord—Jesus, who appeared to you on the road as you were coming here—has sent me so that you may see again and be filled with the Holy Spirit." ¹⁸Immediately, something like scales fell from Saul's eyes, and he could see again. He got up and was baptized, ¹⁹and after taking some food, he regained his strength.

Acts 9:1–12, 17–19

3. If you could compare your spiritual journey to Paul's experience, where are you right now?
   - ❏ on the road to Damascus
   - ❏ starting to hear God call out my name and wondering what God is trying to tell me
   - ❏ experiencing some of the same emotions Paul went through
   - ❏ trying to sort out what has been happening

4. How would you compare your conversion to Paul's conversion?
   - ❏ Mine was more gradual.
   - ❏ Mine was more intellectual.
   - ❏ Mine was different, but just as real.
   - ❏ Mine was even more dramatic.
   - ❏ I'm on my way back to God and I still have a lot of questions.

5. Ananias was sent by God to come alongside of Paul in his crisis. Who has come alongside of you to help you sort out what is going on?
   - ❏ my parent(s) / spouse
   - ❏ my brother / sister
   - ❏ another relative
   - ❏ my group leader / pastor
   - ❏ a teacher
   - ❏ one or two friends
   - ❏ no one
   - ❏ other:_____

6. If you had to explain to little children how God turned your life around, how would you describe it?
   - ❏ It is like getting to know a friend.
   - ❏ It is like waking up one morning and being a different person.
   - ❏ It is like coming into the world as a baby.
   - ❏ It is like a bolt of lightning.
   - ❏ It is like getting a puppy for your birthday.
   - ❏ It is like:_____

7. How were others able to notice the difference in your life after you met Jesus?

8. In what area of your life have you seen the most change since you committed your life to Christ?
   - ❏ my beliefs
   - ❏ my relationships
   - ❏ my goals
   - ❏ my habits / lifestyle
   - ❏ my devotional life (prayer, Bible study)
   - ❏ my priorities
   - ❏ my attitudes
   - ❏ my values
   - ❏ other:_____

9. What changes do you feel God is calling you to make in your life now?

10. How would you like the group to pray for you this week?

DEALING WITH DOUBT

Introduction

Sooner or later, every Christian will have spiritual struggles and doubts—when you feel like your prayers go no higher than the ceiling. Someone you love dies unexpectedly and you wonder if God is asleep on the job. You are disappointed in a relationship—and you wonder if God cares.

This is what this Bible study is all about—spiritual struggles and doubts. The story in the Bible that you will look at is the story of Thomas—often called "Doubting Thomas." For some reason, he was not in the room after the Resurrection when Jesus appeared to the disciples. And he refused to believe them when they said Jesus was alive. Listen to the story. Then, move into groups of 4 and discuss the questionnaire.

1. Who or what would you believe most?
   ❏ news reporter
   ❏ police radar
   ❏ sales advertisements
   ❏ psychic hotline

2. What would convince you to believe that someone really came back from the dead?
   ❏ a death certificate
   ❏ eyewitnesses
   ❏ firsthand knowledge of the person before and after
   ❏ pictures in the *National Enquirer*

3. "Unless I see the nail marks in his hands and put my finger where the nails were, and put my hand into his side, I will not believe it." What was Thomas saying?
   ❏ "You guys are crazy."
   ❏ "I need proof."
   ❏ "I want to believe, but ..."
   ❏ "Don't break my heart again."

4. Who does Thomas remind you of in this story?
   ❏ a science teacher
   ❏ an agnostic
   ❏ an honest person who wanted to believe
   ❏ a friend of mine
   ❏ myself
   ❏ other:_____

5. What is the closest that you have come to going through what Thomas went through?
   ❏ when my parents or I went through a divorce
   ❏ when someone close to me died
   ❏ when I dropped out of Christian fellowship
   ❏ when I tried really hard but failed
   ❏ when I was disappointed and took it out on God
   ❏ other:_____

6. How do you think Jesus feels when we have doubts about our faith?
   ❏ angry—"I can't believe you have doubts!"
   ❏ disappointed—"How could you question me?"
   ❏ ready—"Bring it on, I can handle your questions!"
   ❏ glad—"I'm happy you are curious about me."
   ❏ other:_____

7. What do you rely upon for spiritual "proof"?
   ❏ gut feelings
   ❏ what the Bible says
   ❏ what my church teaches
   ❏ logic and common sense
   ❏ emotional peace
   ❏ Christian family and friends
   ❏ simple faith
   ❏ other:_____

JESUS APPEARS TO THOMAS

²⁴Now Thomas (called Didymus), one of the Twelve, was not with the disciples when Jesus came. ²⁵So the other disciples told him, "We have seen the Lord!"

But he said to them, "Unless I see the nail marks in his hands and put my finger where the nails were, and put my hand into his side, I will not believe it."

²⁶A week later his disciples were in the house again, and Thomas was with them. Though the doors were locked, Jesus came and stood among them and said, "Peace be with you!" ²⁷Then he said to Thomas, "Put your finger here; see my hands. Reach out your hand and put it into my side. Stop doubting and believe."

²⁸Thomas said to him, "My Lord and my God!"

²⁹Then Jesus told him, "Because you have seen me, you have believed; blessed are those who have not seen and yet have believed."

John 20:24–29

8. When you have struggles and doubts in your faith, what have you found helpful?
   ❏ going to the Bible
   ❏ talking it over with my pastor
   ❏ sharing my struggles with my family and friends
   ❏ letting my family and friends share their struggles
   ❏ going to church / small group / youth group
   ❏ going ahead "on faith"
   ❏ spending time alone with God
   ❏ being encouraged by the faith of others
   ❏ other:_____

9. If you could ask Jesus one "hard question" about your spiritual life, what would it be?
   ❏ How do I deal with doubt?
   ❏ How do I deal with guilt?
   ❏ What's wrong when I don't always *feel* like a Christian?
   ❏ Where is God when I'm hurting?
   ❏ Why can't I seem to get closer to you?
   ❏ other:_____

10. How would you describe your spiritual life right now?
    ❏ full of doubt
    ❏ full of faith
    ❏ half and half
    ❏ increasing in doubt
    ❏ increasing in faith

11. How can the group support you in prayer this week?

Spiritual Formation

HEAVY STUFF

Introduction

There comes a time in the life of every Christian when you have to decide who is going to sit on the throne of your life—you or God.

GETHSEMANE

[36] Then Jesus went with his disciples to a place called Gethsemane, and he said to them, "Sit here while I go over there and pray." [37] He took Peter and the two sons of Zebedee along with him, and he began to be sorrowful and troubled. [38] Then he said to them, "My soul is overwhelmed with sorrow to the point of death. Stay here and keep watch with me."

[39] Going a little farther, he fell with his face to the ground and prayed, "My Father, if it is possible, may this cup be taken from me. Yet not as I will, but as you will."

[40] Then he returned to his disciples and found them sleeping, "Could you men not keep watch with me for one hour?" he asked Peter. [41] "Watch and pray so that you will not fall into temptation. The spirit is willing, but the body is weak."

[42] He went away a second time and prayed, "My Father, if it is not possible for this cup to be taken away unless I drink it, may your will be done."

[43] When he came back, he again found them sleeping, because their eyes were heavy. [44] So he left them and went away once more and prayed the third time, saying the same thing.

[45] Then he returned to the disciples and said to them, "Are you still sleeping and resting? Look, the hour is near, and the Son of Man is betrayed into the hands of sinners. [46] Rise, let us go! Here comes my betrayer!"

Matthew 26:36–46

Interestingly, Jesus had to face this very decision. He faced it just before he was arrested and taken away to be crucified. He was in a garden—praying. He knew that Judas had gone to get the temple police to arrest him. Jesus still had time to run away and avoid all the pain. But he had to decide. Immediately.

Jesus took his three closest friends (Peter, James and John) with him to this garden to pray. Listen to the story. Then, move into groups of 4 and discuss the questionnaire.

1. When have you fallen asleep at a very embarrassing moment?
   - ❐ in church
   - ❐ in class or at work
   - ❐ on a date
   - ❐ during a concert or recital
   - ❐ other:_____

2. What was the hardest part of this experience for Jesus?
   - ❐ being let down by his friends
   - ❐ submitting to God's will
   - ❐ preparing for the cross

3. Where is the "Garden of Gethsemane" that you go to when you're faced with making a big decision?
   - ❐ my bedroom
   - ❐ my favorite place outdoors
   - ❐ church
   - ❐ the ballpark
   - ❐ I don't really have a place.
   - ❐ other:_____

4. In the last 12 months, what is the closest you have come to facing your own personal Gethsemane—where you needed to submit to God's will and not yours?

6. What is harder for you?
   - ❏ knowing what God wants me to do
   - ❏ doing what I know God wants me to do
   - ❏ standing alone when my friends or family don't support me
   - ❏ being consistent

7. What have you found helpful in determining the will of God for your life?
   - ❏ studying the Bible
   - ❏ praying
   - ❏ asking the counsel of another Christian
   - ❏ attending church
   - ❏ other:_____

8. When it comes to doing the will of God, how would you finish this sentence? "I desire to do God's will ..."
   - ❏ all of the time
   - ❏ most of the time
   - ❏ some of the time
   - ❏ rarely

9. What decision are you going to face in the near future where you need to seek God's will?

10. How can the group pray for this situation and for other needs in your life?

5. What is the biggest issue you are facing in your spiritual life right now?
   - ❏ sorting out my values
   - ❏ choosing the right friends
   - ❏ making time for God every day
   - ❏ cleaning up my life / breaking some old habits
   - ❏ sharing my faith openly
   - ❏ knowing what God wants me to do with my life
   - ❏ other:_____

Beliefs

GOD THE FATHER

Introduction

This Bible study is designed to help you understand the first statement in the Apostles' Creed: *"I believe in God, the Father Almighty, maker of heaven and earth."* Listen to the story of Adam and Eve. Then, move into groups of 4 and discuss the questionnaire.

1. If you could have a snapshot showing just one moment in this creation story, what would it be?
   ❑ when Adam came to life
   ❑ when Eve came to life
   ❑ a wide-angle view of the unspoiled Garden of Eden
   ❑ the tree of the knowledge of good and evil
   ❑ Adam and Eve seeing each other for the first time

ADAM AND EVE

⁴This is the account of the heavens and the earth when they were created.

When the Lᴏʀᴅ God made the earth and the heavens—⁵and no shrub of the field had yet appeared on the earth and no plant of the field had yet sprung up, for the Lᴏʀᴅ God had not sent rain on the earth and there was no man to work the ground, ⁶but streams came up from the earth and watered the whole surface of the ground—⁷the Lᴏʀᴅ God formed the man from the dust of the ground and breathed into his nostrils the breath of life, and the man became a living being.

⁸Now the Lᴏʀᴅ God had planted a garden in the east, in Eden; and there he put the man he had formed. ⁹And the Lᴏʀᴅ God made all kinds of trees grow out of the ground—trees that were pleasing to the eye and good for food. In the middle of the garden were the tree of life and the tree of the knowledge of good and evil.

¹⁰A river watering the garden flowed from Eden; from there it was separated into four headwaters. ¹¹The name of the first is the Pishon; it winds through the entire land of Havilah, where there is gold. ¹²(The gold of that land is good; aromatic resin and onyx are also there.) ¹³The name of the second river is the Gihon; it winds through the entire land of Cush. ¹⁴The name of the third river is the Tigris; it runs along the east side of Asshur. And the fourth river is the Euphrates.

¹⁵The Lᴏʀᴅ God took the man and put him in the Garden of Eden to work it and take care of it. ¹⁶And the Lᴏʀᴅ God commanded the man, "You are free to eat from any tree in the garden; ¹⁷but you must not eat from the tree of the knowledge of good and evil, for when you eat of it you will surely die."

¹⁸The Lᴏʀᴅ God said, "It is not good for the man to be alone. I will make a helper suitable for him."

¹⁹Now the Lᴏʀᴅ God had formed out of the ground all the beasts of the field and all the birds of the air. He brought them to the man to see what he would name them; and whatever the man called each living creature, that was its name. ²⁰So the man gave names to all the livestock, the birds of the air and all the beasts of the field.

But for Adam no suitable helper was found. ²¹So the Lᴏʀᴅ God caused the man to fall into a deep sleep; and while he was sleeping, he took one of the man's ribs and closed up the place with flesh. ²²Then the Lᴏʀᴅ God made a woman from the rib he had taken out of the man, and he brought her to the man.

²³The man said,

> *"This is now bone of my bones*
>   *and flesh of my flesh;*
> *she shall be called 'woman,'*
>   *for she was taken out of man."*

²⁴For this reason a man will leave his father and mother and be united to his wife, and they will become one flesh.

²⁵The man and his wife were both naked, and they felt no shame.

Genesis 2:4–25

2. What part of creation convinces you the most of God's existence?
   - ❏ the stars in the heavens
   - ❏ the majestic mountains
   - ❏ a newborn baby
   - ❏ a tiny, delicate flower
   - ❏ a beautiful rainbow
   - ❏ a soaring eagle

3. What do you think most of the people around you (job, school, neighborhood) believe about God?

4. When did God become more than just a name to you?

5. Who is the person in your life who shaped you and influenced your early spiritual development the most?
   - ❏ mother
   - ❏ father
   - ❏ grandparent
   - ❏ Sunday school teacher
   - ❏ neighbor
   - ❏ coach
   - ❏ close friend
   - ❏ scoutmaster
   - ❏ brother / sister
   - ❏ uncle / aunt
   - ❏ pastor
   - ❏ youth leader
   - ❏ teacher
   - ❏ other:_____

6. What is something important that person taught you?

7. Which of the following reflects your view of God when you were in grade school?
   - ❏ a kindly old man—like Santa Claus
   - ❏ like my parents
   - ❏ like Jesus—I saw God and Jesus as the same.
   - ❏ a spirit like Casper the friendly ghost
   - ❏ an angry man sending lightning bolts and punishing children
   - ❏ I had no concept of God.
   - ❏ other:_____

8. How has your concept of God changed? Now I view God as:
   - ❏ a judge—determined and declaring right and wrong
   - ❏ Creator—powerful, but not very personal
   - ❏ a loving father or parent—bringing warmth and intimacy
   - ❏ provider—taking care of all my needs
   - ❏ other:_____

9. As a child of God, you inherit all of his promised blessings. What blessing means the most to you right now?
   - ❏ forgiveness (1 John 1:9)
   - ❏ peace (John 14:27)
   - ❏ eternal life (Rom. 6:23)
   - ❏ unconditional love (1 John 4:9)
   - ❏ other:_____

10. How would you like this group to pray for you?

JESUS CHRIST

Introduction

The second statement in the Apostles' Creed is: *"I believe in Jesus Christ, his only Son, our Lord. He was conceived by the power of the Holy Spirit and born of the virgin Mary. He suffered under Pontius Pilate, was crucified, died, and was buried. He descended into hell. On the third day he rose again. He ascended into heaven, and is seated at the right hand of the Father. He will come again to judge the living and the dead."*

The Bible story is about the question that Jesus asked of his disciples: "Who do the crowds say I am?"

PETER'S CONFESSION OF CHRIST

[18]Once when Jesus was praying in private and his disciples were with him, he asked them, "Who do the crowds say I am?"

[19]They replied, "Some say John the Baptist; others say Elijah; and still others, that one of the prophets of long ago has come back to life."

[20]"But what about you?" he asked. "Who do you say I am?" Peter answered, "The Christ of God."

[21]Jesus strictly warned them not to tell this to anyone. [22]And he said, "The Son of Man must suffer many things and be rejected by the elders, chief priests and teachers of the law, and he must be killed and on the third day be raised to life."

[23]Then he said to them all: "If anyone would come after me, he must deny himself and take up his cross daily and follow me. [24]For whoever wants to save his life will lose it, but whoever loses his life for me will save it. [25]What good is it for a man to gain the whole world, and yet lose or forfeit his very self?"

Luke 9:18–25

Listen to the Bible story. Then, move into groups of 4 to discuss the questionnaire.

1. If the typical person in your school, workplace or neighborhood were asked the same question today that Jesus asked his disciples—"Who do you say I am?"—what would they say?
   - ❏ the founder of a religion
   - ❏ the Son of God
   - ❏ the greatest man who ever lived
   - ❏ a social revolutionary
   - ❏ a spiritual philosopher and teacher
   - ❏ a saint (more spiritual than real)
   - ❏ my Lord and Savior
   - ❏ a swear word
   - ❏ a close friend
   - ❏ an enigma (mystery)
   - ❏ other:_____

2. What is *your* answer to the question, "Who is Jesus Christ?" How has your answer changed over time?

3. Which of the following experiences has taught you the most about who you are?
   - ❏ my marriage
   - ❏ my first job
   - ❏ struggling with new ideas
   - ❏ the death of a loved one
   - ❏ living away from my parents
   - ❏ a divorce
   - ❏ a health crisis
   - ❏ a financial crisis
   - ❏ an emotional crisis
   - ❏ other:_____

4. When you compare your Christian life to what Jesus calls you to do—to deny yourself and take up your cross every day—how do you feel?
   - ❏ like starting over
   - ❏ like crawling under the rug
   - ❏ like going for it
   - ❏ like ducking
   - ❏ like yawning

5. What would it mean for you to "deny" yourself?
   ❑ to stop focusing on my problems and think more about others
   ❑ to never do anything for myself
   ❑ to put Christ's desires above my own
   ❑ to trust God to take care of me so I can focus on him

6. If your faith in Christ meant you had to change your lifestyle completely, what would you do?

7. The central affirmation of the early church was "Jesus is Lord," while everyone else was saying "Caesar is Lord." What "gods" compete with your allegiance to Christ?
   ❑ power / influence
   ❑ wealth / possessions
   ❑ pleasure / having fun
   ❑ my spouse / boyfriend / girlfriend
   ❑ my friends
   ❑ my family
   ❑ my health / comfort
   ❑ my work / career / school
   ❑ my reputation
   ❑ other:_____

8. What do you need to do to move closer to Christ in your spiritual life?
   ❑ learn more about Christ's teachings
   ❑ have more faith in Christ's death and resurrection
   ❑ "lose" my life and my self-focus for Christ's sake
   ❑ be more involved in church, youth group, etc.
   ❑ be more consistent in my devotional life

9. How can this group remember you in prayer this week?

Photo Courtesy of Cherry Hills Community Church

THE HOLY SPIRIT

> ⁶So when they met together, they asked him, "Lord, are you at this time going to restore the kingdom to Israel?"
>
> ⁷He said to them: "It is not for you to know the times or dates the Father has set by his own authority. ⁸But you will receive power when the Holy Spirit comes on you; and you will be my witnesses in Jerusalem, and in all Judea and Samaria, and to the ends of the earth."
>
> ⁹After he said this, he was taken up before their very eyes, and a cloud hid him from their sight. ...
>
> **2** When the day of Pentecost came, they were all together in one place. ²Suddenly a sound like the blowing of a violent wind came from heaven and filled the whole house where they were sitting. ³They saw what seemed to be tongues of fire that separated and came to rest on each of them. ⁴All of them were filled with the Holy Spirit and began to speak in other tongues as the Spirit enabled them. ...
>
> ¹⁴Then Peter stood up with the Eleven, raised his voice and addressed the crowd: "Fellow Jews and all of you who live in Jerusalem, let me explain this to you; listen carefully to what I say. ¹⁵These men are not drunk, as you suppose. It's only nine in the morning! ¹⁶No, this is what was spoken by the prophet Joel:
>
> ¹⁷" 'In the last days, God says,
> I will pour out my Spirit on all people.
> Your sons and daughters will prophesy,
> your young men will see visions,
> your old men will dream dreams.
>
> *Acts 1:6–9; 2:1–4,14–17*

Introduction

This Bible study is designed to help you understand the third statement in the Apostles' Creed: *"I believe in the Holy Spirit."* After listening to the Bible story about Christ's ascension and the coming of the Spirit at Pentecost, move into groups of 4 and discuss the questionnaire.

1. If you were one of the disciples when Christ was taken up to heaven, how would you have felt about Jesus leaving you?
    - ❐ terrified
    - ❐ confused
    - ❐ abandoned
    - ❐ angry
    - ❐ excited about what was ahead

2. Had you been present on the day of Pentecost, what would have been your main feeling when it was all over?
    - ❐ That was a once-in-a-lifetime experience.
    - ❐ I hope that wasn't a once-in-a-lifetime experience.
    - ❐ If the Spirit is that powerful, there's no problem I can't face.
    - ❐ Give us five days and we'll take the world!
    - ❐ Nobody at work or school is going to understand this!

3. In comparison to what the disciples experienced when the Holy Spirit came upon them, how would you describe your own experience with the Holy Spirit?
    - ❐ much more tame
    - ❐ similar to theirs
    - ❐ different, but just as real
    - ❐ something I can't explain

4. How would you describe your experience with the Holy Spirit now?
    - ❐ on fire
    - ❐ up in the air
    - ❐ gone with the wind

5. When are you most aware of the Holy Spirit?
    - ❐ reading Scripture
    - ❐ alone with God
    - ❐ sharing in a group like this
    - ❐ spending time in nature
    - ❐ in praise and worship
    - ❐ other:_____
    - ❐ praying with friends

6. The following qualities from Galatians 5:22–23 are called the "fruit of the Spirit." Evaluate your life by circling a number from 1 (very low) to 10 (very high) on each of the "fruit" in the list. Then share which fruit you marked as highest and lowest. Lastly, have each person listen while the others share which fruit they see as that person's highest.

But the fruit of the Spirit is love, joy, peace, patience, kindness, goodness, faithfulness, gentleness and self-control.

LOVE: I am quick to sense the needs of others; I try to respond as Christ would in giving of myself.

1   2   3   4   5   6   7   8   9   10

JOY: I can celebrate life even in the midst of pain and confusion because of my faith in Christ.

1   2   3   4   5   6   7   8   9   10

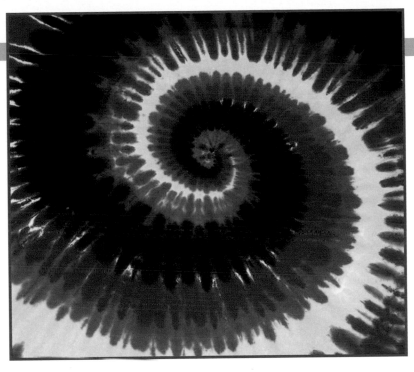

PEACE: I have a quiet inner confidence in God's care of my life that keeps me from feeling uptight and nervous.

1   2   3   4   5   6   7   8   9   10

PATIENCE: I have a staying power that helps me to handle frustration and conflict without losing it when people irritate me.

1   2   3   4   5   6   7   8   9   10

KINDNESS: I act toward others as I want them to act toward me—warm, considerate, generous with praise—always trying to see the best in them.

1   2   3   4   5   6   7   8   9   10

GOODNESS: I have a desire to live a clean life, to set a good example by my conduct wherever I am; I want to be God's man or God's woman.

1   2   3   4   5   6   7   8   9   10

FAITHFULNESS: I stick to my word; I stand up for my family and friends; I can be counted on to stay firm in my commitments to God and others.

1   2   3   4   5   6   7   8   9   10

GENTLENESS: I have an inner strength that permits me to be gentle in my relationships; I am aware of my own abilities without having to make a show of them.

1   2   3   4   5   6   7   8   9   10

SELF-CONTROL: I am learning to discipline my time, energy and desires to reflect my spiritual values and priorities.

1   2   3   4   5   6   7   8   9   10

7. Where in your life do you need the power of the Holy Spirit?

THE CHURCH

Introduction

This Bible study is designed to help you understand the fourth statement in the Apostles' Creed: *"I believe in the holy catholic Church."*

The word "catholic" means "universal" ... so you could say universal church if you wish. The Bible passage describes what happened after Pentecost when so many came into the church (3,000 new believers in one day) that they decided to gather in homes to care for each other.

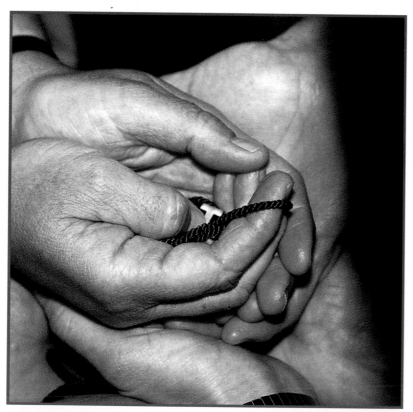

> ### THE FELLOWSHIP OF THE BELIEVERS
> [42] They devoted themselves to the apostles' teaching and to the fellowship, to the breaking of bread and to prayer. [43] Everyone was filled with awe, and many wonders and miraculous signs were done by the apostles. [44] All the believers were together and had everything in common. [45] Selling their possessions and goods, they gave to anyone as he had need. [46] Every day they continued to meet together in the temple courts. They broke bread in their homes and ate together with glad and sincere hearts, [47] praising God and enjoying the favor of all the people. And the Lord added to their number daily those who were being saved.
>
> *Acts 2:42–47*

Listen to the story. Then, move into groups of 4 and discuss the questionnaire.

1. How would you describe the atmosphere when these first Christians got together? (Choose two or three.)

    ❑ chaotic ❑ life-changing ❑ boring
    ❑ fun ❑ predictable ❑ close
    ❑ exciting ❑ unpredictable ❑ too close
    ❑ noisy ❑ warm ❑ caring

2. What made the early church so appealing that thousands wanted to get in?

    ❑ the food ❑ great preaching
    ❑ the miracles ❑ great advertising
    ❑ their openness to others ❑ their spiritual vitality
    ❑ the amazing love they had for each other

3. What is the closest you have come to experiencing the kind of close fellowship that is described here in Acts?

4. If you had been invited to be part of the early church, what would have been your initial reaction?

   ❒ Sounds too much like a cult to me.
   ❒ This is a bit too touchy-feely for me.
   ❒ I have some things I wouldn't sell for anyone.
   ❒ I might give it a try.
   ❒ I would jump at the chance.

5. From your school, workplace and neighborhood, what percentage of people attend church? What's the general attitude about church?

6. If you had to rank your own church or group on the six areas that are described in the early church, what would you say? In your group, read the first area below and let everyone call out a number from 1 (very weak) to 10 (very strong) in that area.

SPIRITUAL NURTURE / GROWTH: *"They devoted themselves to the apostles' teaching and to the fellowship, to the breaking of bread and to prayer."*

> We have given priority to studying the Scripture, to learning more about our faith and to praying for one another.

> 1   2   3   4   5   6   5   7   8   9   10

HEALING: *"Everyone was filled with awe, and many wonders and miraculous signs were done by the apostles."*

> We have seen healing take place in our lives and in our relationships with one another, our families and our friends.

> 1   2   3   4   5   6   5   7   8   9   10

CAREGIVING: *"All the believers were together and had everything in common. Selling their possessions and goods, they gave to anyone as he had need."*

> We look after each other. If someone has a need, we do what we can to care for this person and meet their need.

> 1   2   3   4   5   6   5   7   8   9   10

CORPORATE WORSHIP: *"Every day they continued to meet together in the temple courts."*

> We meet regularly for worship—to celebrate Christ's resurrection and his triumph over sin.

> 1   2   3   4   5   6   5   7   8   9   10

SUPPORT GROUPS: *"They broke bread in their homes and ate together with glad and sincere hearts, praising God and enjoying the favor of all the people."*

> We meet regularly to support one another, praise God, study the Bible, share our needs and pray for one another.

> 1   2   3   4   5   6   5   7   8   9   10

REACHING OUT: *"And the Lord added to their number daily those who were being saved."*

> We keep our church or group open to new people and through our reaching out the Lord keeps bringing others to our fellowship.

> 1   2   3   4   5   6   5   7   8   9   10

7. What aspect of the spiritual life and energy of the early church do you most desire for yourself? For your church and/or this group?

8. How could you help your church and this group be more like the early church?

9. How would you like this group to remember you in prayer this week?

Beliefs

RESURRECTION OF THE BODY

Introduction

This Bible study is designed to help you understand the last statement in the Apostles' Creed:*"I believe in ... the resurrection of the body, and the life everlasting."*

The phrase "the resurrection of the body" actually refers to the resurrection of Christians at the second coming of Jesus Christ. But this is in the future and rather than studying a Scripture about this we are going to study the story of the resurrection of Jesus Christ. The two are connected. If you believe in one, you believe in the other.

Now, listen to the Bible story. Then, move into groups of 4 and discuss the questionnaire.

1. What angle would you expect the *Jerusalem Times* to take on the events of this passage?
   - ❏ "Earthquake Rocks City"
   - ❏ "Cemetery Guards Recount Bizarre Scene"
   - ❏ "Women Claim Professed Messiah Risen From Dead"
   - ❏ "Roman Soldiers Accept Bribe From Jewish Leaders"

2. Imagine that you were one of the women who went to the tomb. How would you have felt when you found the stone rolled back and an angel sitting on it?
   - ❏ scared to death
   - ❏ wondering who took the body
   - ❏ overcome with grief—"I can't take any more heartache."
   - ❏ overcome with joy—"I knew Jesus would come back!"

3. How would you have felt when Jesus suddenly met you?
   - ❏ shocked   ❏ overjoyed
   - ❏ afraid   ❏ full of praise

THE RESURRECTION

28 *After the Sabbath, at dawn on the first day of the week, Mary Magdalene and the other Mary went to look at the tomb.*

2There was a violent earthquake, for an angel of the Lord came down from heaven and, going to the tomb, rolled back the stone and sat on it. 3His appearance was like lightning, and his clothes were white as snow. 4The guards were so afraid of him that they shook and became like dead men.

5The angel said to the women, "Do not be afraid, for I know that you are looking for Jesus, who was crucified. 6He is not here; he has risen, just as he said. Come and see the place where he lay. 7Then go quickly and tell his disciples: 'He has risen from the dead and is going ahead of you into Galilee. There you will see him.' Now I have told you."

8So the women hurried away from the tomb, afraid yet filled with joy, and ran to tell his disciples. 9Suddenly Jesus met them. "Greetings," he said. They came to him, clasped his feet and worshiped him. 10Then Jesus said to them, "Do not be afraid. Go and tell my brothers to go to Galilee; there they will see me."

11While the women were on their way, some of the guards went into the city and reported to the chief priests everything that had happened. 12When the chief priests had met with the elders and devised a plan, they gave the soldiers a large sum of money, 13telling them, "You are to say, 'His disciples came during the night and stole him away while we were asleep.' 14If this report gets to the governor, we will satisfy him and keep you out of trouble." 15So the soldiers took the money and did as they were instructed. And this story has been widely circulated among the Jews to this very day.

Matthew 28:1–15

4. What is the attitude of the people around you (classmates, coworkers, neighbors) toward the resurrection of Christ? Toward life after death?

5. How would you compare the funerals you have gone to when the person who died clearly knew Christ with the funerals of those who may not have known Christ?

6. How would you explain the importance of Jesus' resurrection to a non-Christian? When did the full meaning of his resurrection "dawn" on you?

7. What do you do when you do not understand the resurrection of Jesus or your own resurrection?
   - ❑ fall back on what the Bible says
   - ❑ accept the teaching of my church
   - ❑ go with what I was taught as a child
   - ❑ accept it by faith—"I believe ... help my unbelief!"
   - ❑ other:_____

8. What benefit do you appreciate the most about your own future resurrection?
   - ❑ peace
   - ❑ purpose
   - ❑ courage
   - ❑ hope
   - ❑ comfort
   - ❑ other:_____

9. What difference does the resurrection of Christ make in your everyday life?
   - ❑ not much
   - ❑ quite a bit
   - ❑ a great deal

10. How can this group remember you in prayer this week?

MOUNTAIN TRAINING

Introduction

If Jesus Christ is going to be the Lord of a Christian, the first battle is the battle for the mind. In this Bible Study, you will be looking at three disciples who Jesus took on a mountain trip. Follow along as you hear the story being read. Try to imagine yourself with Jesus as one of the disciples.

Now, move into groups of 4 and discuss the questionnaire.

1. What stands out the most to you from this story?
   ❑ Jesus' transformation
   ❑ Peter's reaction
   ❑ God speaking

2. If you had been Peter when Moses and Elijah appeared, how would you have felt?
   ❑ scared spitless
   ❑ totally awed
   ❑ out of place
   ❑ super high
   ❑ like hiding

3. If you could choose three friends to go with you on a spiritual retreat, who would you choose? Where would you go?

4. When did Jesus appear to you in a special way? If not dazzling light and voices from heaven, how was his glory revealed to you?

5. When you are feeling "down" in your spiritual life, what have you found to be helpful?
   ❑ admitting to God that I'm down
   ❑ praying with a friend
   ❑ getting into a support group
   ❑ reading the Bible
   ❑ going to church
   ❑ getting away by myself
   ❑ other:_____

THE TRANSFIGURATION

²After six days Jesus took Peter, James and John with him and led them up a high mountain, where they were all alone. There he was transfigured before them. ³His clothes became dazzling white—whiter than anyone in the world could bleach them. ⁴And there appeared before them Elijah and Moses, who were talking with Jesus.

⁵Peter said to Jesus, "Rabbi, it is good for us to be here. Let us put up three shelters—one for you, one for Moses and one for Elijah." ⁶(He did not know what to say, they were so frightened.)

⁷Then a cloud appeared and enveloped them, and a voice came from the cloud: "This is my Son, whom I love. Listen to him!"

⁸Suddenly when they looked around, they no longer saw anyone with them except Jesus.

⁹As they were coming down the mountain, Jesus gave them orders not to tell anyone what they had seen until the Son of Man had risen from the dead. ¹⁰They kept the matter to themselves, discussing what "rising from the dead" meant.

Mark 9:2–10

6. How would you describe your relationship with God now?
   - ❐ in the valley
   - ❐ climbing the mountain
   - ❐ on the mountaintop
   - ❐ on the rocks

7. The disciples were told, "This is my Son, whom I love. Listen to him!" What is most effective in helping you to listen to God?
   - ❐ personal Bible study
   - ❐ sermons
   - ❐ group Bible studies
   - ❐ prayer
   - ❐ camps or retreats
   - ❐ I think I'd need a special hearing aid for that!

8. In your private devotional life with God, what is your biggest problem?
   - ❐ finding the time
   - ❐ being consistent
   - ❐ getting to bed the night before
   - ❐ finding somewhere quiet at home
   - ❐ knowing how to get something out of the Bible
   - ❐ keeping from falling asleep
   - ❐ concentrating when I am reading the Bible or praying
   - ❐ desiring to have time with God every day

9. What kind of a realistic goal would you like to set for yourself each day for a "quiet time"—time with God?
   - ❐ 5 minutes
   - ❐ 10 minutes
   - ❐ 15 minutes
   - ❐ 30 minutes
   - ❐ other:_____

10. How could your group or church support you as you plan your spiritual discipline?
    - ❐ hold me accountable
    - ❐ share with me some good ideas
    - ❐ call me every now and then to see how it is going
    - ❐ get off my back
    - ❐ other:_____

11. How would you like this group to pray for you this week?

SPIRITUAL CALLING

THE CALLING OF THE FIRST DISCIPLES

5 *One day as Jesus was standing by the Lake of Gennesaret, with the people crowding around him and listening to the word of God, ²he saw at the water's edge two boats, left there by the fishermen, who were washing their nets. ³He got into one of the boats, the one belonging to Simon, and asked him to put out a little from shore. Then he sat down and taught the people from the boat.*

⁴When he had finished speaking, he said to Simon, "Put out into deep water, and let down the nets for a catch."

⁵Simon answered, "Master, we've worked hard all night and haven't caught anything. But because you say so, I will let down the nets."

⁶When they had done so, they caught such a large number of fish that their nets began to break. ⁷So they signaled their partners in the other boat to come and help them, and they came and filled both boats so full that they began to sink.

⁸When Simon Peter saw this, he fell at Jesus' knees and said, "Go away from me, Lord; I am a sinful man!" ⁹For he and all his companions were astonished at the catch of fish they had taken, ¹⁰and so were James and John, the sons of Zebedee, Simon's partners.

Then Jesus said to Simon, "Don't be afraid; from now on you will catch men." ¹¹So they pulled their boats up on shore, left everything and followed him.

Luke 5:1–11

Introduction

In this Bible study, you will look at a fisherman whom Jesus asked to make a choice—a big choice.

Listen to the story and move into groups of 4 to discuss the questionnaire.

1. Where is the best fishing spot in your area? What is the biggest fish you've ever caught (or the biggest fish story you've ever told)?

2. If you had been Simon Peter when Jesus said, "Put out into deep water, and let down the nets for a catch," what would you have done?
   - ❏ wondered who this guy thought he was
   - ❏ told Jesus I was too tired
   - ❏ suggested another time when the fish were biting
   - ❏ politely told Jesus to stick to his preaching
   - ❏ grudgingly gone ahead with the idea
   - ❏ happily done what Jesus requested

3. When they caught so many fish that their nets began to break, how did Peter probably feel?
   - ❏ overjoyed
   - ❏ dumbfounded
   - ❏ terrible about what he had said
   - ❏ aware of who Jesus was

4. When was the first time you felt the tug of Jesus on your heart?
   - ❏ when I was very young
   - ❏ when there was a crisis in my life
   - ❏ in a church service
   - ❏ when I was at a retreat/camp
   - ❏ just recently
   - ❏ I don't know that I have.
   - ❏ other:_____

5. How would you finish this sentence? "I am committed to know and follow the will of God for my life ..."
   - ❏ all of the time
   - ❏ most of the time
   - ❏ some of the time
   - ❏ on occasion

6. How does the call to leave your nets behind and follow Jesus (in order to "catch men") sound to you?
   - ❏ radical
   - ❏ scary
   - ❏ exciting
   - ❏ crazy
   - ❏ fulfilling
   - ❏ other:_____

7. What would it mean for you to be "catching people" for Jesus?
   - ❏ to share my faith with my friends
   - ❏ to invite friends to my group or church
   - ❏ to show others God's love through *my* love
   - ❏ to start focusing on people rather than things
   - ❏ other:_____

8. In order to "catch people" for Jesus, what do you have going for you that is "good bait" (something that helps draw people to Jesus)?
   - ❏ my ability to make friends
   - ❏ my ability to share my faith
   - ❏ my ability to listen when people have problems
   - ❏ my knowledge of the Bible
   - ❏ my willingness to take risks
   - ❏ my willingness to "walk my talk"
   - ❏ my willingness to help people in need
   - ❏ my openness to people of different cultures and backgrounds
   - ❏ other:_____

9. What would be the greatest thing you would like to do with your life? What is keeping you from doing it?

10. How can this group support you in prayer this week?

POT HOLES

Introduction

Welcome to the real world in the Christian life: the world of super highs and super lows ... and rainy days ... and balmy, boring days. Days when your prayers go no higher than the ceiling ... and you feel as low as a duck's instep. In this Bible study, you are going to see one of those days in action.

The Bible story is about Peter during his down time. At the "Last Supper" when Jesus explained that he would be arrested that night, Peter said, "Lord, I am ready to go with you to prison and to death." Jesus replied, "I tell you, Peter, before the rooster crows today, you will deny three times that you know me." We pick up the story a few hours later when Jesus has been arrested and brought to the palace of the high priest for a pretrial interrogation. Peter followed the police officers and is in the nearby courtyard. Listen to the story. Then, move into groups of 4 and discuss the questionnaire.

1. Imagine that you were a reporter for the *Jerusalem Journal*, and you were assigned to interview Peter after these events. What would be the first question you would ask him?
   ❏ "So, Peter, how does it feel to be a traitor?"
   ❏ "Didn't you ever think about Jesus' prediction?"
   ❏ "How could you have done such a thing?"
   ❏ "How has this changed the way you see yourself?"
   ❏ "What do you plan to do now to make up for this?"

2. If you were in Peter's sandals, how would you have reacted in this situation?
   ❏ kept my mouth shut
   ❏ gone home
   ❏ done the same thing he did
   ❏ stood up for Jesus and argued his case
   ❏ other:_____

PETER DISOWNS JESUS

⁶⁹Now Peter was sitting out in the courtyard, and a servant girl came to him. "You also were with Jesus of Galilee," she said.

⁷⁰But he denied it before them all. "I don't know what you're talking about," he said.

⁷¹Then he went out to the gateway, where another girl saw him and said to the people there, "This fellow was with Jesus of Nazareth."

⁷²He denied it again, with an oath: "I don't know the man!"

⁷³After a little while, those standing there went up to Peter and said, "Surely you are one of them, for your accent gives you away."

⁷⁴Then he began to call down curses on himself and he swore to them, "I don't know the man!"

Immediately a rooster crowed. ⁷⁵Then Peter remembered the word Jesus had spoken: "Before the rooster crows, you will disown me three times." And he went outside and wept bitterly.

Matthew 26:69–75

---

3. What chance would you have given Peter after this event to make a comeback and go on to become a great leader?

4. How do you usually react when you fail?
   ❏ kick myself for days
   ❏ try to make up for it
   ❏ hide my feelings
   ❏ talk to someone about it
   ❏ pray about it
   ❏ shrug it off
   ❏ admit it and move on
   ❏ I refuse to accept failure in anything I do!
   ❏ other:_____

5. What have you found helpful in dealing with failure, and how would you like to react differently?

6. How has failure changed you?
   - ❏ I'm more caring and understanding.
   - ❏ I'm more determined.
   - ❏ I'm more humble.
   - ❏ I'm more realistic.
   - ❏ I don't want to try again
   - ❏ I look out for myself more.
   - ❏ I'm emotionally fragile.
   - ❏ other:_____

7. What failure in your life comes closest to hitting you like Peter's failure hit him?
   - ❏ when I strayed from God
   - ❏ when I deceived my parents
   - ❏ when I went through a divorce
   - ❏ when I "fell off the wagon"
   - ❏ when I messed up at work or school
   - ❏ when I handled a relationship poorly
   - ❏ when I went through financial problems
   - ❏ when I failed to stand up for what's right
   - ❏ when I failed my family
   - ❏ other:_____

8. Have you ever felt that your failures made it impossible for you to serve Christ again? How did you overcome those feelings?

9. Would you give yourself a "plus" or "minus" for each of the following? (Mark one or the other in the blanks.)
   - ____ bouncing back after you blow it
   - ____ forgiving those who fail you
   - ____ standing up for Christ
   - ____ spiritual desire
   - ____ spiritual consistency

10. How can this group remember you in prayer this week?

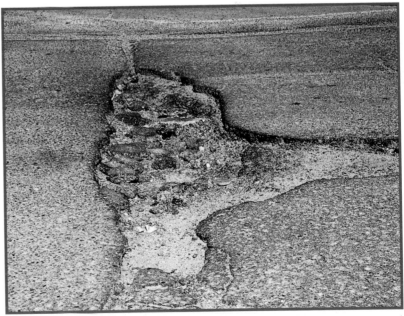

227

Discipleship

REBOUNDING

Introduction

In this Bible story, you will meet Peter after the Resurrection when Peter and his friends were brought back to the team ... and restored to fellowship.

In the process of walking through this story, you will have a chance to talk about your own spiritual comebacks, and help each other see some spiritual principles. Listen to the Bible story. Then, move into groups of 4 and discuss the questionnaire.

1. What do you find most amazing or interesting about this story?
   - ❐ that Peter and the other disciples went back to fishing
   - ❐ that they didn't recognize Jesus at first
   - ❐ that they caught a miraculous number of fish
   - ❐ that Jesus served them breakfast

2. When you are really upset or disappointed, where do you go and what do you do?

3. If you had been Peter and knew you had blown it by recently denying Jesus, how would you feel when he appeared?
   - ❐ terrible—I can't face him.
   - ❐ panicky—He's going to chew me out.
   - ❐ defeated—I'm no good.
   - ❐ hopeful—Maybe there is hope for me.
   - ❐ reenergized—Jesus is alive and I am going for it.
   - ❐ other:_____

4. How would you have felt when Jesus served you breakfast?
   - ❐ awkward
   - ❐ guilty
   - ❐ forgiven
   - ❐ relieved
   - ❐ loved
   - ❐ other:_____

5. What is the closest you have come to "throwing in the towel" and going back on your promise to follow Jesus?

JESUS AND THE MIRACULOUS CATCH OF FISH

21 Afterward Jesus appeared again to his disciples, by the Sea of Tiberias. It happened this way: ²Simon Peter, Thomas (called Didymus), Nathanael from Cana in Galilee, the sons of Zebedee [James and John], and two other disciples were together. ³"I'm going out to fish," Simon Peter told them, and they said, "We'll go with you." So they went out and got into the boat, but that night they caught nothing.

⁴Early in the morning, Jesus stood on the shore, but the disciples did not realize that it was Jesus.

⁵He called out to them, "Friends, haven't you any fish?"

"No," they answered.

⁶He said, "Throw your net on the right side of the boat and you will find some." When they did, they were unable to haul the net in because of the large number of fish.

⁷Then the disciple whom Jesus loved [John] said to Peter, "It is the Lord!" As soon as Simon Peter heard him say, "It is the Lord," he wrapped his outer garment around him (for he had taken it off) and jumped into the water. ⁸The other disciples followed in the boat, towing the net full of fish, for they were not far from shore, about a hundred yards. ⁹When they landed, they saw a fire of burning coals there with fish on it, and some bread.

¹⁰Jesus said to them, "Bring some of the fish you have just caught."

¹¹Simon Peter climbed aboard and dragged the net ashore. It was full of large fish, 153, but even with so many the net was not torn. ¹²Jesus said to them, "Come and have breakfast." None of the disciples dared ask him, "Who are you?" They knew it was the Lord. ¹³Jesus came, took the bread and gave it to them, and did the same with the fish. ¹⁴This was now the third time Jesus appeared to his disciples after he was raised from the dead.

John 21:1–14

---

6. How did Jesus meet you in this experience and bring you back?
   - ❒ through Christian friends
   - ❒ through prayer
   - ❒ through reading the Bible
   - ❒ by talking to a counselor or pastor
   - ❒ I never have gone through this kind of experience.
   - ❒ other:_____

7. What did you learn from this experience?
   - ❒ to trust God
   - ❒ not to expect God to do things my way
   - ❒ the importance of being in a group with other Christians
   - ❒ to come clean with God about sin in my life
   - ❒ other:_____

8. If Jesus showed up today and asked you to go out to eat with him, what would he want to talk to you about?

9. In terms of a weather forecast, how would you describe your future outlook right now?
   - ❒ seven straight days of rain
   - ❒ nothing but sunshine
   - ❒ partly cloudy
   - ❒ bitter cold
   - ❒ other:_____

10. How can the group support you and pray for you this week?

I BELIEVE IN MIRACLES

Introduction

You will be studying a familiar story in the Bible about a wedding in Cana where Jesus performed his first public miracle by turning water into wine. If you have seen *Fiddler on the Roof* you will appreciate this story. Jewish weddings were big occasions. The whole community was invited, and wine was very important. When the wine ran out, it was a great social embarrassment.

Now listen to the Bible story. Then, quickly move into groups of 4 and discuss the questionnaire.

1. If you were the social editor for the local newspaper, what headline would you give this story?
   ❒ "Mother of Preacher Takes Charge at Wedding"
   ❒ "Water Mysteriously Turns to Wine at Reception"
   ❒ "Mother and Son Save Bridegroom From Embarrassment"
   ❒ "Local Wedding Turns Into Wine Tasting Party"
   ❒ "Guests Are Stunned—Groom Saves Best Wine for Last"

2. What's the craziest thing you've ever seen happen at a wedding or wedding reception?

3. How do you imagine Jesus felt about his mother's suggestion that he do something about the wine?
   ❒ annoyed   ❒ honored
   ❒ embarrassed   ❒ reluctant
   ❒ manipulated   ❒ willing

4. If you had been the bridegroom, how would you have felt when you heard about the new wine?
   ❒ relieved—I can't forget about the guests.
   ❒ curious—How did this happen?
   ❒ amazed—This is a miracle!
   ❒ puzzled—The servants must have made a mistake.

JESUS CHANGES WATER TO WINE

2 **On the third day a wedding took place at Cana in Galilee. Jesus' mother was there, ²and Jesus and his disciples had also been invited to the wedding. ³When the wine was gone, Jesus' mother said to him, "They have no more wine."**

⁴"Dear woman, why do you involve me?" Jesus replied. "My time has not yet come."

⁵His mother said to the servants, "Do whatever he tells you."

⁶Nearby stood six stone water jars, the kind used by the Jews for ceremonial washing, each holding from twenty to thirty gallons.

⁷Jesus said to the servants, "Fill the jars with water"; so they filled them to the brim.

⁸Then he told them, "Now draw some out and take it to the master of the banquet."

They did so, ⁹and the master of the banquet tasted the water that had been turned into wine. He did not realize where it had come from, though the servants who had drawn the water knew. Then he called the bridegroom aside ¹⁰and said, "Everyone brings out the choice wine first and then the cheaper wine after the guests have had too much to drink; but you have saved the best till now."

¹¹This, the first of his miraculous signs, Jesus performed at Cana in Galilee. He thus revealed his glory, and his disciples put their faith in him.

John 2:1–11

5. In verse 11 what does John, the author of this Gospel, mean by calling Jesus' miracles "signs"?

6. What "sign" led you to put your faith in Jesus?
   - ❏ the miracles Jesus did in the Bible
   - ❏ a specific miracle Jesus did for me
   - ❏ the wrong direction my life was going
   - ❏ the resurrection of Jesus and the fact that he is still alive
   - ❏ the change in heart I experienced
   - ❏ the changes I saw in others
   - ❏ Nothing else made sense.
   - ❏ other:_____

7. Right now, what is your attitude toward miracles in general, and God's working in your life in particular? What is the most exciting thing in your spiritual life? What in your life feels like stale water in an old jug?

8. What is the "wine level" (zest for living) in your life at the moment?
   - ❏ overflowing
   - ❏ half-full
   - ❏ running out fast
   - ❏ empty

9. In what area of your life do you need a miracle right now?
   - ❏ physical
   - ❏ emotional
   - ❏ relational
   - ❏ school / career
   - ❏ financial
   - ❏ spiritual
   - ❏ other:_____

10. How can this group remember you in prayer this week?

Photo Courtesy of Cherry Hills Community Church

Photo Courtesy of Cherry Hills Community Church

CUSTOMIZE YOUR SERENDIPITY EVENT

FOR ANY OCCASION ...

CUSTOM-MADE EVENTS FOR YOUR CHURCH

Now you can "serendipitize" your church! You can use the activities and Bible studies in this encyclopedia to create your own customized events and offer fun, heartwarming ways for people to build friendships and grow in Christ.

As a resource for much more than small groups, the *Serendipity Encyclopedia* can be used for kick-offs, getting acquainted, celebration, community building or just for fun! You can use this encyclopedia to create dozens of wonderful events, such as:

- A youth retreat on "Living Clean in a Dirty World"
- A family rally on "home devotionals"
- A Valentine's banquet for singles
- A Sunday school class outreach party
- A new member class
- A meeting of the "Upholstery and Carpet Committee"

Whatever your church is doing and any-time people are gathered together, use this encyclopedia to make great things happen. Build relationships and tear down walls of social distance! Let everyone know that your church is a place where truly knowing one another and caring for one another is the highest priority.

Photo Courtesy of Cherry Hills Community Church

Do not let the tasks of a church become more important than the joy of a church. The greatest strength in any congregation is the people. Wonderful people, made new by Christ, who have tremendous capacity for encouragement, honesty, compassion and celebration. Given the simplest nudge, even the engineers and accountants in your church will jump at the chance to answer questions about themselves, play games, laugh and affirm one another!

Use the various activities listed in the *Serendipity Encyclopedia* to instantly create an event for any type of group or function.

Just add people! Whatever your agenda, goals, purposes or content, you can include opportunities to help people "get together." Church programs can be much more than the transfer of knowledge. Any event can happen in an environment of "togetherness" and trust. Let your events, no matter what they are, fulfill the ultimate purpose of a church: loving and edifying one another.

This encyclopedia includes all the activities and ideas you need to help you plan top-notch events! To help you plan a "serendipity" event at your church, choose one of the many different options: everything from Saturday support seminars to a father-son rally. Under each event, you will find a variety of helpful information.

Special Ideas and Suggestions: Set-up ideas, ways to add fun and mischief, suggestions for themes, etc.

Event Agenda: Including suggestions for which Crowd Breakers, Communication Activities, Interactive Exercises and Group-Sharing Bible Studies to use. Also tips on how to include your own Bible study or teaching material.

Planning Hints: Suggestions about how to plan your event, based on the different planning steps included in the next section (beginning on page 295). This includes practical ideas on promotion, evaluation and preparing materials.

So roll up your sleeves and get started! Select the type of event you want to have at your church and let the fun begin!

WHO IS IN YOUR CHURCH?

Wouldn't it be great if your church budget was Fort Knox? You could send limousines door-to-door to pick up visitors and you could hire Steven Spielberg to do the special effects for your Christmas pageant!

Unfortunately, every church has limited resources. Using those resources efficiently is very important. How is your church using its resources? More specifically, to whom is your church devoting its resources?

Your mission statement probably describes a church that helps people develop into devoted servants of God. Those people are the **core** of your church. They are the people who attend regularly, serve as church leaders, give faithfully, and help others become loving followers of Jesus.

The **congregation** consists of those people who attend regularly and might attend a church program or function. These people are the loyal followers who are true to their pastor. The congregation generally will go along with the decision of the core. The congregation gives some money, occasionally ends up on a committee, and leaves discipleship, teaching and leadership tasks to the people in the core.

Each church also has a group that can be called the **crowd**. The crowd is made up of the people who attend a worship service every now and then, rarely give an offering, and seldom attend any other programs or activities. These people do not consider themselves leaders or contributors in any facet of the church. The crowd considers themselves members, and they are kept on the church rolls even though they haven't attended since last Easter. Frequently, the crowd is ignored because they are not always there guiding church programs. Many times they are ignored because they are never asked what they want or need.

Don't forget about the **community**. This is the group of people in your parish or neighborhood who do not attend church. Who are these people? What do they need? What can your church offer them?

You can estimate the number of people in your particular community or parish. Use the following formula to determine the size of your community:

❑ How far will someone drive to visit your church? Choose a time:
  • 5 minutes   • 15 minutes   • somewhere in between

❑ How many people live in the "driving time" radius you have chosen? (You might need a city map and a recent census to determine this amount.)

❑ How many people in this radius would you estimate are already involved in a church? Deduct this number from the previous amount. This number represents your community.

1. Use the diagram below to fill in the various percentages of people in your church.

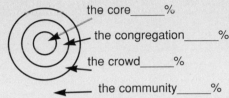

the core_____%

the congregation_____%

the crowd_____%

the community_____%

2. Consider all the programs in your church. These are your most valuable resources. Blood, sweat, tears and money go into these programs. Make a list of all the opportunities for adult involvement (committees, tasks, classes, etc.).

3. Look at your list. Which of these programs are intended for the **core**? The **congregation**? The **crowd**? The **community**? Fill in the blanks below: "Of all our church's programs, ..."

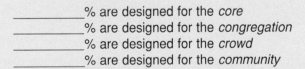

_____% are designed for the *core*
_____% are designed for the *congregation*
_____% are designed for the *crowd*
_____% are designed for the *community*

4. Do the percentages you listed seem like a good use of your church's resources?

5. Do the percentages that you listed fit your church's mission statement?

SMALL GROUPS

Serendipity has always been known for small groups. Serendipity pioneered the small group movement and helped small groups become the important part of church life they are today. This encyclopedia is loaded with exercises and Bible studies to keep any small group alive and kicking for months and months.

A small group can be part of an active small group program, or a small gathering of people at a retreat, party, committee meeting, etc. The same principles that make small group programs so meaningful can also be applied anytime there are 3 to 12 people gathered together.

The Ideal Meeting Agenda

A little planning will turn a good small group meeting into a life-changing meeting. Small groups of 3 to 12 people can become a place where people can "get real" and talk openly about their lives and their faith. Small groups are also the ideal place for Christians to care for one another. In small groups, people learn how to listen, how to pray for one another, and how to affirm and encourage the people in their church. It is in a small group where some of the most important tasks of a church actually happen.

Here are some questions to ask in making your small group meetings more effective:

Where will the meeting be held? Give careful thought to the location of the meeting. Is it free from distraction? Can everyone see each other? Is everyone knee-to-knee and nose-to-nose? Avoid sofas and sitting around tables if possible.

Who is in the group? Do the members know one another? Have they been in a group before? Is the group homogenous? A group of people who do not know each other or have not been in a small group before will need to start slower than a group of friends. Also, a homogenous group, like a group of ninth graders from the same high school, will have more in common than a heterogenous group, which will need more time to get comfortable with one another.

How long will the group stay together? People need to know that their small group won't last forever. Many groups agree on a "group covenant" (p. 54) which details important features about the group: What is the goal of the group? When will the group meet? How long will each meeting last? How many weeks will the group agree to stay together? What are the ground rules for the group (confidentiality, freedom to share, etc.)? What about inviting friends? What about child care?

KEYS TO A HEALTHY SMALL GROUP

1. **A clear purpose:** The group needs to have a shared understanding of the group's purpose and how to accomplish it. The best way to create a purpose is to get two or three people together who have a similar purpose and have them invite others to join with them.

2. **A good beginning:** Groups are growing things and, like other growing things, you need to let the group do their own inviting. Assigning people to groups is usually not an effective way to grow.

3. **Helpful leaders:** A helpful leader is basically one who is prayerful, prepared and active in the life of the group. Good leadership does not just happen. People need to be trained and supported.

4. **Clear communication:** In each of the group meetings, your goal is equal participation by all members. Here is a rule: In the first session, a pattern of communication will be established for the rest of the time, so plan the first session carefully.

5. **Worthwhile content:** The content of the discussion needs to be both interesting and relevant to the group's purposes. We recommend using Serendipity materials. If you choose other small group materials, make sure they are designed not only to do Bible study, but also include group building.

6. **Growing trust and caring:** One of the goals in any small group is learning to love one another. Over a period of weeks and months, intimacy and self-disclosure should grow as the group is guided in that direction. If conflict arises along the way, don't smother it. Deal with it as a group. Correctly handled, it will deepen the trust and care of members.

7. **Centered in Jesus Christ:** One important reminder about Christian small groups. We are called to follow Jesus and his purposes in small groups. If a small group loses touch with why it is meeting, bring it back to the purpose as followers of Jesus. In most groups, this will also mean a time for prayer. Be sure to leave adequate time for prayer requests and caring.

--Roberta Hestenes

What should a group expect? A small group should move toward community, or *koinonia* (fellowship). This is a level of love and trust that will bind that group of people together long after the group has ended. The journey to *koinonia* has several steps. The first step for a group is sharing their spiritual stories. The second step is affirming one another based on what each person has shared. The third step is sharing current needs. A small group meeting should help a group move through the steps toward the goal of *koinonia*.

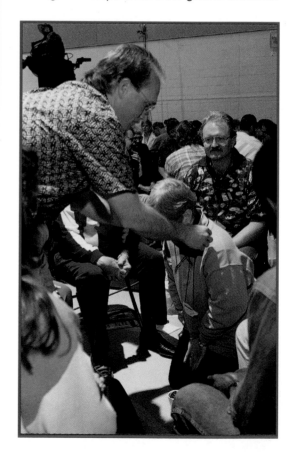

Generally speaking, the ideal group meeting has the following features:

- First, a time of gathering which includes an ice-breaker for getting acquainted or reacquainted.

- Second, a time of discussion which includes a Bible passage. Discussion questions should move from each person's observations about the passage to each person's application of the passage to their own lives.

- Third, a time to discuss group business such as the "group covenant" or the group's ministry project.

- Fourth, a time of caring. This always includes sharing prayer concerns and praying for one another, and possibly a time of affirmation.

You can use the activities in this encyclopedia to plan a balanced small group meeting:

- For the beginning of your meeting, use one of the discussion starters in the Interactive Exercises section (pp. 106–128). Any of the Kick-Off Sentences, Multiple-Choice Options, Self-Disclosure Spectrums, Interviews, Personal Inventories or Rankings would be a tremendous way to begin your meeting. Also, the Conversation Starters, Pop Quizzes, and Guessing Games in the Communication Activities section (pp. 76–86) would be great group starters.

CHURCHWIDE SURVEY FOR SMALL GROUP PLANNING

1. What benefits do you hope to receive from small groups in your church?
    - ❏ They are a way for people to get to know each other.
    - ❏ They encourage a sense of community in our church.
    - ❏ They give people an opportunity for in-depth Bible study.
    - ❏ They are a place where people can really care for one another.
    - ❏ They are a effective way to encourage spiritual growth.
    - ❏ They are a place where hurting people can go for healing.
    - ❏ They are a place to develop spiritual leadership.
    - ❏ other:_____

2. Why do you want small groups in your church? Rank in order of priority.
    - ____ Pastoral Care: Where real empathy can take place.
    - ____ Discipleship: Where spiritual discipline can be fostered by supporting each other and holding each other accountable.
    - ____ Compassion: Where "broken people" can gather and attend to each other's wounds.
    - ____ Edification: The chief means by which new believers can grow into spiritual maturity.
    - ____ Mobilization: The staging area in which people are best equipped and released for ministry in their world.
    - ____ Socialization: Where people can make friends and feel a sense of family.

3. Which type(s) of groups will best meet the needs of the people in your church?

Relationship Groups:
- ❏ Assimilation groups
- ❏ Affinity groups
- ❏ Recreation groups

Discipleship Groups:
- ❏ Bible study groups
- ❏ Christian skills groups
- ❏ Topical study groups
- ❏ Growth groups
- ❏ Accountability groups
- ❏ Prayer groups
- ❏ Sermon discussion groups

Ministry Groups:
- ❏ Service groups
- ❏ Policy setting groups
- ❏ Administrative groups
- ❏ Skill development groups
- ❏ Outreach groups

Need-based Groups:
- ❏ Enrichment groups
- ❏ Support groups
- ❏ Recovery groups

THE ONE ANOTHERS

The Bible lists many different "one anothers," which describe how church members should relate to each other. A small group is a great place for these "one anothers" to happen. Which "one another" do you need right now?

DEVOTION AND HONOR: "Be devoted to one another in brotherly love. Honor one another above yourselves." — Rom. 12:10

ACCEPTANCE: "Accept one another, then, just as Christ accepted you, in order to bring praise to God." — Rom. 15:7

SERVICE: "You, my brothers, were called to be free. But do not use your freedom to indulge the sinful nature; rather, serve one another in love." — Gal. 5:13

KINDNESS, COMPASSION AND FORGIVENESS: "Be kind and compassionate to one another, forgiving each other, just as in Christ God forgave you." — Eph. 4:32

ENCOURAGEMENT: "Therefore encourage one another and build each other up, just as in fact you are doing." — 1 Thess. 5:11

HOSPITALITY: "Offer hospitality to one another without grumbling." — 1 Peter 4:9

HARMONY: "Finally, all of you, live in harmony with one another; be sympathetic, love as brothers, be compassionate and humble." — 1 Peter 3:8

INSTRUCTION: "I myself am convinced, my brothers, that you yourselves are full of goodness, complete in knowledge and competent to instruct one another." — Rom. 15:14

MOTIVATION: "And let us consider how we may spur one another on toward love and good deeds." — Heb. 10:24

• For a new group, try "My Family Supper Table" (p. 118) or "Things That Drive You Crazy" (p. 121).

• For the Bible study portion of your meeting, any of the Group-Sharing Bible Studies (pp. 141–231) will work perfectly. These Bible studies let each person project themselves into the story and answer questions about their personal response to the story. Any of the studies in the Identity or Spiritual Formation categories would be ideal for a new group. A group focusing on spiritual growth could use the studies in the Beliefs or Discipleship categories. Or the group could pick and choose as they go.

• For the caring and sharing time of your meeting, try using one of the affirmation exercises—either the Affirmation Games (pp. 92–103) or the Serious Affirmation (pp. 136–139). For newer groups, try "Child Prodigies" (p. 94) or "Wild Predictions" (p. 103).

Pulling it off ...

Getting ready for a small group meeting requires some planning. First, make sure each participant has the materials they need. Serendipity has a variety of small groups resources for youth and adults which cover dozens of meaningful topics.

These group resources can be ordered by calling Serendipity at 1-800-525-9563 or visit us at: www.serendipityhouse.com.

Outreach Groups

Every church has more than one door. Of course, most people enter your church through the main entrance for a Sunday morning worship service. By offering more opportunities for people to become acquainted with your church, you can create many "doorways" into your church.

Small groups are a great way to make your church more inviting. Outreach groups are small groups specifically designed to appeal to the needs and interests of those people in your community who do not have a church home. Small groups are especially suited for this function because they are flexi-ble and they can be formed quickly around any topic. Small groups are also nonthreatening. Inviting friends and neighbors who are not familiar with church culture into your home for coffee and a Bible study can be easier than inviting those people to church.

Begin your outreach group with a "check-it-out" meeting. This meeting is basically a party or light dinner with several get-acquainted activities and an introduction to the chosen topic. The following is one format for the first meeting of an outreach group. (Use the meeting agenda on page 239 for future meetings.)

- Let everyone get acquainted with "My Favorites" (p. 106).

- Introduce the topic for the meetings and explain the format for each meeting. Assure everyone that they will not be put on the spot to know all the answers or pray out loud.

- Discuss the group covenant (p. 54). Pay special attention to the ground rules.

- Close with "Do-It-Yourself Stress Test" (p. 123). After everyone has shared their scores, close in prayer by using the first option in "Prayer Ideas" (p. 251).

Pulling it off ...

To get an outreach group started, begin with a support seminar (next page), an apartment outreach party (p. 291), or have an event similar to a Sunday school class outreach dinner (p. 281).

Photo Courtesy of Cherry Hills Community Church

Support Seminars

Another way to use small groups to attract people in your community and meet the needs they face is to offer support seminars. Well-suited for a Saturday morning or week-night, support seminars are an introduction to a topic faced by many people. For example, if there are people in your community struggling with stress, unemployment, parenting issues or teen substance abuse, offer a two-hour seminar on one of these topics. Invite a local authority on the subject to speak and answer questions. Here is one agenda for a two-hour support seminar:

- Begin with a fun game like "Serendipity Bingo" (p. 62).

- Divide into groups of about 4 and take turns answering the questions to "My Daily Routine" (p. 107). Use "How to Form Groups" on the next page to help everyone find a smaller group.

- Welcome everyone and introduce the speaker for the seminar.

- At the end of the seminar, ask a church member who is struggling with this particular issue to stand up and announce a new support group on this topic. Pass around a sign-up sheet and some flyers, and an outreach group is born.

Notice how this agenda emphasizes fun and community-building. With proper planning and preparation, you can offer a support seminar that provides practical help and builds new friendships. Then, for your first support group meeting use the agenda outlined on the previous page.

Pulling it off ...

You will need a planning team to effectively launch an outreach group. These people should have small group experience, good social skills and compassion for those who do not know Christ (see "Organize Your Planning Team," pp. 299–304). Specific tasks for this team might be identifying a relevant topic, mailing information to the community (see "Promoting Your Event," pp. 306–311), hosting the meeting and finding a qualified speaker. Another important feature of offering a successful outreach group is knowing what topic is most relevant to the people you are hoping to reach. Besides telling your community that your church cares enough to inquire about their needs, a good survey will indicate seminar topics likely to bring the best response (see "Surveying Your Target Group," p. 302). Finally, be sure to have well-prepared materials. As with any outreach effort, whatever you can do to make everything run smoothly will only help people feel more comfortable (see "Gather and Prepare Materials," p. 303).

HOW TO FORM GROUPS

Anytime you have a large group of people, forming smaller groups quickly is important—and fun! Use the following ideas to create such groups.

1. Name tags can be a good way to form smaller groups. Use different-colored name tags and then group the blues, greens, etc. together. Further divide groups with different symbols, such as smiley faces and stars.

2. Group people by the season or month of the year they were born.

3. Group people by where they would like to go on their next vacation: the mountains, the beach or a city.

4. Group people by the time zone they were born in (Eastern, Central, Mountain, Pacific and "other").

5. Use the following choices to divide groups in two:

   "Would you rather_____ or_____?"

   read a book . . . . play cards
   make your bed . . . . leave it unmade
   go to the opera . . . . go bowling
   ask for directions . . . . keep searching
   do yard work . . . . do laundry
   go on a blind date . . . . go out with friends
   wash the car . . . . wash the dog
   eat sushi . . . . clean the toilet

6. Divide people by the kind of shoes they are wearing: with laces or without laces.

7. Group people by their favorite type of music: Gospel, Jazz, Country, Rock, Pop or Classical.

8. For two other options, look at "Find Your Song Members" and "Find Your Puzzle Members" on page 62.

CHOOSING A LEADER

Sometimes a group of people need to choose a leader for an activity or Bible study. Take turns answering one of the questions and then vote on the best answer. The winner gets to be the leader!

1. How many speeding tickets have you had in the last six months?

2. How many pets do you have and what are their names?

3. Who was born closest to or farthest from this location?

4. Whose birthday is closest to today?

5. Who has celebrated the most momentous milestone in the last year?

6. For youth: Who had to stay after school or go to the principal's office the most times last semester?

7. Who was the youngest person to kiss a member of the opposite sex (besides a family member or relative)?

8. Who has the most interesting story about something that happened to you on vacation?

9. Who has the best story about how their parents met?

10. Who has had the worst job experience?

11. Who has had the most memorable holiday misadventure?

12. Who has had the most embarrassing moment?

13. Who has had the worst experience with bureaucracy?

Group Leaders' Retreat

A retreat for small group leaders can fulfill many different goals. You can have a retreat to let new leaders experience the magic of community and fellowship. You can have a retreat to provide further training for small group leaders. You can also host a retreat for small group leaders to say "thank you" for the job they have done.

Make the effort to determine what would be most beneficial for the small group leaders. By doing so, you can adjust the format of the retreat to meet their needs. For example, if the leaders need more "tools," the retreat could focus on multiplying groups, listening skills or problem solving. If the leaders are new, the retreat could focus on community building, having fun and getting acquainted. If the group leaders are burned-out or feeling overworked, they might need a weekend of affirmation, support and celebration.

The following agenda includes the format for a weekend retreat with three main sessions. This agenda is flexible, depending on the focus of the retreat.

Session 1 (Friday evening)

- Welcome everyone to the retreat and introduce the planning team members.

- Begin with any of the lively Warm-Up Calisthenics, such as "Slap-Downs" (p. 60).

- Next, keep the mood light with one of the Fun Songs, such as "Hokey Pokey" (p. 64).

- Ask everyone to get together with a couple others and take turns sharing their answers to "My Outlook on Life" (p. 106).

- Take a break to let everyone mingle, get a snack or finish settling in.

- After the break, have everyone get in groups of about 8 and play another game like "This Is a Cup! A What?" (p. 73).

- Choose a Bible study that corresponds with your goals for the retreat. If the goal is community building, try "My Uniqueness" (p. 142). If the goal is training, try "The Church" (p. 218). If your leaders need a boost, try "Worries" (p. 184).

- Close with a time of affirmation (such as "Musical Instruments," p. 97), prayer requests and prayer. See "Prayer Ideas" (p. 251) for various methods of prayer that can be used throughout the group leaders' retreat.

Photo Courtesy of Cherry Hills Community Church

245

Session 2 (Saturday morning)

- Prepare "Sonrise Devotionals" for those who want to get up early and have a private time with God.

- Make sure the group is awake by beginning with "Fingers Up" (p. 61) or "Dum Dum" (p. 63).

- After singing and a prayer, this might be a good time for any special presentations or messages.

- Use a group-finding game to create new groups, such as "Find Your Puzzle Members,"p. 62). Or, instead of giving each person a puzzle piece, assign them different farm animals and let them find their group by making the appropriate sound. Oink!

- Get the groups talking with "Warm Memories" (p. 77) or "Find Yourself in the Picture" (p. 78).

- For the Bible study time, use "My Personality" (p. 144) for new leaders who need a taste of community; "Responsibility" (p. 176) for training; or "Down and Dirty" (p. 164) for leaders who feel overworked.

- Close with an affirmation time, such as the "Affirmation Guessing Game" (pp. 98–99). Follow that affirmation time with prayer for one another.

Session 3 (Saturday evening or Sunday morning)

- After a time of singing and worship, have fun with "Shoulder Rub-Down" (p. 60). Have the group stand in one large circle for this activity.

- Use one of the ideas from "How to Form Groups" (p. 243) and then have everyone play "Buzz-Fizz" (p. 72) and "Pass the Balloon" (p. 71).

- Ask each group to take turns answering one of the Biblical Inventories, such as "How's Your Love Life?" (p. 129) or "Be-Attitudes" (p. 132).

- For the Bible study, use "My Spiritual Journey" (p. 202) for new leaders; "Being Real" (p. 154) for training; or "Shattered Dreams" (p. 186) if your leaders are burned-out.

- For an affirmation, use "You Remind Me of Jesus" (p. 137) or try a large group affirmation. For example, each person takes a turn standing in front of a large newsprint pad and writing down positive traits everyone else has noticed about them.

- Close with a time of prayer. Have the group stand in one large circle and take turns completing a sentence prayer, such as "Thank you, Lord, for revealing yourself to me at this retreat by ..."

Pulling it off ...

A retreat is a time to have fun and experience things that are difficult to accomplish at church events. Expect your most powerful memories and life-changing encounters to happen toward the end of the retreat. Most of all, have fun. In an intimate, casual setting, even the stuffiest person enjoys crazy games, laughter and celebration.

Plan your retreat well in advance (see "Create Your Planning Calendar," p. 297). Use your planning team to brainstorm, accomplish particular tasks (pp. 299–301) and make sure each participant has a wonderful time at the retreat. Tasks for your team might include finding a facility for the retreat, inviting all the participants, praise and worship, food and snacks, preparing materials (such as handouts and devotionals), and collecting money. You might wish to have a special events team to organize fun activities like team-building games, skits (including props) and a talent show. A church in Austin, Texas, had a retreat a few years ago for their small group leaders, and had a special team just to welcome each participant and make them feel at home! Finally, be sure to let each person evaluate the retreat (p. 312). They will have great ideas for the next retreat and they would be great candidates for next year's planning team.

Intergenerational Groups

For years, churches have divided people into age-graded programs. This has been popular and successful and provides many advantages. Similar-aged or homogenous groups and classes have an instant appeal for people looking for relationships. Groups like this help people find friends with similar lifestyles. Homogenous groups, however, have limitations. If a group consists of people with similar lifestyles, issues and experiences, the group can tend to see life and God from a similar perspective.

When we interact with people with different lifestyles and in different stages in life, we can be inspired and challenged in new and exciting ways. Intergenerational groups offer these kind of opportunities. For example, in many churches the wisdom of mature believers and the "wildness" of younger believers is separated. However, the younger believers can benefit greatly from the wisdom of others, just as the mature believers can be encouraged and rejuvenated by the "wildness" of a young person's faith.

Mentoring is another built-in advantage of intergenerational groups. While many programs are heavy on "brother-sister" relationships, intergenerational groups offer vertical relationships. This is especially important if a child has only one parent or lives away from grandparents. In addition, younger believers not only observe the faith of older believers, but watch mature believers interact with one another.

Intergenerational or heterogenous groups

are more difficult to get started (though once they begin they are hard to stop!). To make intergenerational groups run smoothly, consider the following principles:

- Pay attention to the model you are using. Imagine your intergenerational group as a rambunctious family sharing their faith and edifying one another. Try to avoid a classroom or lecture model.

- Keep the playing field level. Regardless of the topic, make sure everyone has a chance to respond and contribute in a manner meaningful to each person. If the subject of the meeting is stress, let the children draw pictures of "What drives you crazy?" and "What do you do when you are upset?" while the adults answer discussion questions. Then let everyone discuss their conclusions.

Role-playing and skits are also fun options.

- We all have childhood in common. Allow opportunities for laughter and silliness. Though the entire meeting does not need to be childlike, including activities both children and adults can enjoy will build the foundation for meaningful fellowship.

- Keep it simple. Anyone can pray a sentence prayer. Anyone can relate to a Bible character. Anyone can talk about their day, their friendships and their struggles.

- Use a group covenant (p. 54). You may want to emphasize that everyone is encouraged to participate and that all questions are respected, so that the

younger participants will feel more comfortable; and that the older group members should keep in mind that unsolicited advice-giving can be very detrimental to a group.

- Keep biological families in the same group. After an initial six- or eight-week series of meetings, give family members an opportunity to join other groups. Smaller families, such as a single mother and child, might choose to stay together.

- Keep the group composition balanced. The best intergenerational groups will have equal numbers of younger, older and middle-aged people.

- Do what you can to encourage mentor relationships. Consider "mentor training." Help older believers take advantage of their potential to guide and influence a younger member of their group. For the benefit of other church mem-

bers, highlight those meaningful cross-generational relationships which have come from the intergenerational groups.

Here are some meeting ideas for intergenerational groups:

- Begin with a Crowd Breaker, like "Slap-Downs" (p. 60), "Head, Shoulders, Knees, Toes" (p. 60), "Rabbit" (p. 63) or "It's a Small World" (p. 65). Or start with one of the Group-Building Games (pp. 68–73), such as "Imaginary Ball," "One Frog," or "Pass the Feetball."

- After everyone is seated, let everyone take turns with a Conversation Starter such as "Find Yourself in the Picture" (p. 78) or a Pop Quiz like "Family Fun Times" (p. 81) or "Moon Trip" (p. 81).

- For the Bible study, make sure the younger participants can relate to the topic. Also, surveying each group to

determine the topics they are most interested in is a good idea. Use the listing of the different Bible study topics (p. 141) as a ballot for group members to vote on the topic they would enjoy the most. For younger members, have plenty of crayons, modeling clay and other materials for them to use to express themselves.

- Use one of the Affirmation Games on pages 92–103. Affirmation is an especially valuable part of an intergenerational group.

- Close with prayer (see p. 251), making sure that everyone in the group can contribute to the prayer time if they choose to do so.

Pulling it off ...

Include intergenerational small groups within the context of your current or upcoming small group program. Simply expand your planning and promotional efforts to include children, youth, singles and families. You might wish to recruit some of the people from your planning team (p. 299)—and their children—to join an intergenerational group to "test the waters." These people can help with promotional efforts, such as interviews during a worship service or other church event (p. 309). Also, make sure any effort you make to survey your congregation (p. 302) includes topics that members of all ages can relate to.

See the next section, "Small Group Kick-Off" for a full description of how to begin a small group program.

Small Group Kick-Off

A full-scale, churchwide kick-off is a great way to start a small group program. You can even begin your small group program with a variety of different types of groups: discipleship groups, support groups, outreach groups, intergenerational groups ... whatever your church needs!

The *Serendipity Encyclopedia* offers dozens of valuable ideas and tools to help you launch your small group program successfully. You already have "The Ideal Meeting Agenda" (p. 237), "How to Decide on a Beginner Group Covenant" (p. 54) and "Prayer Ideas" (p. 251). Now you need to get the groups started ...

Pulling it off ...

In a nutshell, you cannot plan too much to effectively kick off a small group program. Begin by creating your planning calendar (pp. 297–298). Many churches have had good results with a fall kick-off, corresponding to the semesters of the school year. Give yourself plenty of time to complete each part of the planning process.

As you gather your planning team (p. 299), find people who appreciate the small group concept. These are people with small group experience, but not necessarily group leaders. Be sure to include small group components in your planning meetings, including your introductory meeting (p. 299). You can also lead a six-week trial run (p. 300) to assure that all of your team members know exactly what small groups can provide. After a brainstorming ses-

sion (p. 300), begin to identify the different tasks (p. 301) that need to be done to kick off your small group program. The teams that need to be recruited (p. 302) might include:

- Group Leader Training Team
- Survey Team
- PublicationsTeam
- Promotion Team
- Phone Team
- "Small Group Sign-Up Fair" Team
- Support Seminar / Outreach Team
- Intergenerational Small Group Team

Meanwhile, add each task to your planning calendar! This way you can monitor your

teams (p. 304) and give them the attention and support they deserve.

After you have begun to train your small group leaders, you can start gathering the materials (p. 303) you plan on using in your small group program.

About eight weeks before the first groups begin, you can begin promoting (pp. 306–311) your program. Any of the ideas listed in this section will help you promote your small group program. Work with the promotion team to schedule the different promotional events you plan to use. Specifically, be sure to let potential group members have a "taste" of a small group experience as much as possible. For example, when presenting the small group

CHECKLIST FOR SMALL GROUP LEADERS

BEFORE THE MEETING

A. Pray for the Group: Pray for every member of the group by name.
- be specific
- be personal

B. Prepare: Here are six areas to focus on as you think about the meeting:
- People: Who is coming and why?
- Arrangement: What needs to be done—seating, temperature, Bible study, child care, music, materials, etc.? Who will do it? Are you sure?
- Relationships: How will you help people feel cared for? What can you do to break the ice? How can you help the group relax, feel comfortable, open up?
- Study / task: What is your agenda? What questions are you going to use in the Bible study? What else do you want to accomplish?
- Prayer: What are the goals for your prayer time? How much time? What kind of prayer? What about those who feel uncomfortable praying aloud?
- How much time is available? How are you going to use it? What is the *real* starting time? Closing time? Are you attempting too much? Too little? Who could take some of the segments?

DURING THE MEETING

A. Use of Time: Keep the group within limits. There are situations where the time use will change according to the need of the moment, but there needs to be an agreed-upon beginning and end to the meeting, as well as approximate time limits for each segment.

B. Flow of Discussion: One of the tasks of the small group leader is to keep the flow of the discussion moving. This is an art picked up by practice, but here are some ground rules for leading good discussions.
- ❏ When you ask a question, give time for people to think.
- ❏ You're the discussion leader ... not the answer person or the final authority on all matters.
- ❏ Assist people to participate, but avoid forcing anyone to answer.
- ❏ Refrain from monopolizing, or being the authority figure.
- ❏ Pace yourself. Getting through all your questions isn't nearly as important as permitting everyone to participate.

C. Interpersonal Communication: During the discussion process, there may be interactions that require you to do some follow-up later on. For example, one person dominates the group, and they do not respond to your redirecting. Make a mental note of these and follow up later on.

AFTER THE MEETING

Care for the members. There are four types of people that especially need to be followed up on:
- those who were absent
- those who were ignored or were silent during the meeting
- anyone who was "attacked" during the meeting
- anyone who is hurting in a special way

Obviously, this model for group meetings is best if you have highly trained small group leaders. But if you do not have this luxury, this model is probably less effective because it is totally dependent upon the skills of the leader. And if the leader is not skilled, or is not in tune with the VISION for the total small group program of the church, the leader may well take the group in another direction or no place at all.

--Roberta Hestenes

concept at a leadership meeting (p. 307) begin the presentation with an ice-breaker and close with an affirmation game. This is the same principle at work in the "Interactive Worship Service" (p. 292)—which is another tremendous way to promote small groups, because it is a large group event modeled after a small group format. Finally, anytime you offer printed materials about your small group program, include a listing of the small groups and a description of each group and how to join.

Don't forget to evaluate your program (pp. 312–313) periodically. Since small groups encourage meaningful communication among church members, use good communication with your team members and small group participants. The same principle is true regarding recognition (p. 314). Just as affirmation is an important component of a warm small group, be sure to affirm your group leaders and team members by giving them the recognition and appreciation they deserve.

PRAYER IDEAS

Many of the events described in this section include opportunities for people to pray together. Some people, however, might not feel comfortable praying out loud in a group. Use this list to choose a method for prayer best suited for a particular group of people.

1. Let a previously assigned person close the group in prayer. Encourage each group member to pray for one another in the coming week.

2. Read a prayer together, such as the Lord's Prayer (Matthew 6:9–13) or the Serenity Prayer.

3. Ask the group to take turns sharing their answers to the question, "How can we pray for you this week?" Have a previously assigned group member pray for the different prayer concerns.

4. Ask the group to share their prayer concerns, then ask for a volunteer to pray for what was shared.

5. As each person shares their prayer concerns, ask for a volunteer to pray for that person. Then take turns going around your group letting each volunteer pray for the concerns which were mentioned.

6. After prayer requests have been shared, ask each person to pray for the person on their right (or left) silently or out loud. After an appropriate amount of time, have a volunteer close the prayer time.

7. During your prayer time, ask each person to take turns completing one of the following sentences. These "sentence prayers" are a good way to encourage someone to begin praying aloud.
   "Lord, I want to praise you for ..."
   "Lord, show me what to do about ..."
   "Lord, I want to thank you for ..."

252

FAMILY EVENTS

Perhaps you have heard people say, "That church is like a family to me!" When was the last time you heard someone say, "My family is like a church to me!"?

In a world where families struggle to stay together, the church is the only institution which can serve as an example for healthy family life. Our churches should set the standard for love, forgiveness and role models. This is especially important for those people who do not have biological families they can turn to for love and support.

This section includes activities and ideas which build on the idea of the church as a family. This means that these events are perfectly suited for biological families. By providing practical ways to help families be better families, a church can fulfill its opportunity to demonstrate what a family can be.

Any of these events can also be used to build intergenerational relationships in your church. Simply include single adults, kids living with one parent, widows and widowers, orphans and couples without children. For example, a church can host a mother-daughter celebration and invite all women. For more information about intergenerational opportunities, see the introduction to "Intergenerational Groups" (p. 247).

Family Fun Night

The key word in this event is fun. Many families are so busy and task-oriented that they need to be reminded how much fun they can have together. A church is the perfect place to provide an opportunity for families to laugh, play and pray.

Though you do not need a reason to offer a wonderful event like this, it can be used for specific purposes. For example, you can have a family fun night if you are going to kick off intergenerational groups (p. 247) or a home devotional emphasis (p. 261).

A family fun night is an event which includes activities appropriate for all ages. Any participant can accomplish each activity; the common denominator is fun. The format is fast-paced. There is no time for boredom or inattentiveness. Also, teaching times are kept short.

Here is a sample format for a family fun night.

- Begin with high-energy large group activities, like "Shoulder Rub-Down" (p. 60). Follow that with some fun songs, like "Row, Row, Row Your Boat" (p. 64) or "It's a Small World" (p. 65). Then do something like "Fingers Up" (p. 61), as you gradually help the group get focused and work off some of their "excitement energy."

- Divide into smaller groups of 8–10 people, using one of the group finders, such as "Find Your Song Members" (p. 62).

Photo Courtesy of Cherry Hills Community Church

Photo Courtesy of Cherry Hills Community Church

Good planning is just as important for a one-time event like a family fun night as it is for beginning an entire program. As you plan this event, you might recruit teams (p. 302) to help gather and prepare materials (p. 303) and promote the event (pp. 306–311) to families in and outside your church. Mailed invitations, phone calls and personal invitations might encourage attendance by a family who are not members of your church. Be sure to include parents and leaders in your church's children's program as you plan this event. You might even consider assembling a panel of young "experts," inviting children and teens to submit their ideas.

Family Retreat

A family retreat can be the perfect way to kick off or strengthen a family or intergenerational ministry. In either case, a family retreat is a wonderful way to emphasize how fun and inspiring family interaction can be.

A key issue regarding a family retreat is the main emphasis. Is the retreat intended to focus on biological families? Or is the retreat open to anyone—either designed to adopt people without biological families (widows, orphans, singles, etc.) into existing ones or a retreat emphasizing the "church as a family"? This decision determines how much "intermingling" is scheduled during the retreat, as opposed to creating more time for biological families to spend together.

The format of this retreat includes three

- Once groups have formed, ask them to pick a name for their group (just for fun). Then play "Pass the Balloon" (p. 71) and "Pass the Feetball" (p. 73). Announce winners and give them a gag gift. Then play a round or two of "One Frog" (p. 72) or "This Is a Cup! A What?" (p. 73).

- Continue to get everyone more focused by moving toward quieter, less active games. Staying in their (named) groups, have them do "Fire Drill" (p. 80). Next, try "I Am More Like ..." (p. 113).

- Remaining in their groups, do the Bible Study "True Friends" (p. 156). For the younger participants, have paper and crayons on hand for them to draw a picture of one of their friends and then explain why that person is a true friend.

- Many of the Affirmation Games (pp. 92–103) will work very well for the mixed ages at an event of this kind. Take a look as well at "Valued Values" and "You Remind Me of Jesus" (pp. 136–137).

- Choose one of the prayer methods described in "Prayer Ideas" (p. 251). Then close the entire evening with one of the Celebration Dances, such as "We Are One in the Spirit" (p. 64).

sessions which can be adapted for a mixed group or a retreat consisting only of biological families. In addition, the following activities can be included in the retreat schedule.

- Fun skits and Bible-story skits
- Campfire activities (stories, S'mors, etc.)
- Praise songs and activity songs
- Noncompetitive large-group games
- Talent show
- Quiet times
- Nature walks and scavenger hunts
- Board games
- Team games and relays, with prizes for everyone

Choose the activities which complement your group and their particular goals and abilities. Don't underestimate the power of a retreat setting to help anyone "let their hair down" and have a fun and uplifting weekend! And don't forget to bring the necessary props, costumes, balls, gunnysacks and prizes!

Session 1

This session is designed for a family retreat which includes either biological families or a church family:

- First, settle in with some family time. If your retreat includes people who did not bring their biological family, assign them one! Put a single person and a widower with the Jones family and add Mr. and Mrs. Whozit to the Smith family.

- Start with a game, such as "Rhythm" (p. 70), "One Frog" (p. 72) or "Pass the Feetball" (p. 73). Next, spend some time getting acquainted. For biological families begin with "My Outlook on Life" (p. 106). For a mixed group use "My Daily Routine" (p. 107) or "My Favorites" (p. 106).

- Once the family groups have had a chance to connect, begin several large-group activities for everyone to join. Begin with some of the Calisthenics and Tension Breakers like "Slap-Downs" (p. 60) and "Fingers Up" (p. 61). Next, do some Nonsense Rhymes and Fun Songs, such as "Dum Dum" (p. 63) and "Hokey Pokey" (p. 64). When these activities are complete, welcome the group, introduce the emphasis of the retreat, and make any important logistical announcements.

- After a short break, move back into the family groups. Ask each group to do one of the Biblical Inventories, such as "Be-Attitudes" (p. 132).

- Close with an Affirmation Game within each of the family groups. "Automotive Affirmation" (p. 94) or "Musical Instruments" (p. 97) are good choices.

- Remind each group to close by sharing their prayer concerns and then close with someone leading a prayer for the entire group, while the family groups stand in a circle and hold hands.

Photo Courtesy of Cherry Hills Community Church

Session 2

The final two sessions begin with large-group activities and then move to family-group activities.

- Begin with everyone gathered in a single large group. Have fun with a song like "Hokey Pokey" (p. 64) or a dance like "It's a Small World" (p. 65). Rhymes like "Rabbit" or "Harry" (p. 63) are also great ways to get large groups loosened up.

- Moving to the family groups, begin with a Conversation Starter, like "Find Yourself in the Picture" (p. 78). Then do an activity like "Magazine Collage" or "Wire Sculpture" (pp. 87–88). A biological family might enjoy "Your Family Crest" (p. 89). If time allows, ask each group to make a "Group Banner" (p. 90). Be sure to let each group explain their creation.

- Next, ask each group to complete one of the Bible Studies, such as "My Abilities" (p. 148). You might wish to have each group choose a leader by taking turns responding to one of the questions under "Choosing a Leader" (p. 244).

- Do another affirmation exercise. "Colors" (p. 92) or "Strength Bombardment" (p. 93) are two possibilities.

- Close with each group sharing their prayer requests. Ask for a volunteer in each group to close the session by praying for the concerns expressed in their group.

Session 3

It is a good idea to remain flexible during this final session. Give the Holy Spirit plenty of freedom to work in the lives of each person and each family group. Remain sensitive to those activities which seem to be especially meaningful, so you won't end a great experience just to remain on schedule.

- With everyone in one large group, begin with some Warm-Up Calisthenics or Tension Breakers, such as "Shoulder Rub-Down," "Morah," or "Mirror" (pp. 60–61). Then sing some songs, including "Love Round" (p. 64). Close your large-group time with "We Are One in the Spirit" (p. 64).

- Back in family groups, try some Group-Building Games, such as "Motormouth" (p. 68), "Categories" (p. 70) or "Sculpturing" (p. 71). Groups that are composed of biological families might

Photo Courtesy of Cherry Hills Community Church

256

do "Reminiscing Choices" (p. 77), and mixed groups might do "Warm Memories" (p. 77). Depending on the available time, one of the Sensory Exercises can be powerful, such as "Trust Walk" (p. 74) or "Choose Your Apple" (p. 75).

- For the Bible study time, try "Being Real" (p. 154) or "My Spiritual Journey" (p. 202) for mixed groups. For groups composed of biological families, use "Family Expectations" (p. 160).

- Allow extra time for the affirmation and prayer time during this session. For affirmation, try "You Remind Me of Jesus" (p. 137) or "Thank You" (p. 138).

- For the prayer time, you might bring the groups together and ask questions like, "How has God spoken to you during this retreat?" and "How can the group pray for you?" Instruct the group to pray for one another by standing in a circle and taking turns completing the sentence prayer, "Lord, I want to praise you for ..."

Pulling it off ...

To successfully plan your family retreat, follow the "Pulling it off" guidelines for the "Group Leaders' Retreat" (p. 246). Try to develop a planning team which consists of leaders from the various age-group programs which will be represented. Also, additional tasks for your planning team might include gathering props and game materials and organizing the different "family groups" (if the retreat is open to more than biological families).

Father-Son Rally

Like any "family" event, a father-son rally can be literal or figurative. As a literal father-son event, a rally like this can be valuable if the fathers in your church need help parenting their sons. This rally can be offered to begin men's prayer groups, a father-son camp out, or even ministry teams (such as home repair or prison ministry).

When conducted as a figurative event, a father-son rally can be used to begin a "mentoring" emphasis, which builds relationships between older and younger men. These relationships provide guidance for the younger men while taking advantage of the wisdom of

older men. In this case, any male in your church can attend (though a lowest-age limit might be suggested). If you include single men, widowers, or young men without a father "on the scene," take special care to pair up the participants in order to make an effective match.

Options for this event include inviting specific groups to "fill the gaps." If you need more older men, invite widowers or retired men who live away from their biological families. Or invite young men or boys who are church members but live with their mothers. You could even use a father-son rally so older men could "adopt" young men from an orphanage, youth shelter or boys' ranch. Finally, you can invite men of all ages and organize them into multigenerational groups.

This would involve organizing the rally by forming groups consisting of a boy under 12, a teenage boy, a young man, a middle-aged man and an older man.

The format for this event is a single session, lasting approximately two hours. This session can be conducted as a church event, at a retreat, or at a church-sponsored barbecue, fishing trip or skeet shoot.

- Begin with several large-group events. Depending on your group of men, it might help to have a musician or amateur comedian get everyone laughing or singing. If the group begins with singing, ease them into a few fun songs, such as "Row, Row, Row Your Boat" (p. 64) or "Head, Shoulders, Knees, Toes" (p. 60). You can also get the group loosened up with "Harry" and "Dum Dum" (p. 63).

- After everyone is either laughing or embarrassed, begin a game of "Serendipity Bingo" (p. 62). Then get everyone organized in groups according to their biological families. If your rally is open to men in addition to biological families, use matching name tags to help everyone find their partner(s) (see the first suggestion in "How to Form Groups," p. 243).

- Next, have everyone gather in groups of 6–10. Play a couple of games like "Buzz-Fizz," "One Frog" (p. 72) or "Motormouth" (p. 68) if you have more than a few young boys. Then have each person take turns with some get-acquainted activities such as "My Favorites" (p.

106), "My Temperament" (p. 114) or "Reminiscing Choices" (p. 77).

- Follow with one of the Group-Sharing Bible Studies. Different groups will require different topics, but "Being Real" (p. 154), "Friendships" (p. 152) and "Priorities" (p. 172) are good choices.

- Do not miss the time for affirmation. "Strength Bombardment" (p. 93) and "Automotive Affirmation" (p. 94) are good. Then have the actual father-son pairs sit together. Ask these pairs to take turns affirming one another by adapting the "Power People" (p. 124) and "Valued Values" (p. 136) exercises.

- Finally, ask all the pairs to return to their groups of 6–10 and close by sharing their prayer concerns. You may want to ask the oldest member of each group to close by praying for the concerns that were shared.

Pulling it off ...

For your planning team (p. 299), be sure to gather a group of men of different ages. You can even include an older boy or teenager on the team. Test some of the proposed activities with your planning team, by conducting a trial run (p. 300). Some of the specific tasks (p. 301) of your planning team might involve planning the fishing trip or cookout which will include the rally, inviting men and boys from different church programs, and grouping young men and older men in appropriate pairs.

One sure-fire way to promote your event

(pp. 306–311) is to put a flyer about the rally above the urinals in the men's restrooms in your church!

Mother-Daughter Celebration

Just like the father-son rally, the mother-daughter celebration can be limited to biological mothers, daughters and grandmothers, or it can be open to any woman. This event can be offered to strengthen families, begin or strengthen a women's ministry, start a women's Bible study or support group, or simply be offered periodically on a stand-alone basis.

While women might be more comfortable with social conversation with other women, both men and women need encouragement to communicate with one another in ways that are inspiring and biblically edifying. This mother-daughter celebration encourages affirmation, responding to Scripture, and group prayer. It can open doors between women and between mothers and daughters, encouraging them to share their faith with one another on an everyday basis.

Options for this event include building the event around particular themes. For example, the celebration can have a holiday theme, include a crafts presentation, a cookie or recipe swap, or even a fashion show. Also, consider the particular topic of the Bible study time. Relevant themes might include relationships with men, relationships with other women, expressing emotions, spiritual growth, or support and recovery issues. Be aware that a theme like parenting will exclude some of the participants.

This event includes the following format, which will take about two hours. Be sure to keep the celebration tightly structured to avoid slipping into a merely social gathering.

- Begin with some Warm-Up Calisthenics and Fun Songs, such as "Head, Shoulders, Knees, Toes" (p. 60) and "Hokey Pokey" (p. 64). Follow with a Nonsense Rhyme like "Rabbit" or "Dum Dum" (p. 63).

- To help everyone find a small group (6 to 10 women), write the name of different songs on the back of each person's name tag and have them whistle that song until they find their group members who are whistling the same song (see "Find Your Song Members," p. 62). Make sure the mother-daughter pairs and the mother-daughter-grandmother trios are kept in the same small group.

- Next, play a Group-Building Game, such as "Rhythm" or "Categories" (p. 70). Then help everyone get acquainted with "My Outlook on Life" (p. 106) or "Miss America" (p. 113). Follow that with "Wallet (Purse) Scavenger Hunt" (p. 76). For the Bible study, try "My Personality" (p. 144) or "Worries" (p. 184).

- Go around the circle for the affirmation

time, with each person affirming the person on their right with "Recognition Ceremony" (p. 93). Then get each mother-daughter pair to affirm one another by choosing an animal, a vehicle and a boat to affirm one another from "Affirmation Guessing Game" (pp. 98–99).

- Close in prayer by returning to the groups of 6 to 10 and taking turns sharing prayer concerns. You might want to

ask the oldest member of each group to pray for the concerns that were shared.

Pulling it off ...

Successfully planning this event is similar to planning the previous event, "Father-Son Rally." Use your planning team (pp. 299–304) to add the finishing touches, such as decorations and snacks, which can make this event thoroughly special.

Home Devotional Kick-Off

Many churches know the value of having a weekly or monthly home devotional. A home devotional is a time when the family gathers together for prayer and Bible study. This kick-off is a time to demonstrate, to each family member, what a home devotional consists of.

The kick-off is approximately an hour to an hour-and-a-half "trial run" of a typical home devotional meeting. The church supplies the materials and simply walks the family through the format.

- To get everyone settled, begin with a few Crowd Breakers (pp. 59–65). Then give an introduction of the concept and a prayer.

- Next, in an open area with plenty of space between groups, ask each family to sit in a circle, knee-to-knee.

- Begin with a fun activity, like "Imaginary Ball" (p. 68), "Buzz-Fizz" or "One Frog" (p. 72). (Mention that after a few meetings, families can skip directly to a discussion starter.)

- Then ask each group to take turns answering a discussion starter such as "Family Fun Times" (p. 81) or "Precious Time" (p. 109).

- Move quickly to a Bible study such as "My Uniqueness" (p. 141) or "Family Expectations" (p. 160). Mention that

each family can choose their own Bible study topic when they begin their home devotionals. Ask the parent with the most speeding tickets to lead the Bible study, but encourage each family to share the leadership role.

- Close with a time of affirmation and prayer. Go around the circle affirming one another with "Strength Bombardment" (p. 93). Finally, take turns sharing answers to the question, "How can we help you in prayer?" Ask the leader to pray for the different concerns that were shared. Mention that each family can choose to close in prayer using any of the methods mentioned in "Prayer Ideas" (p. 251).

Pulling it off ...

One important feature regarding the successful implementation of home devotional meetings is making sure each family has sufficient materials (p. 303). One way to solve this issue is to provide each family with a *Serendipity Encyclopedia* and a simple listing of suggested exercises for the meeting format:

- Discussion Starter
- Bible Study
- Affirmation Exercise
- Closing Prayer

Or, you can create home devotional booklets each week which contain the materials each family will need for each meeting.

If finding time to meet is a struggle for some families, encourage each family to discuss the "group covenant" (p. 54). Besides helping families discuss meeting times and priorities, they can also discuss ground rules like confidentiality and advice-giving.

Also, be sure to get feedback (p. 312) from each participating family. Ask the children if they enjoyed the meetings. You might need to add special activities to keep the younger children interested, such as crafts or games. Contact each participating family periodically to make sure everything is going smoothly.

YOUTH EVENTS

Serendipity and youth events have a long, wonderful history. Many youth programs enjoy Serendipity material and enjoy great meetings, rallies and retreats. The material in this section will help any youth leader design excellent, life-changing events.

The fun and excitement that teenagers bring to a youth program (and their faith in general) is a tremendous asset to any church. The *Serendipity Encyclopedia* encourages different age groups within a church to share their strengths, and a youth group is no exception. For this reason, try to include other age groups in your youth events. By inviting different adult church members to participate in your youth events, you can avoid the limitations of a "15-year-old body of Christ," which occurs when a youth group becomes too isolated from the church as a whole. The *Serendipity Encyclopedia* focuses on what people have in common and encourages people to get together based on the commonality of their faith, their everyday lives and their capacity to have fun.

Please note the process of the youth events. Each meeting or session gradually moves toward a time of trust and openness. This is especially important for teenagers. Many young people are insecure or feel awkward as they make the transition between childhood and adulthood. Unfortunately, middle schools, junior high schools and high schools can be places of insults, cliques and bravado. A youth event needs to be a safe place, without put-downs and rejection, where

Photo Courtesy of Cherry Hills Community Church

a young person can feel loved and accepted. Keep the Serendipity process in mind as you plan and orchestrate the various events described in this section. A youth event which moves gradually to a warm affirmation activity and a time of mutual prayer can have a remarkable impact on a teenager.

In addition, following a tight schedule, even if it includes "wacky" activities, will help kids feel safer and secure (especially middle schoolers). What a young person experiences at a church function can be more meaningful than what they hear or learn.

Here are some suggestions which might provide some helpful ideas as you consider planning a youth event. First, consider the location of your meetings. Make sure there is sufficient space for any large group activity and good space for the small group time. If possible, arrange chairs in small circles so each person can sit close to their small group members and talk freely without having to speak too

loudly or risk being overheard. Developing trust begins when you arrange the furniture!

Second, occasionally mixing different ages and genders can be valuable. Older kids need to see themselves as role models and leaders for younger kids, and younger kids need to observe older kids "in action." Also, letting guys and girls talk with one another, especially about personal topics, can help each participant experience healthy interaction with members of the opposite sex.

Finally, be sure to add your own pizzazz to any of these meetings. Pull out the guitar and sing or let some kids do some funny skits. Take advantage of the talent and enthusiasm of the kids in your youth program!

Awesome Bible Study Meetings

If your youth program includes frequent Bible study meetings, this encyclopedia will be a tremendous addition to your efforts. By following the format listed below, and choosing games and Bible study topics best-suited for your young people, each meeting will be a priceless opportunity for spiritual growth, friendship and smiling faces.

- Begin your meeting with a Crowd Breaker, like "Hokey Pokey" (p. 64) or "Serendipity Bingo" (p. 62).

- Getting everyone from one large group to several small groups (4 to 6 members) can be fun. See "How to Form Groups" (p. 243) or give everyone a slip of paper with an animal or appliance written on it. Then tell everyone to find their group members by acting like the animal or appliance. No talking, sound effects only!

- When the groups are formed, do some Group-Building Games like "Pass the Balloon" (p. 71) or "One Frog" (p. 72).

- Next, spend a few moments getting acquainted—with one of the self-disclosure spectrums, such as "Mr. / Miss America" (p. 113) or one of the multiple-choice exercises, like "TV Quiz Show" (pp. 110–111).

- For the Bible study, choose one of the Group-Sharing Bible Studies for each group to discuss. "Being Real" (p. 154) or "Worries" (p. 184) are good choices if you do not have a particular topic in mind.

- After the Bible study time, have each group close with a time of affirmation. "You and Me, Partner" (p. 96) or "Automotive Affirmation" (p. 94) are two possibilities.

- For the prayer time, choose one of the prayer methods listed under "Prayer Ideas" (p. 251).

Pulling it off ...

Having a planning team (p. 299) assist with something as frequent as a weekly Bible study meeting can be a tremendous help. Also, getting input from others helps keep the

Photo Courtesy of Cherry Hills Community Church

event fresh and lively. Try to include young people in the planning process. Teenagers might not tell you if something is boring, but they might tell a teenage member of your planning team.

Gathering and preparing materials (p. 303) is important to an effective Bible study meeting for youth. Giving each participant the material they need will help them feel confident that the meeting is well-planned and predictable. A young person who is unsure about what to expect during the meeting might feel unsettled and less likely to let his or her guard down.

"Hot Issues" Retreat

A youth retreat can fulfill a variety of different functions in a youth program. A retreat is a great way to kick off a new semester or welcome a new group of fifth or sixth graders as they advance into the youth department. A youth retreat is also a tremendous way to introduce the young people to new leaders or adult participants. The retreat setting is also a super way to give older teenagers an opportunity to develop their leadership skills. Letting a high school junior or senior lead a Bible study or group discussion can be less intimidating in an informal setting.

The informal, away-from-church setting of a retreat has other advantages. A retreat can be the ideal place for a group of young people to talk openly about the critical or "hot" issues facing them in their everyday lives.

The following schedule is for a weekend retreat which includes four main sessions. This allows for a Friday evening session, a Saturday morning session and then recreation on Saturday afternoon. This is followed by a Saturday evening session and a Sunday morning session.

Session 1 (Friday evening)

This session is primarily a time for everyone to work off some excess energy, learn about the retreat format and say "hello." Supplement the activities listed below with plenty of music, snacks and time for "settling in."

- Begin with some singing and Warm-Up Calisthenics, like "Slap-Downs" (p. 60). Then try one of the Nonsense Rhymes such as "Dum Dum" (p. 63).

- To get everyone mingling, try a game called "Who Am I?" Each person has a name of a famous person or character (Tiger Woods, Winnie-the-Pooh, Sleeping Beauty, Santa Claus, etc.) taped to their back. Each person tries to be the first to guess who they are by asking one another only yes or no questions about their identity.

- Find a fun way to get everyone into small groups of 4 to 6 people. Try one of the group-finding Mixers (p. 62) or an activity from "How to Form Groups" (p. 243). Have several methods for forming groups ready because this first session will involve a lot of "group-switching" to help everyone connect with one another.

- For the first small group activity, play Group-Building Games like "Motormouth" (p. 68) and "Rhythm" (p. 70).

- Move everyone into new groups and try one of the Kick-Off Sentences, such as "My Favorites" or "My Outlook on Life" (p. 106).

- Next, change groups again and take turns answering "Who Influences You?" (p. 122) or "Lifestyle Checkup" (p. 115).

- In the final new group, use the Biblical Inventory "The Armor of God" (p. 130), and let the group members affirm one another with "Broadway Jobs" (p. 95).

- Close with a time of prayer (see "Prayer Ideas," p. 251).

Session 2 (Saturday morning)

The next two sessions follow a similar format, focusing on Bible study and discussion of the "hot issues" most important for your group.

- Begin by getting the group settled and focused by singing "Head, Shoulders, Knees, Toes" (p. 60) and then playing "Mirror" (p. 61).

- Use "Find Your Song Members" (p. 62)

YOUTH RETREAT IDEAS:

Magazine Collage: Give the group the following instructions: "Leaf through a pictorial magazine or daily newspaper and tear out some pictures, words, slogans, want ads, etc. that reveal who you are: (1) Your interests, (2) your self-image—how you see yourself, (3) your special abilities, and (4) your outlook on life. After 10 minutes, collect your "tear-outs" and paste them on a sheet of newsprint or poster paper. Then, get together with one or two others and explain your 'self-portrait.'"

Blind Volleyball: Divide the players into two equal groups. The two teams then get on different sides of a volleyball court and sit down on the floor in a row, as in regular volleyball. The "net" should be a solid divider that obstructs the view of the other team, such as blankets hung over a regular volleyball net or rope. The divider should also be low enough that players cannot see under it. Then play volleyball. Use a big, light plastic ball instead of a volleyball. Regular volleyball rules and boundaries apply. A player may not stand up to hit the ball. The added dimension of the solid net adds a surprise element to the game when the ball comes flying over the net.

Suitcase Relay: Divide the group into equal teams—as many boys as girls. Give each team a suitcase. In each suitcase is a lady's dress and a man's suit—complete with shirt and tie. On the word "GO," a first couple (guy and girl) from each team must run with their suitcase to the opposite end of the room, open the suitcase, and put on everything in the suitcase—the guy putting on the lady's dress and the girl putting on the man's suit. Then they carry their suitcase back to the starting line and take off the dress and suit. Put the clothes back into the suitcase and hand the suitcase to the next couple. The first team to complete the relay wins.

to get everyone into groups of 6 or so for the small group time. Be sure to choose fun songs!

- Once small groups have been formed, play a short game like "Buzz-Fizz" (p. 72) or "This Is a Cup! A What? (p. 73).

- Spend a moment taking turns talking by answering "Risky Business" (p. 116) or "My Best and Worst Side" (p. 109).

- Choose any of the Bible Studies in the Values or Issues categories (see p. 141) which fit the needs of your group. Supplementing the topic with a skit can be fun and helpful.

- After the Bible study, let the group members affirm one another with "Wild Predictions" (p. 103) or "You and Me, Partner" (p. 96).

- Let each group close in prayer using one of the methods under "Prayer Ideas" (p. 251).

Session 3 (Saturday evening)

As the retreat progresses, be aware of the need to adjust the schedule to meet the needs of the participants. Adding a snack break, a time for questions, a special prayer session or an invigorating round of calisthenics or active games can help keep the group on track.

- A song or rhyme is a great way to get the group going after a day of recreation. Try "Hokey Pokey" (p. 64) or "Harry" (p. 63).

- To help everyone find their group for this third session, use "Find Your Puzzle Members" (p. 62).

- Since each new small group needs to spend some time "connecting," play "Sculpturing" (p. 71) or "Pass the Feetball" (p. 73) to get them started. Then do "Three Facts / One Lie" (p. 85) or "Family Fun Times" (p. 81).

- Choose another "hot topic" for the Bible study.

- For the affirmation time, use "Recognition Ceremony" (p. 93). Close with group "sentence prayers" (see point 7 on p. 251).

Session 4 (Sunday morning)

The format of this session will be different from the previous two sessions. This session will remain a large group format, much like a worship service. The secret to this session is to allow plenty of singing and plenty of opportunities for sharing.

- Begin with prayer and singing. By this stage in a retreat, worship will be very important.

- Give a short presentation on the "hot issues" facing your group. Give everyone a chance to respond to how they will face those issues in the future.

- Read the Scripture passage for "A High Standard" (p.131). Have everyone work on a copy of this Biblical Inventory on their own.

- Give each person an opportunity to share what they have learned during the retreat in general, or this exercise in particular, or what they would like prayer about. Pray in response to what was shared.

- Affirmation can still happen in a large group. Stand or sit in a circle. The group will take turns affirming each person in the circle. Give everyone copies of "Valued Values" (p. 136) and "You

WEEKEND RETREAT:

Objective: (1) To build a close-knit community inside of the youth group, and (2) to deepen the spiritual life of the youth group.

Time: Friday night through Sunday noon.

Leadership: The youth pastor or leader should build a youth ministry team to assist in this retreat.
- Retreat Director
- Group Coordinators—a counselor for every 4 to 7 kids
- Recreation Coordinator
- Cook
- Music Director

FRIDAY NIGHT
Group Building
Game Plan

- Crowd Breakers / 40 minutes
- Groups / 50 minutes
  - Group-Building Games
  - Communication Games
- Singing / Wrap-Up Talk / 20 minutes

SATURDAY MORNING
Groups / Bible Study
Game Plan

- Singing / Calisthenics / 10 minutes
- Groups / 50 minutes
  - Concentration Games
  - Communication Games
  - Bible Study
- Wrap-Up Talk / 20 minutes

SATURDAY AFTERNOON
Dog Patch Olympics

Have the Olympics well organized so that no time is wasted finding the equipment, etc. The group coordinators and camp speaker should be involved directly in some way.

SATURDAY NIGHT
Affirmation Bible Study
Game Plan

- Calisthenics / Skits / 10 minutes
- Groups / 60 minutes
  - Group-Building Games
  - Affirmation Games
  - Bible Study
- Wrap-Up Talk / 20 minutes

SUNDAY MORNING
Worship / Commissioning
Game Plan

- Singing / Calisthenics / 30 minutes
- Groups / 60 minutes
  - Final Talk
  - Lord's Supper
  - Commissioning

Remind Me of Jesus" (p. 137). Go around the circle and affirm one person at a time. Let three or four people step forward and affirm that person using one of the descriptions listed in these activities.

- Remaining in a circle, hold hands and close in prayer. A leader can pray, "Lord, we praise you because ..." and let people in the group, beginning at your right or left, complete the phrase.

- Close this session and the retreat with one of the Celebration Dances, such as "We Are One in the Spirit" (p. 64).

Pulling it off ...

As you select and gather your planning team (p. 299), try to include a variety of people who have retreat experience. This way, when the planning team has their brainstorming session (p. 300) about the retreat schedule, they can speak from their own retreat experience. As you consider the different tasks (p. 301) for your team members (see also the "Pulling it off" instructions for the group leaders' retreat (p. 246), assign someone to recruit older youth to be leaders during the retreat. These leaders can lead small groups, lead recreation time and take on other responsibilities. Recognizing these leaders, affirming them and praying for them will help them understand their opportunity to be a role model for others.

Surveying your group (p. 302) to determine what issues are most critical to them is an obvious way to make the topics of the Bible studies more relevant. Also, preparing materials (p. 303) is important to the success of this retreat. Putting together a booklet of the various activities you plan on using for each session can help everything run smoothly. Finally, prepare an evaluation form (p. 312) for each person to complete before they return home, or mail the evaluation form to each participant with a return envelope.

Outreach Party

One of the most appealing features of your youth program is the group itself. Young people are going to judge a church more by what they experience than by what they hear in a sermon or Bible study. An outreach party lets nonattending or unbelieving teenagers see God at work in your youth group. This event is fun and gives everyone plenty of opportunities to get acquainted and make new friends.

This outreach party is not designed for a full-blown Bible study or sermon, though a brief Gospel presentation might be appropriate. The event should be fun and include music, skits, snacks and a variety of group activities. Two hints which will help make this outreach party a success: First, keep the format moving along quickly. "Dead time" with nothing happening can make newcomers nervous and bored. Second, make sure everyone is greeted and given something to do when they arrive. No one, especially a teenager, wants to stand around by themselves before things get started.

Location is another important factor when planning an outreach party. Having the event on "neutral ground" (like a lake house, park clubhouse, recreation center, etc.) is a great way to meet people halfway. You can even include the suggested format with a swimming party or other active, fun event.

The following format can be used anytime your youth group has invited their friends and classmates to an event. Recognizing that young people are deeply social, emphasizing relationship-building is a great way to expose a newcomer to your group.

- After welcoming everyone, present a funny skit by some of your youth group members.

- "Serendipity Bingo" (p. 62) is a great Crowd Breaker, especially if some of the participants are new to the group and might not be ready for singing or dancing.

- Using name tags or a similar equivalent (see "How to Form Groups," p. 243), put everyone in groups of 6 or so. Quickly do "One Frog" (p. 72). Then move to "Mystery Person" (p. 86). Be sure to have pencils and pieces of paper available for this exercise.

- Next, either in new groups or in the same groups of 6, play another Group-Building Game, such as "This Is a Cup! A What?" (p. 73), and then do "My Favorites" (p. 106), perhaps asking each person to answer three of the 10 questions.

- Moving quickly between activities (and groups), do "Find Yourself in the Picture" (p. 78) or "I Am More Like ..." (p. 113). Now you can do a short Bible study using the same quick format. Have each group discuss "How's Your Love Life?" (p. 129).

- This would be a good time for a Gospel presentation. Or ask one of your youth to tell how their encounter with Jesus

Photo Courtesy of Cherry Hills Community Church

has affected their life.

- Keeping everyone in their most recent groups, close with a time of affirmation. "You and Me, Partner" (p. 96) or "Automotive Affirmation" (p. 94) will both work in this situation. Finally, let each person answer the question, "How can we pray for you?"—and then have a volunteer in each group pray on behalf of everyone in their group.

Pulling it off ...

Besides including teenagers on your planning team (p. 299), this might be a good opportunity to get another church group involved in the youth program and outreach. Perhaps some single adults or senior adults would be interested in helping with the planning of this event.

To get a feel for the event itself, walk through the outreach party. A trial run (p. 300) will help you and your planning team make any necessary improvements and adaptations.

As you delegate the different tasks (p. 301) for your planning team, consider jobs like finding a facility, preparing materials (p. 303), skits and music, and promotion (p. 306). Creativity is the key for promoting an event like this. Ideas include windshield flyers (for high school students), distributing "free tickets," a school newspaper ad, or putting up flyers in school hallways. Personal invitations, however, are always most effective.

SOAR LIFE GROUPS

Old Time Sects and Violence, a LIFE Group studying the gore stories from the Bible and doing other fun stuff.

His Hands, a LIFE Group committed to service projects and studying the Scriptures.

Servants, a LIFE Group committed to community service projects.

Athletic Supporters, a LIFE Group of kids supporting other kids by attending each other's sporting events, plus Bible Study.

Families in Flux, a LIFE Group ministering to teens affected by divorce.

Action, a LIFE Group studying current events and a Christian perspective on such events.

Hikers, a LIFE Group for hikers studying friendship and planning a few hikes.

Plant Jesus, a LIFE Group about being a Christian in today's world (to save the world, you gotta know the world).

Goal Keepers, a LIFE Group of soccer players studying the Scriptures and playin' the game.

Rock-A-My-Soul, a LIFE Group looking at different styles of rock music and some Christian bands that offer the same sound but with a Great Message!

Crown, a LIFE Group studying the biblical principles of money management and stewardship.

Spirit-filled Hard Core, a LIFE Group of students interested in the Christian hard-core music scene, playing CD's, videos, and looking into the message of the lyrics.

Girl Talk, a LIFE Group about being a beautiful young lady (on the inside and out).

Jesus Jam Unplugged, a LIFE Group of student musicians and singers who want to jam praise songs and write new music together.

--East 91st Street Christian Church, Indianapolis, IN

Prayer and Share Groups

Helping a young person establish a habit of a daily devotional time with God is not easy. A prayer and share group, composed of 4 to 8 young people, is one way to begin this spiritual discipline. These groups can meet for about 30 minutes and do not require an adult leader. An older teenager can lead younger ones. The concept is simple: A group meets before school on the bus, in a classroom, on the school yard or any quiet place. They begin with an opening discussion starter, read a Scripture passage and answer four or five questions about the passage, and close with a time of prayer. By simply putting the material in the hands of the participants in an easy-to-use format, you can help the teenagers at your church take their faith into their everyday lives.

Here is an example of the format for one session of a prayer and share group:

- Begin with a simple discussion starter. "I Dream of Genie" (p. 112) and "Mr. / Miss America" (p. 113) are examples of fun ways to get a group talking.

- Then move to a Bible study. Choose a topic which would be appropriate for your group. Since these groups involve taking their Christian faith into their weekday lives, "Peer Pressure" (p. 158), "Sharing Your Faith" (p. 168), and "Morality" (p. 178) are obvious possibilities. After reading the Scripture passage, answer the questions that follow.

- Close with a time of prayer. In addition to asking, "How can we pray for you?" encourage prayer requests based on

the topic of the lesson. For example, if the study is about peer pressure, ask, "How can the group pray for you as you deal with peer pressure?"

Pulling it off ...

Of all the different ways to prepare for an event, there are two ways to make sure these prayer and share groups go well. First, prepare your materials (p. 303) properly. Give each prayer and share group leader handouts which include a discussion starter, a Bible study with the appropriate discussion questions, and appropriate prayer request questions. By simply copying the various activities from this encyclopedia, you can give each prayer and share group the material they need for a great meeting. Second, evaluate your efforts regularly (p. 312). Ask the participants of each prayer and share group how

much they are enjoying their experience. Since you will not be there to observe each group, evaluation is extremely important.

Parents' Night

Inviting parents and older adults to an event which encourages interaction with teenagers is a lot of fun and rewarding as well. One way to approach an event of this kind is to promote it to parents as an opportunity to experience a youth meeting first hand. The benefits of this are obvious. It can be a great way to encourage support for the youth program among older church members. It can also help recruit additional youth leaders. Giving parents a chance to meet one another and enjoy a time of fun and sharing can also help build relationships among the parents who can be developed into leadership teams and support committees. In addition, a parents' night can help draw younger or uninvolved teenagers into the youth program in the future.

Letting adults and parents experience the fun and craziness that goes on at a youth meeting can also stimulate the faith of these older visitors. Many people, especially those who grew up in church, look back fondly on the fun they had when they were involved in youth programs as teenagers.

The following format for a parents' night can be used in two different ways. One way involves putting parents and their own children in small groups at the appropriate time of the meeting. The other option puts kids and adults together in a random fashion. The advantages of each choice are obvious. If the young people need some quality, guided time with their own parents, keep families together. If the teenagers would benefit from interacting with adults other than their parents, use a random method for forming small groups.

• After an official "welcome," announcements, singing and/or skits, begin with a Fun Song like "Hokey Pokey" (p. 64) and a Nonsense Rhyme like "Dum Dum" (p. 63). Add to the fun with a round of "Serendipity Bingo" (p. 62), and offer a gag gift to the winner.

• Depending on the format you have chosen, form small groups of 6 or so according to families, or use a random group-making method like "Find Your Song Members" (p. 62), or a combination of the ideas listed in "How to Form Groups" (p. 243).

• Help each small group get acquainted and loosened up with some Group-Building Games like "Pass the Balloon," "Sculpturing" (p. 71) or "Buzz-Fizz" (p. 72).

• Use a Conversation Starter to get the groups talking. "Find Yourself in the Picture" (p. 78), "Things That Drive You Crazy" (p. 121) or "Life Signs" (p. 120) are some suggestions. Use one of the methods listed under "Choosing a Leader" (p. 244) if you need to identify someone to keep the group on track.

• For the Bible study, choose any topic which you feel is suited for your group, or use "Family Expectations" (p. 160), "My Uniqueness" (p. 142), "Friendly Fire" (p. 166) or "My Spiritual Journey" (p. 202). The Bible study you choose

might depend on whether or not your small groups have been formed according to families or formed randomly.

• A time of affirmation is an extremely valuable part of an event of this kind. Use "Automotive Affirmation" (p. 94) or "Valued Values" (p. 136).

• Close in prayer by asking each group to take turns answering the question, "How can we help you in prayer?" Ask a parent or teenager in each group to close the meeting in prayer.

Pulling it off ...

Certainly, the most important task as you plan an event like parents' night is promoting the event (pp. 306–311). Keep this in mind as you recruit your planning team (p. 299). Recruiting teenagers and adults with strong social skills is a good idea. Also, look for people who might not be the most active churchgoers. Sometimes people who are less active church members have more friends and acquaintances who do not have a church affiliation. An event like this is a great way to introduce your youth program to kids and their parents, so direct your promotional efforts beyond your congregation. Similarly, this event is a tremendous way to attract inactive parents whose children are involved in the church and to attract inactive teens whose parents are active church members.

SINGLES EVENTS

Church-based programs for single adults meet important needs in many people's lives. Besides providing valuable opportunities for social interaction, singles programs encourage spiritual growth and Christian fellowship. Churches of every heritage have opened their doors to single adults, whether they are divorced, widowed, or never married.

One important challenge for any singles program is to balance opportunities for socializing and spiritual growth. Too many well-intentioned singles programs have lost their vision of discipleship and over-emphasized social events. The *Serendipity Encyclopedia* includes many activities which can be used to plan events which are socially valuable and spiritually edifying.

Great Bible Studies

One important secret to a successful Bible study is to stop and appreciate the lifestyles of the participants. Single adults enjoy meeting others and they enjoy talking about themselves. (Who doesn't?!) Therefore, plan a Bible study for singles with plenty of opportunities for mingling and discussion. Keeping a tight agenda is also helpful, making it easier for everyone to contribute to the discussion. This is especially important if the single adults in your group include both "Bible scholars" and people without much church experience.

As with any group event, keep the process of the event in mind. Schedule each

activity with a particular goal in mind. In most cases, that goal will be a time of sharing, prayer and affirmation. The Bible studies included in this encyclopedia, for example, use a similar process. Discussion begins about the story (If you had been Peter when Jesus said, "Put out into deep water, and let down the nets for a catch," what would you have done?); and moves to questions about our own lives (How does the call to leave your nets behind and follow Jesus sound to you?).

- Once the group has arrived, begin with some singing. You can also welcome everyone and make announcements.

- Next, try some Fun Songs such as "Row, Row, Row Your Boat" and "Hokey Pokey" (p. 64). Follow this with some

Tension Breakers, like "Fingers Up" and "Morah" (p. 61). By letting everyone pair off for these activities, opportunities are provided for people to meet others.

- To help everyone get in groups of 4–6, try a fun group-finder like "Find Your Puzzle Members" (p. 62). If you have time (and your group is large enough), you might wish to form groups several times, doing an activity or two each time. If so, be sure to check "How to Form Groups" on page 243.

- Once the groups have been formed, start with a game like "One Frog" (p. 72), then use an activity to start discussion. "Reminiscing Choices" (p. 77), "Family Fun Times" (p. 81), and "The Old

Neighborhood" (p. 117) are good choices. Use one of the questions under "Choosing a Leader" (p. 244) to help each small group choose someone to facilitate the discussion.

- The Bible study the groups discuss depends, of course, on the needs and interests of the group. Some groups might benefit most from a study on "Forgiveness of Sins" (p. 204) or "Sexual Desires" (p. 198). Others will benefit from a study on "Spiritual Calling" (p. 224) or "Rebounding" (p. 228).

- Close with a time of affirmation and prayer. For an affirmation activity, "Valued Values" (p. 136) and "You Remind Me of Jesus" (p. 137) are especially uplifting. As people share their prayer concerns, encourage them to ask for prayer related to the topic of the Bible study.

Pulling it off ...

One of the more important things to keep in mind when planning a Bible study for single adults is to seek their input. For example, be sure to survey the group (p. 302) to discover the topic(s) of study which would be most valuable to them. Request feedback (p. 312) frequently to determine if the format and activities are effective and enjoyed by the group participants.

FUN MIXERS FOR SINGLES RETREAT

Scavenger Hunt: Use whatever is in your wallet, purses or pockets. This game is played like an "old-fashioned" scavenger hunt, except this time the teams have to produce the items from things they have in their possession. Forms teams of 6 to 8.

One person acts as the referee in the center of the room. Each team sits in a cluster, equidistant from the referee. The referee calls out an item, such as a shoestring ... and the first team to bring this item to the referee is the winner. Points are awarded to the team based on the "difficulty factor" in obtaining the items. The referee keeps score and periodically announces the score. (If one team is ahead, the referee can equalize the score by awarding a few extra points for the next item.)

Here is a list of items and suggested points. Call out one item at a time. For 1,000 points, the first team to bring to the referee: a sock with a hole in it; picture of Thomas Jefferson (on a 25-cent piece); something that smells; guy with lipstick on; baby picture; love letter; dirty comb; seal of the United States (dollar bill); used ticket; 1982 dime.

For 2,000 points, the first team to bring to the referee: eight shoestrings tied end to end; three shirts on one person backwards and buttoned up; 89 cents in change; three different-colored hair tied together; four shoes that total 29 in shoe sizes ... tied together.

For 3,000 points, the first team to bring to the referee: two people inside one shirt ... all buttoned up; one person with 4 belts, 3 shirts, and 8 socks on; first team to line up in a row according to shoe size.

For 5,000 points, the first team to bring to the referee: the whole team surrounded by a rope made out of socks.

Song Choreography: This activity will help a team work together on a project that is "group building" for themselves and entertaining for others. Form teams of 6 to 8.

Prepare beforehand slips of paper with song titles: old or new. They should be familiar and short. Gather the following props: broom, mop, bucket, an old sheet or blanket (or come up with your own). Give one slip of paper to each team and show them the props they'll be able to use. All the teams are to quickly create a choreography or musical drama—or comedy—out of their song titles using the four props in any way they like.

After 5 or 10 minutes, call everyone together. Then, one by one, have each team put on its act before the entire group. Either the retreat leader or the leadership team could choose the best team. The competition should be judged on the basis of originality, the best use of props, and the overall production.

What's the Product: Beforehand think of 20 well-known advertising slogans. When you are ready to play the game, read most of the slogan, leaving off the name of the product it is promoting. The participants have to supply the name. The player with the most right answers wins. Example: "Just do it."—Nike.

Valentine's Banquet

Valentine's Day can be a fun time for single adults, but it can also be a lonely day. The purpose of a Valentine's banquet is to give single adults of all ages an opportunity to go out and have a great time with other singles.

The format of this event is fairly simple. A dinner is provided and everyone sits together around tables. After the dinner, announcements, and an "official" welcome, the tables are cleared and everyone moves to an open area in the same room. After a series of large group activities, which give everyone the chance to get acquainted, smaller groups are formed around the tables. The event concludes with a time of prayer.

- It's hard to beat "Serendipity Bingo" (p. 62) to get a group like this going. Next, liven things up with Fun Songs like "Row, Row, Row Your Boat" or "Hokey Pokey" (p. 64).

- Forming groups is important because it gives people a chance to get better acquainted and meet someone they've been wanting to get to know. Avoid putting people in the same group they ate with. Try the different ideas from "How to Form Groups" (p. 243).

- Staying with the Valentine's Day theme, get your newly formed small groups talking with "Mr. / Miss America" or "I Am More Like ..." (p. 113). Then go to a Conversation Starter that gives each person a chance to talk about their past, such

as "Three Facts / One Lie" (p. 85). If you have time, do one more activity. "Choosing Friends" (p. 126) is a good option.

- Instead of a full-blown Bible study, have each group use the Biblical Inventory "How's Your Love Life?" (p. 129). This is a challenging discussion which reminds everyone that real love comes from God.

- Let the group affirm one another with "Musical Instruments" (p. 97). Then ask each person to answer the question, "How can we pray for you?" Ask a volunteer to pray on behalf of their group to close the evening.

Pulling it off ...

Gather your planning team (p. 299) and do the necessary brainstorming (p. 300) to prepare the perfect event. Your planning team will need to decide what food to serve, how much to charge for the banquet, details about the dress code (formal, semiformal or casual) and whether or not bringing dates will be emphasized.

Use the typical methods for promoting (pp. 306–311) the banquet at your church, but consider ways to use an event like this to reach new people. Adding live music or a "big band" sound might make your banquet more attractive to nonmembers. Consider using invitations made in the form of Valentine's Day cards to promote the event. Since you will probably be using R.S.V.P., these invitation cards could even be given away at nearby nightclubs, coffee shops or other locations where single adults can be found.

Mingling Party

This event is simply a "get acquainted" party. It can be used at large churches to help people in large singles groups get to know one another. The mingling party is also a terrific outreach event. By taking advantage of the desire of single adults to meet new people, a church can host a mingling party away from the church building and invite single adults from the community to come and meet other single adults.

The basic format of this event is a two-hour, evening party which includes refreshments. The mingling party consists of many fast-paced ways for people to form small groups and take turns sharing their answers to a variety of get-acquainted activities. By the end of the evening, everyone has met everyone else and many new friendships and relationships are formed. Highlight the evening by asking a spiritually mature member of your singles program to share the story of their encounter with Christ. You can even present songs and skits during each "break" to assure a balance between socializing and a spiritual emphasis.

The secret of hosting a successful mingling party is keeping the pace of the meeting fast. Since the event consists of frequent and nonstop formation of small groups (of about 6 people), having a variety of ways to form groups quickly is important. The clever use of name tags can be very helpful. For example, prepare all the name tags in advance, keeping the side where the names are written blank until people arrive. On the back of each name tag, write the name of a song, an animal, a color, an automobile, the seven dwarves, etc. Throughout the evening, people will have to find matches for these different categories in order to form groups. As the evening progresses, have people sing the song on their cards or make the sound of the animal listed on their cards to find their group members. Using the ideas listed in "How to Form Groups" (p. 243) can also help you form groups quickly.

- Get everyone loosened up with some Nonsense Rhymes and Fun Songs (pp. 63–64), followed by a fun game of "Serendipity Bingo" (p. 62).

- Form groups of about 6 people and play "Motormouth" (p. 68), and then discuss "Lifestyle Checkup" (p. 115).

- Form new groups and play "Categories" (p. 70), and then discuss "Lessons in Conflict" (p. 119).

- Form new groups and play "Buzz-Fizz" (p. 72), and then discuss "Things That Drive You Crazy" (p. 121) or "My Temperament" (p. 114).

- Form new groups and play "One Frog" (p. 72), and then discuss "Risky Business" (p. 116).

- Form new groups and take turns answering two or three of the questions under "My Outlook on Life" (p. 106), and then discuss "Life Signs" (p. 120).

- Form new groups and do "Ranking Careers" (p. 125) and "Do-It-Yourself Stress Test" (p. 123).

- Continue like this as time allows, and then conclude with "The One Anothers" (p. 240). Ask each person to choose the "one another" they need most right now. Close by inviting each person to find the "one another" they need at your church, and then lead the group in a prayer.

Pulling it off ...

Use your planning team to test each activity you use to make sure it will work well with your group (pp. 299–301). The greatest challenge for planning a successful mingling party is promotion (pp. 306–311). Promoting this event outside your congregation is almost essential. Radio ads, regionalized mailings or even a billboard will help get the word out about this event. Once you have hosted a mingling party, future mingling parties will be easier to promote.

Spiritual Growth Retreat

Keeping spiritual growth as a priority in a singles program can be a challenge. Offering a spiritual growth retreat is another way to balance the tendency some single adult programs have to over-emphasis social functions at the expense of discipleship and Bible study.

A spiritual growth retreat for single adults does not need to be a cloistered, contemplative or overly-serious event. As a matter of fact, limiting religious discussions to the Bible study and prayer time can help achieve a healthy balance for an event like this. Use activities, songs, skits, talent shows, camp-fires, recreation and discussion starters to encourage a great time of fun and relationship-building.

For the basic format of the spiritual growth retreat, use the agenda listed under "Group Leaders' Retreat" (pp. 245–246). However, for the Bible studies, use "God the Father" (p. 212) for session one, "Jesus Christ" (p. 214) for session two and "The Holy Spirit" (p. 216) for session three. You could even have another retreat later in the year and use "The Church" (p. 218), "The Forgiveness of Sins" (p. 204) and "Resurrection of the Body" (p. 220) Or survey your singles group to see what topics related to spiritual growth would be most helpful to them.

Photo Courtesy of Cherry Hills Community Church

Photo Courtesy of Cherry Hills Community Church

SUNDAY SCHOOL EVENTS

Sunday morning Bible study, or Sunday school, continues to have a tremendous impact on people's lives. Many churches focus on Bible teaching and discussion during the "Sunday School Hour," but encourage social activities and fellowship during other times. Since the friendships made in a Sunday school class are so important to many churchgoers, making a special effort to encourage those relationships can be tremendously rewarding. In addition, a lecture-style class will engage more lifestyle issues if group interaction is encouraged. By giving attention to the relationships among the class members, they will be more likely to bring their "whole selves" in contact with the Scripture.

This section includes several ways for a Sunday school class (or classes) to offer events which supplement the teaching time and help class members build meaningful relationships with one another. A new class kick-off, outreach dinner, multiclass rally, intergenerational Sunday school and a class retreat are discussed in this section.

New Class Kick-Off

Any time a new Sunday school class is formed, it is a worthy investment to devote the first meeting to helping the class members get acquainted. The familiarity that is created will

encourage more discussion, which should make the new teacher happy as well!

This one-hour event focuses on helping everyone get more comfortable with one another while avoiding the awkwardness of the first meeting. This format can also be used to "liven up" a class that needs a boost or help a class get acquainted if several new members have joined.

- Certainly the size of the new Sunday school class is an important consideration as you choose the particular activities for your new class kick-off. For a group of over 10 members, begin with a fun song, such as "Head, Shoulders, Knees, Toes" (p. 60) or "Row, Row, Row Your Boat" (p. 64). For a smaller group, try one of the Nonsense Rhymes, such as "Rabbit" (p. 63).

- To put everyone into groups of 6 or so, try one of the fun Mixers, like "Find Your Song Members" (p. 62). If you form groups several times more people can get acquainted, so you will need to have other group-finding games in mind (see "How to Form Groups," p. 243).

- Play a quick Group-Building Game each time a group is formed. Try "Categories" (p. 70) the first time. Then do "TV Quiz Show" (pp. 110–111).

- For the next group, play "Buzz-Fizz" (p. 72) and then discuss "How Do You Feel About ..." (p. 108).

- For the next group (if time allows), discuss "Things That Drive You Crazy" (p. 121) or "Life Signs" (p. 120).

- After a brief presentation, including an introduction of the new teacher, let everyone share their answers to the question, "What do you hope to get out of this class?"

- Close in prayer, with each small group sharing their answers to the question, "How can we help you in prayer today?" Then have everyone stand in a circle, holding hands while the teacher prays on behalf of everyone.

Pulling it off ...

Organizing a planning team (p. 299) to help kick off a new Sunday school class is a great way to get more people to have "ownership" in the class. Encourage your planning team to discuss how to attract class members (without simply "borrowing" people from other classes). Also, as you promote this event (see pp. 306–311), mention that the class will begin with a get-acquainted party!

Photo Courtesy of Cherry Hills Community Church

Class Retreat / Teachers' Retreat

When a Sunday school class goes away for a weekend, wonderful things can happen. The casual, fun setting of a retreat can provide the perfect balance with a classroom setting. There are several reasons why a Sunday school class might decide to go on a retreat together. A class might simply need to get better acquainted and build community. Or a class might want to focus on a particular topic for a few sessions during a retreat. Also, a class might need to huddle together during a crisis, such as a trauma in someone's life, a teacher leaving town, or a solution to an inter-class conflict.

For the agenda of a Sunday school class retreat, use the format for the group leaders' retreat (p. 245), the single adults' spiritual growth retreat (p. 277) or the youth weekend retreat (p. 264). Adapting these events is important because each Sunday school class will have different needs and issues.

A class retreat has the advantage of being an event for a group that has a history and future together. With this in mind, consider adapting the formats of the other retreats to include some of the Show-and-Tell activities (such as "Group Banners" or "Community Construction" on p. 90) or an affirmation exercise that emphasizes groups rather than individuals (such as "Thank You," p. 138).

The teachers in your Sunday school program or department might need to "get away from it all." This is usually a one-night event, unless special plans are made for a "teacher-less" Sunday school time—like offering a multiclass rally (p. 282) as a large group Sunday morning event for those classes without teachers. A retreat of this kind is a great way to kick off a new Sunday school year, can encourage burned-out or unappreciated teachers, or introduce teachers to one another or a new Sunday school director.

Use the schedule for the group leaders' retreat (p. 245) for the Sunday school teachers' retreat. This format includes several options for the schedule, depending on the needs of the teachers.

Pulling it off ...

For the class retreat, use the class members themselves for the planning team (p. 299). This way, a portion of each class period can be devoted to brainstorming (p. 300) and delegating tasks (p. 301). Specific tasks might include finding a location, planning the recreation, meals and snacks, devotionals, etc.

For the teachers' retreat, expecting the already-busy teachers' to plan their own retreat is not recommended. A planning team can be formed from each of the teachers' classes. This will result in a planning team that is motivated by their gratitude for their teacher. Give the planning team opportunity to brainstorm and invent creative ways to host a retreat that will bless the lives of the Sunday school teachers.

Photo Courtesy of Cherry Hills Community Church

Outreach Dinner

Many Sunday school classes would like to reach out to friends and family who are not active in a church, but they don't know how to get started. By hosting a dinner party for the purpose of outreach, a class can get organized and rally around the event.

This event is a simple evening dinner or party for the purpose of introducing friends to members of the Sunday school class. After dinner or dessert, an announcement is made that everyone is going to do some activities to get better acquainted. After a few activities, everyone is invited to attend the Sunday school class. A class member might also talk briefly about how the class has impacted his or her life or share about their encounter with Christ.

• As with any outreach event, proceed with caution. Songs and nonsense rhymes might be too embarrassing for someone not affiliated with a church. "Serendipity Bingo" (p. 62) is a great way to get a group going. Or if the group is small enough, jump right into a discussion starter, like one of the Kick-Off Sentences on pages 106–107—such as "My Outlook on Life." Ask each person to take turns sharing their answers to three or four of the questions listed with the activity you have chosen. "TV Quiz Show" (pp. 110–111) is another good option.

- Either in small groups (for an event like this, simply ask everyone to gather in groups of 5 or 6) or in a single large group, play "Final Jeopardy" (p. 126) or "Things That Drive You Crazy" (p. 121). Two great activities to use if you keep the whole group together are "Old-Fashioned Auction" (p. 79) and "Medical History" (p. 120).

- Close with "Life Signs" (p. 120). Then thank everyone for coming, introduce the subject of your class and invite everyone to attend. At this time you can ask someone to talk about their experience in the class.

Pulling it off ...

The main key to success in an event like this is helping everyone encourage one another as they consider inviting their friends. Devote sufficient time during your planning meeting (p. 299) or Sunday school class meetings to letting people talk about some of their reservations or anxieties about inviting people to a church event. By allowing empathy, encouragement and prayer, the group can find strength from one another. Then you can brainstorm (p. 300) and delegate different tasks (p. 301).

Multiclass Rally

Sometimes it's just fun to gather everyone together for a great time. Sunday school, especially age-graded programs, tends to iso-late people according to their age and life stage (such as parenting). A multiclass rally, held periodically, can introduce people from different Sunday school classes and help build relationships.

A multiclass rally can be offered in several ways. You could find an open, unoccupied space and gather all the classes from a particular department for a multiclass rally. Or you could combine two different generations, such as young adults and senior adults, and encourage the building of mentoring relationships. A multiclass rally could also be offered for several classes of all different age groups and life stages, resulting in a truly mixed group.

Since this event has definite time constraints, starting on time and moving quickly through the activities is essential.

- Begin with Warm-Up Calisthenics, like "Slap-Downs" or "Shoulder Rub-Down" (p. 60). Encourage everyone to join activities with people who are not in the same Sunday school class.

- Sing a Fun Song like "Love Round" (p. 64) or "Head, Shoulders, Knees, Toes" (p. 60). Follow this with a Nonsense Rhyme (p. 63).

- Help everyone find a group, either using "Find Your Song Members" (p. 62) or with the help of a coded name tag. Forming smaller groups of 6 or less will keep each activity moving quickly. Then try a Group-Building Game, such as "This Is a Cup! A What?" (p. 73). Ask each group to take turns answering one of the Kick-off Sentences like "My Daily Routine" or "Down Memory Lane" (p. 107).

- Continue forming new groups as you have time, being sure to remind everyone to meet people outside their own Sunday school classes. Each time a group is formed, play a quick Group-Building Game like "Categories" (p. 70), "Buzz-Fizz" or "One Frog" (p. 72). Follow the games with any of the discussion activities, such as "Robinson Crusoe" (p. 108) or "The Old Neighborhood" (p. 117); though you might wish to move to more serious activities as the rally progresses, such as "Do-It-Yourself Stress Test" (p. 123) or "Lessons in Conflict" (p. 119). "The One Anothers" (p. 240) can be especially meaningful when everyone is asked, "Which of the 'one anothers' do you need most today?"

- Close by asking each group to share their prayer concerns and then choose one of the "Prayer Ideas" (p. 251).

Pulling it off ...

To get started, form a planning team (p. 299) composed of people from the various classes who will be a part of the multiclass rally. Encourage the teachers of these classes to see the value of these events and remind the teachers that these rallies will rarely interrupt their teaching efforts.

Most likely, once the first rally or two has been conducted, grassroots enthusiasm will help the most when it comes to promoting (pp. 306–311) this event. Since your target groups are clearly defined, let members of your planning team—or preferably people who have already participated in a multiclass rally—share their experience with classes scheduled to participate in upcoming rallies.

Be sure to gather feedback (p. 312) as each class participates in a multiclass rally. Since asking people to leave their normal Sunday school routine is a significant request, evaluating feedback will help keep the multiclass rallies meaningful and effective.

Intergenerational Sunday School

An intergenerational Sunday school class is similar to an intergenerational small group (p. 247). All of the principles of intergenerational interaction listed on pages 247–248 hold true when people of different ages gather for a Sunday school class. Pay special attention to the fact that a lecture-style meeting will not be effective for younger participants.

The biggest difference between an intergenerational small group and an intergenerational Sunday school class is the amount of time available for each meeting. Typically, Sunday school classes have about 50–75 minutes to conduct their meetings. This will mean adapting the proposed format on page 248 in order to fit the available time. Not doing a Crowd Breaker and a Group-Building Game will probably result in a meeting format that will fit in the time allowed.

Try a test run (see p. 300) before opening the doors to new intergenerational Sunday school classes. Resist the temptation to pick

active, socially-adept church members for your trial run. Form a test group that is representative of the Sunday morning attenders.

This will give you a more accurate picture of how the classes will operate when everyone is invited to join.

OTHER EVENTS

What is the most valuable asset in your church? The people and the relationships they share with one another! Anytime believers are gathered together is a time to build relationships. And anyone with the love of Christ to share has something wonderful to offer! Take advantage of every opportunity to build trust, encourage affirmation, and invite kindness and laughter.

In addition to the small group, family, youth, singles and Sunday school events already described in this encyclopedia, other events can also be done with an emphasis on relationships. This section tells how to conduct a new member orientation, recognition banquet, weeknight prayer supper, committee meetings, apartment outreach party and an interactive worship service.

New Member Orientation

A new member class or new member orientation can be much more than teaching someone about your church. New member orientation is a tremendous opportunity to prepare members to be a vital part of your church. One key question must be answered: In addition to the information you want to give and receive from new members, what do you want them to experience?

If you want your church to be a place where people can develop and enjoy mean-

ingful relationships, you can use new member orientation to set a precedent. By including relationship-building activities in your new member orientation, two things happen: Your new members get to build relationships during the orientation itself *and* they learn how to develop other relationships in future church events. If new members learn from the very beginning that your church places a high priority on relationship-building, they will carry that expectation with them throughout their church involvement. You can show, right off the bat, that your church is much more than sitting passively in a classroom or worship service. You can demonstrate that church is a place where faith is expressed as each member shares their lives with one another.

As you plan your new member orient-

ation, you will need to consider the experience you want each new member to have as well as the information you would like to present to them. Use the activities in the *Serendipity Encyclopedia* for the "experiential" components of your new member orientation, including having fun, getting acquainted, prayer and affirmation. The "informational" components of the orientation can easily be combined with the experiential ones. Here is some of the information you can include in your new member orientation:

- An introduction to the church staff and leadership.
- A walking or video tour of the facilities.
- A summary of the different ministries and how to get involved.

- An explanation of your church's beliefs
- A presentation on denominational history
- Membership requirements
- Assessments: Life issues, talents, spiritual gifts, etc.
- Testimonies and introductions of current church members
- How to get information about church activities
- Church finance and giving information

Each church has a different format for their new member orientation. One session will be outlined below, but different activities can be plugged in to fit the number of sessions offered at your church.

- Regardless of the size of the group in your new member orientation, begin with an activity to help everyone relax. Tension Breakers (p. 61), Fun Songs (p. 64) and Nonsense Rhymes (p. 63) will certainly do the trick. If the group is fairly large, a game of "Serendipity Bingo" (p. 62) will also get everyone laughing and mingling. Two other games you could use before breaking up into smaller groups are "Old-Fashioned Auction" (p. 79) or "Medical History" (p. 120).

- When you form groups, keep in mind that large group presentations can be done while everyone is sitting in small groups of 5 or 6. "Find Your Puzzle Members" (p. 62) is a great way to form groups. Use "How to Form Groups" (p. 243) for future sessions. Also, consider inviting current members of different ages to attend a session of your new member orientation.

Certainly new members need to meet more than other new members!

- Once the small groups have been formed, spend a moment encouraging everyone to get acquainted. One of the Kick-Off Sentences (pp. 106–107), such as "My Fantasy World," is a good choice.

- At this time you can begin to present information. Switching to small group activities, such as Multiple-Choice Options (e.g. "Precious Time," p. 109), Self-Disclosure Spectrums (e.g. "Lifestyle Checkup," p. 115) and Personal Inventories (e.g. "My Risk Quotient," p. 123) balances lecture with interaction.

Balancing the presentation of information with interactive activities reinforces the idea that your church is a place of relationships as well as learning.

- Be sure to close with a time of affirmation and prayer. Many of the Affirmation Games can be used, such as "Strength Bombardment" (p. 93) or "Wild Predictions" (p. 103). Use the prayer time wisely. Choose one of the options listed in "Prayer Ideas" (p. 251) to close each session of your new member orientation. Have a goal in mind of the prayer experience you would like each new member to gain before they finish new member orientation.

Pulling it off ...

Since promotion is not a big concern with this event, you can pay extra attention to your planning team (p. 299). Members of the church staff and other leaders might be part of the planning team, but strive to include input from other church members. For best results, include church members who have been members for various periods of time. Long-time members and relatively new members can each provide valuable insight into the assimilation process.

Your planning team can each take on the different tasks you identify (p. 301). Some of these tasks might be informing membership candidates about upcoming new member orientation, preparing orientation materials, recruiting current members to be involved in a session, and following up to assure that new members have found their niche in the church.

In regard to gathering and preparing materials (p. 303), it is recommended that a booklet be produced which includes everything a new member would need during the orientation. This booklet should include all the group-building activities and their own copy of the information that is presented. Try to make the informational material creative and interesting. Rather than simply listing the staff members of the church, you could include a "Match-the-Minister-with-the-Ministry" game. Some churches have included spiritual gifts assessments and other self-discovery tools in their written materials.

Evaluation (p. 312) is also important. Plan on asking new members one month, six months and one year after they have completed the orientation if the new member orientation was effective in preparing them for their church experience.

Recognition Banquet

Let's face it, a church is run on volunteer energy. Paid staff members can only do so much, and it is the time and effort offered by laypeople that make any church thrive.

Unfortunately, it is hard for an overworked minister or church leader to take the time to recognize and affirm a layperson's hard work. Taking a volunteer for granted can weaken any organization. Whatever the cause, from the Lions Club to working to promote God's kingdom, anyone who donates their time appreciates a hearty "thank-you."

A recognition banquet is an event designed to let the volunteers and lay ministers at your church know how much they are appreciated. Everything from the meal to the entertainment to the activities should be considered a gift to all those people who work hard for your church and its programs. Have a nice meal in a nice setting. Include some wonderful music or other entertainment. Let the ministers say "thank you." Let the people who have been helped by the work these people have done also say "thank you." Give trophies, door prizes, gift certificates, pins, coffee mugs—anything to bring a smile and express your gratitude (it doesn't need to be expensive).

Of course, add some fun and relationship-building to your recognition banquet. Sometimes people get so busy with their particular task or program that they do not get to

know people hard at work in other parts of the church. The following activities will not take very long and will be a wonderful addition to the banquet.

- Begin with a fun Crowd Breaker (pp. 59–65). You could play "Old-Fashioned Auction" (p. 79) with the whole group.

- Quickly form small groups of 4 to 7. Use one of the methods found on page 62 or in "How to Form Groups" (p. 243).

- Then ask each person in each small group to take turns responding to one of the activities listed under Kick-Off Sentences, such as "My Favorites" or "My Fantasy World" (p. 106).

- End by asking the groups to take turns answering the question, "Why are you being recognized for your church involvement?" After everyone has shared their story of volunteering, close with a time of affirmation. "You Remind Me of Jesus" (p. 137) or "Valued Values" (p. 136) are ideal choices. This affirmation in small groups assures that every volunteer in your church will be given a verbal, face-to-face affirmation. When this is done, ask everyone to stand up and give everyone a standing ovation!

Pulling it off ...

Put the details of planning this event on a calendar (pp. 297–298), so that nothing will be overlooked. Regarding the formation of a planning team (p. 299), the greatest difficulty will be finding people to volunteer to help organize the event who don't already have responsibilities. You certainly do not want to ask people to plan their own recognition banquet! This is one event in which the church staff will probably have to be heavily involved.

Brainstorm (p. 300) with your planning team about ways to honor these committed volunteers. Fun and creativity are most welcome at an event like this! As tasks are identified and delegated (p. 301), they might include identifying everyone (don't forget anyone!) who should be invited, planning the meal, securing speakers, providing awards, gifts and prizes, and getting some whiz-bang entertainment. Keep in mind that an event like this will require some money to be successful.

Weeknight Prayer Supper

Since the earliest days, the church has enjoyed wonderful fellowship around the dinner table. Many churches have weeknight dinners which include Bible study and prayer. To recapture the joy of seeing church members eat together and then inspire and encourage one another, use the *Serendipity Encyclopedia* to make those dinners even more special.

This event includes a dinner and a large group ice-breaker, followed by a small group time of Bible study, affirmation and prayer. After several weeks of different small groups, your church family will be strengthened by dozens of new and warm relationships. Serendipity has a tablet of placemats for church suppers which you can order by calling 1-800-525-9563.

Decide if you want to keep families together or encourage people to mix and mingle, making new friends. Regardless, you will need to keep groups small and close togeth-

er. Asking everyone to sit around a long, "lunchroom" style table to engage in meaningful conversation will prove difficult. Just make sure that each discussion group is no larger than 5 or 6 people and everyone can hear each other using normal voices.

- Begin with everyone at the supper singing some Fun Songs (p. 64) and enjoying a Nonsense Rhyme (p. 63) or two.

- In small groups, get everyone involved in a Group-Building Game (such as "Rhythm," p. 70) and a Multiple-Choice Option ("My Best and Worst Side," p. 109, for example).

- If you are including younger people, choose a Bible study that someone of any age can enjoy. Any of the Bible studies included in this encyclopedia will work well. Use one of the questions under "Choosing a Leader" (p. 244) to identify someone to facilitate each group.

- Next, ask each group to do one of the Affirmation Games, such as "Colors" (p. 92) or "Automotive Affirmation" (p. 94).

- Close with prayer. Let each group member answer the question, "How can we support you in prayer this week?" Share several options from "Prayer Ideas" (p. 251) and let each group choose how they will pray.

Pulling it off ...

Use your planning team (p. 299) to provide ideas for this event. Identify ways to make the transition to a new way of doing an established event (a prayer meeting). Try this new format once and then request feedback (p. 312) to find out how people felt about the event.

Another important component to pulling off a weeknight prayer supper is the proper preparation of materials (p. 303). A fun way to make the materials available to each person is to make placemats. Using 11" by 17" paper, print the material for the evening and put one at every seat. You could even put coloring activities or games on the back for younger children. Or you could order placemats designed for all ages from Serendipity. Order one tablet for every eight people.

After the first successful supper, be sure to promote the event (pp. 306–311) to the rest of the church. People will want to know if something fun is going on!

Committee Meetings

A committee meeting? Adding fun and relationship-building activities to a committee meeting? Isn't a committee meeting a time to make decisions, determine policy and plan the budget? What good would games, conversation starters and affirmation do in a committee meeting?

Actually, quite a lot. A church should never operate under the assumption that administration is more important than edification. Besides, a committee will function with greater effectiveness if the committee members learn to appreciate one another as friends and fellow believers, rather than mere acquaintances on the same committee. At any rate, what is the real "business" of a church if it is not love, encouragement and heartfelt communication?

Adding relationship-building activities to a committee meeting is different than adding activities to other events. Most committees function on their own with a set agenda. To make the most of a committee meeting, you can give the resources and encouragement to the head of the committee and ask them to include a few quick components in their meeting. You could visit each committee, perhaps at the beginning of the year, and explain the nature of the meeting additions.

- The new format is very simple. An icebreaker is used at the beginning of the meeting. (See the listing of exercises on pages 67–68 and 105.) "Find Yourself in the Picture" (p. 78) is a great activity for a committee to do. Similarly, "Sculpturing" (p. 71) is a great activity

for a task-oriented group like a committee. A Kick-Off Sentence, Personal Inventory or Ranking could also be used (see p. 105).

- Helping a committee close their meeting properly is also important. Any of the Affirmation Games, especially "Frog Temperaments" (pp. 100–101) are good choices, as are the Serious Affirmations, including "Valued Values" (p. 136) and "You Remind Me of Jesus" (p. 137).

- Finally, by providing tips on how to close a meeting in prayer (see "Prayer Ideas," p. 251), the committee meetings at your church will become a time of spiritual growth in addition to a time of decision-making.

Pulling it off ...

Helping the committee chairperson understand the importance of adding these activities to their meetings is the secret to improving the committee meetings at your church. This can be done by explaining that every church event should include a few moments of edification and these activities don't need to take much time. In addition, would you mind if the word got around that committee meetings were an uplifting and enjoyable experience?!

Photo Courtesy of Cherry Hills Community Church

Give each committee chairperson a page of instructions including information about the specific activities they can use. You might even wish to give each committee leader a copy of the *Serendipity Encyclopedia* with recommendations about the activities which are well-suited for a committee meeting.

Apartment Outreach Party

This event is another way to take your church to the people who need it most. Great concentrations of people live in apartment complexes, and if you have a church member who lives in the same complex you can invite those people to your church.

One way to accomplish this is to plan a party with some people from your church and a church member who lives in the complex as host. Have the party in the clubhouse or other common area and invite everyone to attend if they want to find out about your church. This party is designed to help people get acquainted and let those people who are interested in finding a church home get to know members of your church.

Be sure to explain in advance that the party will include some fun and nonthreatening games and activities. Notice that the agenda following does not include much religious language or the kind of religious activities you would find in a church setting. Instead, you can demonstrate the importance of building relationships and demonstrate that your church cares about the felt needs people

face. You can address these needs by choosing activities which focus on the real-life issues all of us face everyday, such as stress.

- Get everything rolling with a game of "Serendipity Bingo" (p. 62), and encourage the church members who are in attendance not to try to win the game by interacting with one another. Give a prize to the winner.

- Using color-coded name tags, form groups which consist of both church members and guests from the apartment complex. Make sure the groups consist of no more than 8 people.

- Take a moment to let everyone share their answers to a discussion starter, such as "Down Memory Lane" or "My

Daily Routine" (p. 107).

- Then move to the "Do-It-Yourself Stress Test" (p. 123). This is a simple, voluntary way for people to let their guard down about what is really going on in their life. "Find Yourself in the Picture" (p. 78) is a similar option.

- Close by inviting everyone to your church and, if possible, handing out flyers or brochures about your church. If you have time and your guests aren't too restless, have a previously chosen church member tell their story about what your church means to them. End the party with a prayer, remembering to mention, in general terms, the events in our lives which cause stress.

Pulling it off ...

Your planning team (p. 299), most likely needs to include a resident of the apartment complex where you are hoping to host your party. This team needs to include people who are outgoing, spiritually mature and who have a heart for sharing Christ with people who are not involved in a church. Some of the tasks (p. 301) of this team might include providing refreshments, decorations, promotion, prayer and follow-up.

Promotion (pp. 306–311), of course, is critical to an event like this. Though many apartment complexes do not allow door-to-door solicitation, you can place flyers around the complex and even mail invitations to each resident. Your mailing could also include a survey (p. 302). Be sure to include the name and, preferably, a photograph of each church member who is a resident of the complex and helping host the event. If possible, encourage every invited person to call those church members who are residents of the complex if they have any questions. Also, if the phone numbers of the entire complex can be obtained, residents can be invited with a phone call.

Interactive Worship Service

This is a wonderful event you can do in place of your normal Sunday morning worship service. An interactive worship service basically brings a small group agenda to the entire con-gregation. This event is easier to accomplish at some churches than others, but it can be adapted to show the whole church the wonderful things that happen in a small group.

An interactive worship service can be used to help kick off a new small group program or small group emphasis. This event can also be offered for a "fellowship" or "community" emphasis.

The set-up for an interactive worship service is important. First of all, consider the seating in your sanctuary or worship space. If you have pews, consider having this event in another location, such as the fellowship hall.

However, this event can be a tremendous success, pews or no pews! Also, you might need to set up a few microphones throughout the room. An interactive worship service encourages sharing and some churches will need microphones for everyone to hear one another.

- Begin your interactive worship service with some Fun Songs, such as "Love Round" (p. 64). Then, as you sing songs and hymns throughout the service, let people raise their hands or go to the microphones to request the songs that they would like the congregation to sing.

Photo Courtesy of Cherry Hills Community Church

292

- Then play a game of "Serendipity Bingo" (p. 62). You could even customize this game to match your congregation. For example, you can change some of the boxes to read "Has been on a church retreat," or "Has parked in a visitor parking space."

- If space allows, gather everyone into groups of 4 to 6. Do this quickly by saying, "Find three or four people you don't know very well and sit in a tight circle." After a game of "Serendipity Bingo" this will be easier than it sounds.

- In the small groups, play a quick game of "One Frog" (p. 72), and then ask everyone to take turns sharing their answers to three or four of the questions in "Down Memory Lane" (p. 107).

- Choose one of the Bible studies (such as "The Church," p. 218). Instead of a minister reading the Scripture passage, ask for a volunteer to go to a microphone and read the passage. You can ask several people to read different parts of the same passage.

- Next, as you go through the questions, let volunteers come to the microphone and share their answers. Or if everyone is already in small groups, let them share their answers in their groups.

- For affirmation, combine all the different options in "Affirmation Guessing Game" (pp. 98–99) and ask people to think of church members they know. (You might read 1 Corinthians 12:22–23 to remind everyone to remember the less noticeable people in the church.) Then let volunteers go to a microphone or stand up and read the three qualities they chose to describe someone and then give that person's name.

- Finally, open the floor for everyone to share their prayer requests. Close by asking everyone to hold hands and pray for one another. End the service by singing "We Are One in the Spirit" (p. 64), with or without the dancing.

Pulling it off ...

An event like this is surprisingly easy to pull off, especially when you consider the tremendous rewards an interactive worship service can bring.

The two greatest concerns for your planning team (p. 299) will be making sure the room is prepared and, in place of the normal "Order of Worship," create the materials (p. 303) everyone will need to participate. Other tasks might include having team members carry microphones to each person who wants to speak (which also keeps someone from dominating the time) and volunteering to "go first" if members of the congregation are reluctant to speak.

Photo Courtesy of Cherry Hills Community Church

PLANNING YOUR SERENDIPITY EVENT

Photo Courtesy of Cherry Hills Community Church

STEPS FOR EFFECTIVE PREPARATION

PLANNING YOUR EVENT

A smooth, successful event does not happen by accident. A two-hour rally can take weeks of planning and a top-notch retreat will demand months of preparation. This section contains suggestions and ideas for successful event planning. Simply use the different planning methods in the order they are presented. For specific planning ideas, each event in the previous section includes tips for planning that particular event in the suggestions sub-titled "Pulling it off."

Many of the events described in the previous sections will be new to your church. Consequently, the planning required to prepare for these events will be new as well. Take the opportunity to revitalize the typical event planning at your church by planning these new events thoroughly and effectively. Many times, the difference between average event planning and great event planning is how significantly someone's life has been touched.

The essential component to any effort to plan a church event is prayer. Prayer, in this case, captures your dependence upon God to share his power and purposes in the lives of the participants. As you plan, pray frequently and ask God, in his sovereignty, to let your efforts be blessed by the presence of his Spirit. It can be too easy to maintain a reliance on our own ideas and energy to achieve the kind of results which are far beyond our ability or comprehension. Remind yourself and your planning team that God cares deeply about the event you are working so hard to accomplish. Finally, be sure to include prayer in any planning meeting.

This section is divided into three main areas: "Planning Your Event," "Promoting Your Event" and "Preparing for Future Events"—which discusses "post-event" tasks that serve to improve the quality of the event each time it is offered.

Photo Courtesy of Cherry Hills Community Church

In this section pay special attention to two things: your calendar and your planning team. Having a calendar in your hands throughout the planning process will be extremely helpful. In regard to the planning team, select the people carefully, monitor their progress frequently and give your planning team plenty of thanks and recognition.

Create Your Planning Calendar

Once you have chosen the date you are going to have your event, it is time to start filling in your planning calendar. As different tasks are identified, add them to the calendar so you can keep an accurate assessment of the progress your team is making. Add every detail of your planning process, including phone calls to your planning team members as you monitor their progress and double-check their efforts. Also, keep your planning calendar handy, perhaps posted on a wall, and give your team members a copy of the planning calendar as well.

Two sample calendars have been included. The one below is a planning calendar for a father-son rally. The one on the next page is a portion of a year-long planning calendar for a small group program kick-off.

Sunday	Monday	Tuesday	Wednesday	Thursday	Friday	Saturday
1 Preliminary Meeting at Lunch	2	3	4	5 Trial Run and Brainstorming Session	6	7
8 Identify Tasks and Delegate	9 Begin Phone Surveys	10 Post Info. on Bulletin Board	11 Announce at Church Supper	12 Submit Bulletin Ads	13 Secure Space for Rally	14 Mail Flyers
15 Announce at Sunday School	16 Write Ad for Church Newsletter	17	18 Announce at Civic Club Meeting	19 Follow-Up Phone Calls	20 Call Team and Say Thanks	21
22 Present at Worship Service	23	24 Prepare Materials	25	26 Get Refreshments	27	28 Father-Son Rally!!

A SAMPLE SMALL GROUP CALENDAR
Here is a sample small group calendar.
Notice how this small group program "kicks off" in September.

July	August	September
• Executive leadership team all-day planning session • SURVEY sent to all church members • Follow-up call to all members to get SURVEY returned	• SURVEY results analyzed for future groups • BROCHURE describing all groups created and sent to all members • Curriculum ordered • One-day orientation for leaders	• Sign-up campaign begins • Leaders commissioned • Huge poster in foyer describing groups, pictures of leaders shown • Monthly LEADERSHIP meeting
October	**November**	**December**
• Thank-you cards sent to leaders • Short-term groups encouraged to sign up for new period or join existing groups • Overnight retreat for leaders	• Midterm evaluations sent to leaders • Plans for second semester kick-off made • Special Advent groups announced • Monthly LEADERSHIP meeting	• SURVEY about Interest Groups created for "Christmas crowd" • Photo exhibit of small groups in foyer • Curriculum ordered • Christmas party for leadership
January	**February**	**March**
• New BROCHURE about small group opportunities • New leaders commissioned • Sign-up campaign for new groups • Old covenant groups asked to renew covenant for new semester • Monthly LEADERSHIP meeting	• Special Lenten groups offered—six weeks only • Leadership team overnight planning retreat • Newsletter started—ideas for groups • Valentine cards sent to leaders • Monthly LEADERSHIP meeting	• Plans for small group graduation banquet announced • Midterm evaluation sent to leaders • Group leaders reminded of commitment to "birth" new group • Monthly LEADERSHIP meeting
April	**May**	**June**
• Lenten groups finish—invited to join existing groups • Countdown for all covenant groups begins • Needs assessment questionnaire given to all groups • Monthly LEADERSHIP meeting	• Recognition of group leaders in Sunday morning worship service • Group leaders asked to sign contract for another year • Graduation banquet for all groups—together	• Summer four-week special interest "fun groups" announced • Leadership team evaluates entire small group program • New leaders recruited

For long-term, large-scale events, like a kick-off for a new small group program, use a year-long calendar the same way you would use a month-long calendar.

Organize Your Planning Team

As you consider recruiting a team of people to help you plan your event, there are several things to keep in mind:

- Try to include people who represent your target group. Potential participants will have the best insight into an event designed to appeal to themselves and their peers. In the case of outreach events, try to include new members or others who are new to the Christian faith.

- Similarly, include a variety of different people. If your event is for single adults, gather a planning team of single adults from different lifestyles, ages, careers and personality types. This will help make the event more inclusive (less cliquish) and attract team members with a greater variety of skills, experience and interests.

- As you recruit planning team members, give them as much specific information as possible. Explain what joining the planning team will involve, the number of meetings you foresee, and the length of time they will need to be committed to the planning team.

- Also, consider other qualifications. Is the person an active church member? Have they supported similar programs in the past? Do they have the time and emotional energy to contribute effectively?

Once you have chosen your planning team (and they have agreed to help!), send them a letter thanking them for agreeing to serve. Include information about the introductory meeting in the letter.

Host an Introductory Meeting

Your first meeting with the planning team is crucial to getting your efforts off to a good start.

- Begin by making sure everyone is aware of the meeting. A reminder telephone call the day before is always helpful. Also, be sure they know how long the meeting will last and where the meeting will be held.

- Make sure the meeting room is set up properly. This includes putting a sign on the door, providing refreshments, supplying name tags and pens, setting up chairs and tables and distributing any handouts (planning calendar, meeting agenda, etc.).

- Once everyone has arrived, begin with an ice-breaker activity. You can choose one of the activities you plan on using for the actual event, or try a Kick-Off Sentence, such as "My Daily Routine" (p. 107). Be sure to give everyone an opportunity to introduce themselves and answer a question like, "Why did you offer to help plan this event?"

- The informational content of the meeting will need to include the following components. Feel free to supplement your presentation with overhead images or a handout summarizing your main points.

- Begin with an opening prayer.

- Give a brief summary of the agenda for the meeting.

- Share why the particular event is important, including who is being targeted and how the event can impact their lives.

- Explain the "Who, What, Where and When" of the event. Give any details you can about the schedule of the planning efforts and what will be expected of the planning team members. Also distribute blank planning calendars at this and future meetings, filling in the appropriate dates for different tasks as they are determined.

• As best you can, share what it will take to get the event off the ground. What logistical steps, promotional efforts, decision-making, etc. will need to be done?

• Use an overhead transparency or other audiovisual aid during your meeting.

• Include a time for questions, comments and suggestions.

• Next, take a moment to let everyone share their responses to "Find Yourself in the Picture" (p. 78). This will help everyone begin thinking about their role on the planning team.

• Give everyone the opportunity to officially sign up and commit themselves to helping plan the event.

• Announce your next meeting and close in prayer.

After the meeting, send each person a thank-you note for their willingness to contribute to the planning team. You can also remind them about the next meeting.

Conduct a Trial Run

In any letters or reminder calls, explain to your planning team that this second meeting will provide the opportunity to conduct a trial run of the actual event. The purpose of this meeting is to give everyone a better idea about what the event will be like. Conducting a trial run will also help build enthusiasm for the event and give your planning team a basis for improvements and suggestions. (Note: for

<table>
<tr><td>

Basic Requirements for the Family Fun Night Planning Team

• **3 Planning Team Meetings**

• **Your Particular Tasks**

• **10 Phone Calls**

• **Attending the Family Fun Night**

</td></tr>
</table>

retreats, this meeting will take longer since several sessions will need to be tested.)

Pretending like your planning team are participants at the actual event, walk through the event from start to finish. Each activity does not need to be done completely, just enough that everyone has a feel for what is going to happen. Also, do not fail to reproduce the "little moments" of the event, such as what happens when someone arrives or when everyone sits down to eat. The more accurate your trial run, the more effectively your planning team can evaluate the format, materials, and the activities themselves.

Brainstorming! Evaluate and Improve

Either after the trial run or at a separate meeting, give the planning team the opportunity to do some brainstorming. Effective brainstorming opens the discussion and gives everyone the chance to share their ideas and insights

---

Youth Retreat
Planning Team Commitment Card

Name: _____

Address:_____

Phone: _____

❑ **Yes, I want to be a member of the planning team.**

❑ **I'm not sure. Call me in a week.**

❑ **Sorry. I can't commit to this project.**

about the event. Remind the group that any idea is valuable and nothing is too outrageous. Moderate the event by making sure all the relevant topics are addressed while you are brainstorming. If necessary, occasionally drop in questions like, "What about the 'flow' of the event?" or "How would a first-time attender feel as they participated?" Ask someone to jot down the various suggestions as they are shared.

Identify and Delegate Tasks

The trial run and brainstorming process will help everyone on the planning team get a better idea about the various tasks required to successfully prepare for the event. Begin by identifying the different tasks that will need to be completed. Use a large newsprint pad or overhead projector and write down the different tasks as the planning team calls them out.

Here are some of the different tasks already identified in the descriptions of the various events included in the previous section:

- Find and reserve an appropriate facility
- Contact local officials for proper event permits
- Promote event in church publications
- Write and perform a skit about the event
- Announce the event in church meetings
- Develop materials for the event
- Gather props for the activities and games
- Organize food and snacks
- Welcome each person to the event
- Conduct a survey of the target group
- Facilitate groups during the event
- Prepare and send postevent evaluation forms
- Register participants and collect money
- Create and mail brochures

The next step in this process is delegating the various tasks to the different planning team members. Who is going to prepare the materials for the event? Who is going to see that information about the event is included in the church newsletter? Who is going to make announcements at the appropriate Sunday school classes? Who will gather props and prizes? Your planning team might be able to discuss the various tasks and divide them among themselves very easily. Or you could let each person list their choices on a piece of paper and then match them with the various tasks, making sure that each task is covered. Above all, try to divide the different tasks equally among the team members. Once the different planning tasks have been delegated, talk with each team member and "flesh out" the particulars of their responsibilities.

Recruit Teams

The next step is helping each member of the planning team recruit other church members to help them complete their particular tasks. Most likely, each planning team member has a few friends and acquaintances they can call on to help. Or, you can recruit people and assign them to the tasks that need assistance. Encourage the planning team to give potential helpers as much information as possible about what will be required to fulfill their responsibilities. Everyone wants to know what the job they are committing to will require. If you have given your planning team written information and planning calendars, provide copies to any additional helpers so everyone will know the relevant details about the event.

The new teams formed to fulfill the different planning tasks will probably need to have at least one meeting. Remind each team leader to begin each meeting with prayer and an ice-breaker activity and close the meeting with a time of affirmation and prayer. You can attend these meetings or simply ask each team to record the specific details and corresponding dates for the different steps they are taking to complete their task. Remember to provide encouragement to your planning team as they recruit others to help.

Survey Your Target Group

One of the best but most neglected ways to make sure your event is a success is to ask your target group what they need. For example, if you are planning a youth retreat, it is wise to survey the youth group and ask them what issues and concerns they are facing in their lives. Surveying potential event participants not only reveals valuable information about their lives, but also introduces the event. In addition, it is a simple act of love to ask someone about their needs and concerns.

Surveying the target group might be one of the tasks identified and delegated by your planning team. A survey team has several options for gathering information about the target group.

- First, they can attend any gatherings of the target group, like a singles Bible study, and simply ask, "What issues are you facing in your life that you would like to address at this spring's retreat?"

- An on-site survey card could be prepared and distributed to the target group, such as the senior adults, or enclosed in the church bulletin for the entire congregation. A survey card should include a thorough listing of choices (see sample on p. 311). The sample shown on the next page, in addition to the general issues listed at the top, includes options which correspond with Bible studies included in this encyclopedia. For instance, if many of the people you surveyed for a week-night prayer supper marked Stress as a topic, you have a good idea what Bible study to use during the prayer supper.

- A survey can also be mailed to your target group. Keep in mind that an accompanying letter will need to be enclosed and should take into account if the recipient is a church member or not. Including a stamped, self-addressed envelope will increase the response rate. Your survey team could even follow up the mailed survey with a phone call, gathering information verbally from those people who did not return the survey.

- Surveys can also be delivered. This is especially useful for outreach events. Survey forms with return envelopes are delivered to people's homes and the recipients are told:

    "Our church is trying to help the people in our community, but we need to know what you need. If you will complete this confidential survey and mail it back to us, it will help us offer events and resources which are relevant and effective. Please do not sign your name and address, unless you would like us to send you a copy of the survey results."

- If no one is home, the survey is placed on the doorknob with a letter which includes a similar message. After the results have been tabulated, send everyone information about those events which have been planned based on the survey results.

- Phone surveys are another option. Here is one format for conducting a telephone survey:

    - Begin by introducing yourself and stating your affiliation with the church.

WEEKNIGHT PRAYER SUPPER: TOPIC SURVEY

The planning team is preparing for our Weeknight Prayer Supper. We need to know what discussion topics would be most valuable to you. Please take a moment to record your choices and return this survey. Thanks!

1. Generally speaking, I am interested in learning more ...
   ❑ about who I am and how I feel about my life
   ❑ about my lifestyle and values
   ❑ about my spiritual life

2. When it comes to who I am, I am most interested in studying about ...
   ❑ my uniqueness   ❑ my personality
   ❑ my values   ❑ my abilities
   ❑ my future   ❑ being real
   ❑ my friendships   ❑ peer pressure
   ❑ tough love   ❑ family expectations

3. When it comes to my lifestyle and values, I am most interested in studying about ...
   ❑ priorities   ❑ possessions
   ❑ worries   ❑ old habits
   ❑ stress   ❑ moral issues
   ❑ forgiving others   ❑ racism and prejudice
   ❑ serving others   ❑ sexual desires

4. When it comes to my spiritual life, I am most interested in studying about ...
   ❑ my spiritual journey   ❑ basic Christian doctrines
   ❑ my spiritual calling   ❑ dealing with doubt
   ❑ rebounding from failure   ❑ sharing my faith

- Make sure the person you are calling has time for a short conversation.

- Briefly describe your reason for calling: "We are planning an all-church retreat and want to be sure the topic of the retreat is relevant and helpful."

- Use open-ended questions for your phone survey:

- "What church programs are you and your family currently involved in?"

- "What is most valuable about your involvement?"

- "What support could our church offer to better serve you and your family?" (Read some topics from the survey on this page or page 311 if necessary.)

Gather and Prepare Materials

For most of the events listed in this encyclopedia, preparing printed materials is extremely helpful. This is true for a weekend retreat booklet or a basic handout for family fun night. Providing each event participant with printed agenda and activity information helps them feel comfortable knowing that everything is "under control." This is especially true for events which include teenagers and non-members.

Preparing materials might be a task identified by your planning team. Use the following checklist to help you determine what to include in any materials you distribute at your event:

- event schedule
- crowd breakers
- discussion activities
- Bible studies
- words to songs and rhymes
- prayer options
- affirmation activities
- recreation information
- aids to choosing discussion leaders
- aids to forming groups

This information can be reproduced in a variety of formats, including booklets, placemats or single-page handouts. Serendipity encourages churches to photocopy any of the activities in this encyclopedia, though some church leaders will benefit from having their own copy of the *Serendipity Encyclopedia*.

Monitor Your Teams

Try to stay abreast as each member of your planning team oversees the completion of the different tasks. The comparatively little effort required to monitor the various teams results in a valuable windfall. In addition, all the team members appreciate that their hard work is noticed and appreciated.

Monitoring the different teams begins with making sure each team has at least one meeting to identify and select the specific tasks. The promotion team might select one person to make announcements at church meetings, select someone else to put event information in the church publications and select the other team members to do mailing and phone calls. Once you know the different tasks each team has agreed to do, record those tasks on your planning calendar. This way, you can contact the team to see if the tasks have been completed or are on track.

Say "Thank You"

Throughout the planning process, do not forget to express your gratitude to your planning team and other team members. Short, simple and frequent thank-yous are all it takes to let people know that you notice and appreciate the work they are doing. Taking the time to write a little note, make a simple phone call or share an encouraging word to someone on a Sunday morning will keep everyone on your planning team motivated and content. You can also introduce all the volunteers helping plan an event during a worship service. Your church would probably enjoy knowing the people who are currently at work on an upcoming event.

Friday Night
Small Group
"Get Acquainted" Questions

1. Tell your name, the Home Group(s) you have been part of and three things from the following list:
   - ❏ The most unusual thing about my hometown.
   - ❏ My favorite vacation.
   - ❏ The best present I ever got.
   - ❏ What I like most about my best friend.
   - ❏ What I like most about my favorite hobby.
   - ❏ What has inspired me most about my grandparents.
   - ❏ The greatest thing about my child / children.

2. What I expect to get out of this event:

3. The obstacles I had to overcome to get here are:

4. Something unusual about me is:

This is from a booklet prepared for a small group leaders' retreat.

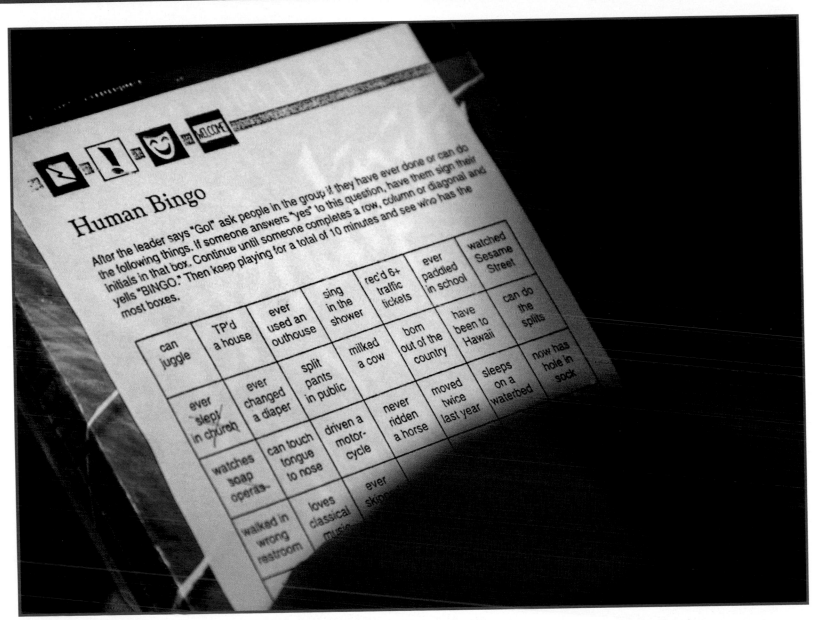

Human Bingo

After the leader says "Go!" ask people in the group if they have ever done or can do the following things. If someone answers "yes" to this question, have them sign their initials in that box. Continue until someone completes a row, column or diagonal and yells "BINGO." Then keep playing for a total of 10 minutes and see who has the most boxes.

can juggle	TP'd a house	ever used an outhouse	sing in the shower	rec'd 6+ traffic tickets	ever paddled in school	have been to Hawaii	watched Sesame Street
		split pants in public	milked a cow	born out of the country			can do the splits
ever slept in church	ever changed a diaper		driven a motor-cycle	never ridden a horse	moved twice last year	sleeps on a waterbed	now has hole in sock
	watches soap operas	can touch tongue to nose					
	walked in wrong restroom	loves classical music	ever skinny				

This is a sample of a handout you can distribute for a shorter event. A single 8.5" x 11" page is well-suited for a crowd breaker, discussion starter, Bible study or affirmation activity.

PROMOTING YOUR EVENT

The members of your planning team devoted to helping promote your upcoming event have a very important job. A great event, built upon hours and hours of planning, will be useless if your target group does not have adequate information. Consider the following principles as you begin to promote your event:

- Be sure to use a VARIETY of promotional methods. Personal invitations, phone calls, announcements, flyers, bulletin inserts—different people will find information in different ways. You might even choose to form several teams to handle different promotional tasks. Remember, different target groups respond to different promotional methods.

- Emphasize the PURPOSE of the event as much as you emphasize the event itself. Remember that most people are not very interested in the idea of another church activity, but they are interested in something that meets their needs.

- Be CREATIVE! Promoting an event is more than telling the what, where, when and why. Use your imagination to develop promotional methods which grab people's attention!

- Take advantage of every opportunity to give potential participants a "sneak preview" of the event. In addition to giving a presentation or announcement at a meeting or worship service, give everyone a chance to do a fun song, discussion starter or other activity. Then explain that the upcoming event includes many more similar activities. One example of promoting an event in this way is the interactive worship service described on page 292.

- Remember that effective promotion costs time and money. Include promotional costs in the budget of your event. And schedule your promotional efforts. Put your promotional efforts on your planning calendar.

- Always proofread everything you produce as you promote your event.

- Make sign-up sheets available anytime the event is announced.

Photo Courtesy of Cherry Hills Community Church

The following different ways to promote your event are discussed in this section:

- Meeting presentations
- Church publications
- Sermons
- Worship service interview
- Skits, puppets, slide shows, etc.
- Phone teams
- Display table
- Brochures, flyers and posters
- Mailing
- Month-long emphasis

Meeting Presentations

Announcing your upcoming event at various church meetings is a great way to get the word out. If possible, begin with meetings of church leaders, including boards, sessions, elders, deacons, committee meetings—any meeting of church staff or lay leaders. In most cases these people, who are very active in the church, have opportunities to tell others about the event. It can also be helpful if the leaders of your church know that your planning team made a special effort to inform them of the event before other promotional methods have been used.

As the date of the event draws closer, focus your efforts on other meetings. You can announce the event at Sunday school, church suppers, youth meetings, small groups and choir practice. Distribute a flyer or other written summary which includes all the relevant information about the event. If possible, give a brief "taste" of what the event will be like, guiding the group through an activity similar to one planned for the event.

Give extra attention to the purpose of the event and include an opportunity for people to sign up. Also, allow time for a few questions. Remember, the more prepared you are during a meeting presentation, the more your audience will assume that the event itself will also be done well.

Church Publications

Your church already has effective ways to share information about your event. The Sunday morning bulletin can be used, as well as the church newsletter. Here are some guidelines to help you make the most effective use of these resources:

- Don't hesitate to use a clever gimmick to get someone's attention. Remember, the main goal is getting someone to read what you have to say!

- Keep your theme and approach positive. Emphasize the good things the event will accomplish.

- Keep your message clear, strong and simple for maximum effect.

- Make your copy "reader-friendly." Use a minimal number of type faces. Avoid small fonts and writing with too many bells and whistles, such as words that are capitalized, italicized, underlined or bold.

- Use photographs when you can, but make sure the image is sharp and you can clearly see smiling faces.

- Strive for readability. White space is helpful and common in most professionally produced advertisements.

- Adding color by using colored ink or colored paper can be attention-getting.

Sermons

Preaching a special sermon, or series of sermons, related to the upcoming event can be a valuable way to inform the congregation. Children's sermons can also be used to promote events that are designed for children, their families or the entire church.

A sermon related to your upcoming event indicates that event has received the blessing of your pastor and the church staff. A sermon also helps connect the event with the entire life of the church and helps identify the event with the overall church vision. A sermon can also provide valuable biblical support for the event, convincing the congregation that the event is solidly included in God's purposes.

Practically speaking, a sermon or series of sermons devoted to the upcoming event can give the congregation the time to fully consider participating in the event. Ample time is also given for sharing important details about the event. Also, a survey of the congregation (see "Survey Your Target Group," p. 302) can be combined with a sermon.

PROMOTING YOUR PROGRAMS AND EVENTS

PERSON-TO-PERSON INVITATIONS: This is the most effective method, but limited by the number of people you know.

BROCHURES: A simple trifold brochure, made on 8.5" x 11" paper is an effective tool. Try not to fill it too full of information, and use attractive fonts and graphics.

CATALOGS: A catalog of your various small groups, either in brochure or booklet form, is an impressive promotional piece. Some churches ask the leaders to write their own descriptions of their groups and put them in the catalog. Here is an example from the HOME GROUP ministry:

> **"Parents and Tragic Loss."** Parents who have lost a child face difficult feelings. This Home Group will provide a place for parents to come and find support from other parents who have lost their children. Grief, anger, hope, getting on with your life and other issues will be addressed. This group will also spend time together outside the group in a variety of enjoyable activites. This Home Group is open to couples or individuals.

A catalog listing small groups should also explain the basic features of the small group program.

NEWSPAPER ARTICLES or ADVERTISEMENTS: Newspaper ads are great, but expensive. If you write a press release describing your event or program, listing a contact person, your local newspaper might put the information in the newspaper free of charge.

WRITTEN ANNOUNCEMENTS IN THE CHURCH BULLETIN: Even better, put an insert in the bulletin that people can take home and put on their refrigerator. You could also include a card they can fill out and put in the offering plate if they are interested.

VERBAL ANNOUNCEMENTS IN THE WORSHIP SERVICE: This is best when there is corresponding written information in the bulletin.

BULLETIN BOARDS: If they are effective, use them! You could even post a sign-up sheet.

POSTERS: Placed strategically around the church, posters can be inexpensive, visual reminders for your program or event.

DRAMA / SKITS: If your church is used to drama, this can be a powerful way to promote small groups in general, and your upcoming event in particular.

VIDEO PRESENTATION: Videos can be a wonderful method of promoting events. Using either video or photographs, you can put together a video or slide presentation showing "real" people enjoying your program or event.

DIRECT MAIL: Even at bulk rates, direct mail is expensive. If you survey an area, however, sending them a small group catalog in response would be a valuable investment.

RADIO or TV ADS: If you have the money, your church can reach vast numbers of people this way.

PHONE TEAM: This is a fun job for your leaders and other helpers before their program or event ever starts. Meet at the church or someone's business after hours (where you have access to more than one line) and make a party out of it!

Worship Service Interview

Instead of merely announcing your event during a worship service, conduct an interview. Choose either someone who has participated in the event in the past, or is currently helping plan the event. This provides a first-hand account about the event and helps personalize it as well.

During the interview, emphasize the effect the event has had on the person you are interviewing. Focus on their life before and after the event. By highlighting life change, you can portray the relevancy of your event. Also, use humor and don't be afraid to let the person you are interviewing share their emotions.

Here are some questions you might consider asking during a worship service interview:

"How long have you been a part of our church?"
"What brought you to our church?"
"When did you first attend this event?"
"Why was this event so valuable to you?"
"In your opinion, what kind of person would benefit from this event?"
"What would you say to someone who isn't sure whether or not to attend this event?"

Following the interview, announce all the details of the event.

Skits, Puppets, Slide Shows ...

A skit, puppet show, slide show, interpretive dance or special music can be an effective way to give your event the kind of attention it deserves. Discuss some of these possibilities with your planning team to see what unique skills and talents they have which can be used to create an unusual and unforgettable promotional opportunity.

Using a skit or slide show, for example, to promote your event can give you tremendous creative freedom. Whether your efforts result in a serious skit or lighthearted puppet show, you can choose a theme best-suited for your event. Identify the major needs your event will address (see "Survey Your Target Group," p. 302) and let those needs be the theme of your skit or slide show.

Phone Teams

A phone team makes telephone calls to inform people about an upcoming event. An excellent follow-up to a survey that has been mailed to your congregation or community (see "Survey Your Target Group," p. 302), a phone call can provide valuable repetition when combined with other promotional methods.

Photo Courtesy of Cherry Hills Community Church

When you call, introduce yourself, make sure the person you are calling has time to take the call, and invite them to attend the event. Try to recruit a phone team consisting of people who have participated in the event in the past and can give a first-hand account of what to expect. For fun, have your phone teams gather at a location with several phone lines. Order pizza and have a calling party!

Display Table

A display table or bulletin board in a high-traffic area at your church is a good way to promote your event for several reasons. First, it doesn't require an attendant to be effective, though having someone standing nearby to answer questions can be very helpful. Second, it can be used over an extended period of time, exposing potential participants to important information on several occasions. Finally, a display table or bulletin board can be a good way to distribute literature. Including a brochure in a holder marked "take one" gives easy access to information and gives people the opportunity to take several copies and give them to friends and family members.

Include a sign-up sheet at your display table. And photos, in addition to the essential event information, are also valuable. Again, with any promotional method, be sure to include a description of why someone should attend the event.

Brochures, Flyers and Posters

Use a variety of printed materials to promote your event. Consult the list of guidelines for church publications (p. 307) for ways to help you create brochures, flyers and posters which are effective.

Brainstorm with your planning team to identify ways to use brochures, flyers and posters. Brochures can be mailed, inserted in the bulletin or passed out to a Sunday school class or other group. Brochures can even be made to hang from a doorknob. Flyers can also be mailed, handed out or used like "mini-posters." Give away flyers and brochures at meeting presentations, display tables and bulletin boards. Make posters and put them up at church. Remember, repetition is an important part of advertising. Flyers and posters can also be used at other locations. Community bulletin boards and store windows are two possibilities.

Consider hiring a graphic-design specialist to help you make a top-notch brochure or flyer. This is especially important if you plan to mail or distribute the brochure or flyer outside your church. Quality printed material can portray a sense of competence and excellence to an outsider, who might feel anxious about attending a church event.

Mailing

Though expensive, mailing information about your event can be an effective promotional tool. Mailing is especially helpful for large churches and for those events which include nonmembers.

Make sure the material you mail is complete, including all the necessary information about the event. Correcting mailed information is difficult, expensive and awkward. If the mailing is going to people who are not church members, a quality layout, free of errors, is especially important.

If you wish to send your information to people in your community, you can target specific types of people or a specific area. Many companies sell data or mailing labels based on certain demographic criteria. These services are helpful, but add costs in addition to postage, printing and layout production. Consider enclosing a letter with your brochure or flyer. Since a mailing to a nonmember tells the recipient that your church cares about them, a mailing can have value even if the recipient does not attend the event.

Month-Long Emphasis

Discuss with your planning team the possibility of a month-long effort to promote the event. This is especially useful if the event is a major one, such as a churchwide retreat or the kick-off of a new program. A promotional emphasis of this kind relies on a combination of promotional methods which thoroughly inform the target group about the event. Depending on your event and your target group, your planning team can devise a strategy which includes a carefully chosen combination of the promotional methods described in this chapter. In general, use a full spectrum of methods which appeal to each segment of your target group. Also, go from methods which have a broadscale impact on your target group to promotional methods designed for smaller groups and individuals.

Home Group Survey

Check the Home Groups you would enjoy:

SUPPORT GROUPS:
- ❏ Grief and Loss
- ❏ 12 Steps
- ❏ Stress Management
- ❏ Parents of Young Children
- ❏ SIDS Support Group
- ❏ Single Parents
- ❏ New Mommies
- ❏ Aging Issues / Retirement
- ❏ Parents of Teenagers
- ❏ Divorce Recovery
- ❏ Health and Nutrition
- ❏ Parents of Children with Special Needs
- ❏ Alzheimer's Support
- ❏ Unemployment Support
- ❏ Career Assessment
- ❏ Blended Families
- ❏ Adult Children of Divorce
- ❏ Grandparents Raising Grandkids
- ❏ Bankruptcy Recovery
- ❏ Adults Caring for Their Parents
- ❏ Widows / Widowers
- ❏ Midlife Issues

STUDY GROUPS:
- ❏ Women's Study Group
- ❏ Men's Study Group
- ❏ How to Pray
- ❏ Basic Christian Beliefs
- ❏ Christian Families
- ❏ Small Businesses
- ❏ Christian Discipleship
- ❏ How to Study the Bible
- ❏ Discovering Your Spiritual Gift
- ❏ Marriage Enrichment

SUPPORT GROUPS (singles):
- ❏ Twenties
- ❏ Thirties
- ❏ Forties +
- ❏ Christian Artists
- ❏ Walkers & Runners
- ❏ Shooters
- ❏ Cyclists

PREPARING FOR FUTURE EVENTS

After your event is over, there is a small amount of work left to do. Making the effort to prepare for future events by gathering feedback and recognizing your team members serves several valuable purposes. First, a little feedback goes a long way when you are planning next year's event. If you know what works and what does not work for an event, you can plan accordingly the next time the event is offered. Second, asking participants and planners about their ideas and experiences concerning the event places value on their input and helps provide closure. Third, the process of gathering feedback is a great opportunity to identify potential planning team members for future events. And, of course, giving everyone who helped plan the event a pat on the back builds community, affirms their Christian service and increases the likelihood that they will help plan future events.

This section includes the following topics:

- Sending an evaluation form
- Interviewing participants
- Having an evaluation meeting
- Recording ideas for the next event
- Recognizing team members

Send an Evaluation Form

One effective way to gather feedback is to send an evaluation form to everyone who helped plan or participated in the event. Though this form can be submitted to each person before the event is actually finished (such as during the last session of a retreat), mailing the evaluation form does not interfere with the event itself and gives each person time to reflect on their experience.

Send the evaluation form with a cover letter, explaining why gathering feedback about the event is helpful. Thank each person profusely in advance and put postage on the return envelope. Remember that these people are doing you a favor by completing and returning the form. You could even include a coupon for a discount at a local restaurant as an expression of your gratitude.

An example of an evaluation form for small groups is found on the next page. Use a variety of different types of questions, such as multiple-choice, open-ended and rate-on-a-scale questions. Ask for ideas about format, setting and topic, and be sure to ask if the respondent would like to help with next year's event.

Interview Participants

Face-to-face interviews can complement the use of an evaluation form. Interviewing event participants is more time consuming, but provides detailed information. You can learn things by talking to someone that you cannot learn from a form. In addition, you can choose to interview a representative sampling of the people who actually attended the event. By

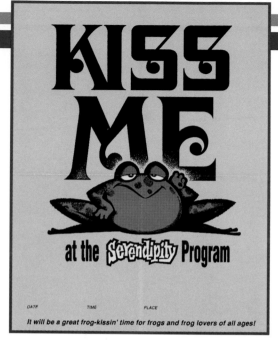

It will be a great frog-kissin' time for frogs and frog lovers of all ages!

asking each member of your planning team to interview three or four participants, a valuable amount of feedback can be gathered without any one person doing all the work.

For the interview itself, prepare a list of questions like the ones used in the evaluation form. As each component of the event is discussed, ask follow-up questions to clarify their response.

Have an Evaluation Meeting

After the feedback has been collected, gather your planning team for the final meeting. This meeting is important, and if it is included in each team member's job description, attendance should not be a problem. This final event helps provide closure for a team that has worked hard together and takes advantage of everyone's experience during the planning process.

Evaluation Questionnaire— After Each Stage of a Long-Term Group:

1. As I see it, our purpose and goal as a group was to ...

2. We achieved our goal(s):
   - ❏ completely
   - ❏ somewhat
   - ❏ almost completely
   - ❏ We blew it.

3. We agreed at the beginning of this group to a covenant (see page 54). Did we keep this covenant?

4. I found the approach to the group sessions:
   - ❏ very helpful
   - ❏ intellectually stimulating
   - ❏ challenging
   - ❏ irrelevant for my life
   - ❏ life-changing
   - ❏ new to me
   - ❏ boring
   - ❏ so-so
   - ❏ other:_____

5. One of the most significant things I learned was ...

6. In my opinion, our group functioned:
   - ❏ smoothly, and we grew
   - ❏ pretty well, but we didn't grow
   - ❏ It was tough, but we grew.
   - ❏ It was tough, and we did not grow.

7. The thing I appreciate most about the group as a whole is ...

8. If I were to suggest one thing we could work on as a group, it would be ...

Here is a suggested meeting agenda:

Begin with an opening prayer. Then let everyone share their answers to "Find Yourself in the Picture" (p. 78). If you used this exercise as recommended in your planning team's introductory meeting (pp. 299–300), everyone can share how they have changed since then, perhaps as a result of the planned event.

Ask everyone to give their overall impression of the event.

Review the feedback collected from the evaluation forms and interviews.

Discuss the particular components of the planning process and the event itself, focusing on ways to improve the event and the planning process. Issues you might wish to discuss include:

- Attendance at the event
- Involvement and support by church staff
- How well planning tasks were completed
- Impact on participants' lives
- Value of event in regard to church mission
- Promotional efforts

Give everyone a chance to share their experience as a member of the planning team.

Close with an affirmation activity, such as "My Gourmet Group" (p. 139) or "You Remind Me of Jesus" (p. 137).

Be sure to take notes during this meeting. What is discussed will be priceless as you plan future events!

Record Ideas for the Next Event

You have valuable data when you combine your experience, the feedback from your planning team, and the results of the evaluation forms and interviews. While it is still fresh, sit down with this information and write down your ideas for the next time the event is offered. Use your planning calendar to adjust the planning schedule, if necessary. Also, make sure you have all the names of people who might be interested in helping plan the event in the future. To assure good support from the church staff and other church leaders in the future, write a brief report about the event and give each church leader a copy. Include the results of the event and your ideas to improve future events.

Recognize Team Members

In many cases, after a volunteer devotes many hours of effort to help plan an event they are lucky to receive a statement like, "Hey, thanks for all your hard work. I really appreciate it."

Certainly your planning team and other volunteers deserve more than that! Actually, there are a variety of ways to let these helpers know how much you appreciate their dedication to planning a meaningful event.

- Let the entire church express their gratitude. Introduce all the team members during a worship service and ask the

congregation to give them a standing ovation or a couple of hearty "hip hip hoorays!"

- Profile your planning team in the church bulletin or newsletter, letting the congregation know who these people are who worked so hard.

- Write each person a special note, acknowledging their particular input, and then follow up with a phone call.

- Take your planning team to dinner. Reserve a room or large table at a nice restaurant and have a great time!

- Invite everyone to your home for a party. Play games and enjoy snacks together. Encourage them to bring family members or friends.

- Give each person a special gift, such as a custom-made award certificate, a trophy, or a gift certificate to a local Christian bookstore.

Your recognition ideas can be implemented during a worship service, at a party or dinner, or even during your concluding evaluation meeting (p. 312).

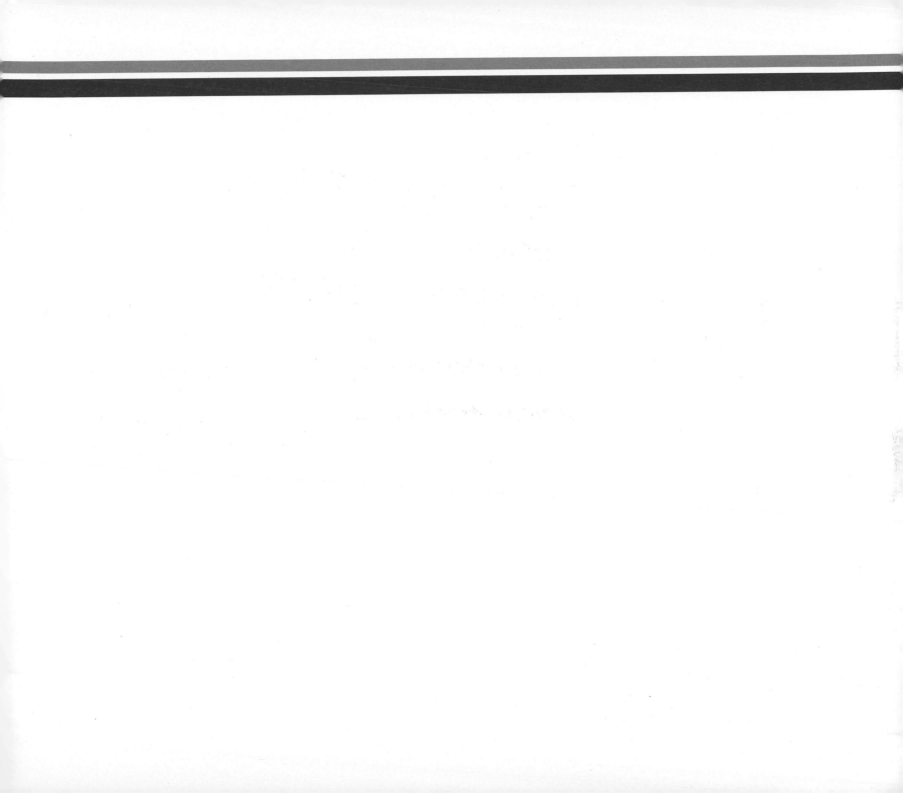